Criminal Justice and Corruption

Graham Brooks

Criminal Justice and Corruption

State Power, Privatization and Legitimacy

palgrave
macmillan

Graham Brooks
University of West London
London, UK

ISBN 978-3-030-16037-1 ISBN 978-3-030-16038-8 (eBook)
https://doi.org/10.1007/978-3-030-16038-8

Library of Congress Control Number: 2019935509

Cover credit: Alamy EG5JKA

This Palgrave Macmillan imprint is published by the registered company Springer Nature Switzerland AG
The registered company address is: Gewerbestrasse 11, 6330 Cham, Switzerland

Contents

1
Introduction

This book sets out to examine the impact of corruption *in* and *on* criminal justice systems and the public acceptance and legitimacy, or lack of it, of the state's power to punish, particularly once exposed as corrupt. The inspiration for this book comes from cases of corruption that regularly surface around the world that discredit criminal justice in democratic and non-democratic nations. Whilst corruption is perhaps expected under dictatorships and/or an absolute monarchy (Greitens 2016; Yadav and Mukherrjee 2016) for at least some of the population in these states, it is perhaps most disappointing if or when corruption occurs in democratic nations where there is the expectation that criminal justice and the law is impartial and objective.

Most of the international literature on criminal justice corruption examines law enforcement, or more specifically, the police (Punch 2003; Del Pozo 2005; Ivkovic 2005; Alpert and Noble 2009; Skolnick 2010; Tankebe 2010; Campbell and Campbell 2010; Caldero and Crank 2011; Kane and White 2013; Bacon 2014; Stanford 2015; Greitens 2016; Miller 2017; Beare 2017). The police, however, are only one

G. Brooks, *Criminal Justice and Corruption*,
https://doi.org/10.1007/978-3-030-16038-8_1

agency in any criminal justice system, and whilst powerful, with the discretion conferred upon them by the state, and some of the public, depending on the country and/or sections of it, they are not the only agency that is sometimes corrupt. Law enforcement is sometimes accused of institutional and cultural racial bias but the whole criminal justice system—law courts; prison and probation services—in democratic nations have also appeared to 'accept' such practice(s) (Brown and Frank 2006; Michelle 2010; Rodriguez 2010; Tonry 2010, 2011; Tyler 2014; Spohn 2015; Gottschalk 2015).

A note of clarification is needed before reading this book, though. I use the term 'criminal corruption' (Brooks 2016) to indicate that a criminal act has occurred rather than one that falls under some moral code. In addition I refer to law enforcement rather than the police. I make this distinction here because referring only to the police is a somewhat understated reach of a states' law enforcement capacity. Border and immigration and revenue, customs and excise also 'police' both its borders, citizens and threats to state security, and can also be corrupt. Finally, I prefer to use narcotic(s) to describe the use of and/or manufacture of illegal substances in this book; the reason is to make a clear distinction, if possible, between proscriptive and prescriptive substances and illegal and legal consumption of some kind of medication and/or alcohol. Narcotics are associated with corrupt 'narco' states (Grillo 2011) and corrupt criminal justice systems, which is the theme in the book.

However, where relevant I will explicitly state that different types of corruption also influence criminal justice, and sometimes lead to criminal corruption. These are:

Unethical corruption—an unethical but still legal act or one that is on the cusp of illegality but presented as an 'error' or 'mistake', e.g. lawyers holding on to information in a case that clears a suspect of the crime (see Chapter 10).

Corruption of process/procedure—where 'rules' of policing are breached, e.g. arrest suspect on limited evidence and/or fail to follow set process at arrest, interview and charging stage(s) (see Chapters 3 and 4).

Corruption of an ideal—the ideal of rehabilitation in probation is marginalized in favour of punishment in the community (see Chapter 8).

These often unethical acts lead to a criminal act(s) and individuals and organizations are victimized by the system that is there to protect them and offer redress as a victim of crime. Acts of corruption hit the poorest in our midst the hardest, but all of us, even those that are lucky enough to spend our life without any direct encounter or recourse to use criminal justice are still victims, particularly in democratic nations, if our system of 'justice' is built on corruption.

This book is an attempt to address this issue. This is not a criticism of the corruption literature of which there are excellent texts available. I am unable to name them all here but I recommend (Rose-Ackermann 1978; Johnston 2005; Rothstein 2011; Graycar and Prenzler 2013; Heywood 2015; Miller 2017; Banks 2017). This book is a contribution to the debates regarding corruption but primarily criminal justice systems and the impact this can have on the public and ultimately legitimacy of power exercised by a state (Bottoms and Tankebe 2012). Criminal justice on a national and international scale is open to substantial corruption be it a public agency or private sector or a combination of both and this is a threat to local, national and international criminal justice.

Furthermore, and still under-researched in sociology and criminology is the unethical and criminal corruption that is part of awarding criminal justice contracts to the private sector. There is excellent literature on private sector involvement in criminal justice but the majority of this literature tends to consider the impact of privatization on provision of police services (South 1988; White 2014, 2015; Diphoorn 2016), prison systems (Burkhardt 2014; Gottschalk 2015; Eisen 2017) and probation services (Fitzgibbon and Lea 2014; Fitzgibbon 2016), instead of the private sectors attempts to secure public legitimacy (Fitzgibbon and Lea 2017) in the field of criminal justice. This is understandable but the reach of corruption is such that it can occur before a contract is awarded. A contract can be awarded to a private company by a public body due to aggressive lobbying, 'sponsorship' of events, or employing ex-public sector employees with contacts working in the criminal justice system or simple straightforward bribery to secure a contract. Before a contract is signed, a brick is laid as a foundation for a prison, immigration centre, or probation offices, and/or computer systems installed in law enforcement officers there is the potential for corruption. It is here as well as the end result of providing services in criminal justice that is in need of more attention from criminology.

There is literature on state power (Foucault 1977), or abuse of it, privatization of criminal justice services (Fitzgibbon 2016) and legitimacy (Beetham 1991; Coicaud 2002; Bottoms and Tankebe 2012) and trying to prevent and reduce acts of fraud and corruption (Brooks 2016) but little on business practices where criminal justice contracts are secured via corruption. A contract secured by corruption can lead to the corruption of services provided to the police, e.g. manipulation of emergency telephone calls data to reach a contracted threshold of emergency calls (White 2015; Fitzgibbon and Lea 2017). This is a corruption of criminal justice and one that affects us all.

Such corruption though is no different to any type of business, but criminal justice systems and those that work in them are vested with power to alter the shape of an individual's and family current and future life. As a victim of fraud or some type of corruption, which we sometimes not might be aware (e.g. price fixing a product or service we purchase) we still maintain our liberty and have no criminal record. Once defined and labelled as a 'criminal' ex-offender our employment prospects often narrow (Schmitt and Warner 2011; Flake 2015) as do our relationships with others. This is not an attempt to excuse individual or organizational criminal acts; this, in fact, is my concern here. Corruption of criminal justice is and should be about more than miscarriages of justice. I highlight here how criminal justice is itself a victim and purported notions of justice are sometimes a sham, a system that is rigged and abused by those working in it, but also the private sector to secure criminal justice contracts.

The numbers of criminal justice services involved in putting individuals—innocent or suspected—under surveillance, and/or transporting innocent or suspected offenders to a court or prison, processing cases in a court, analysis of police data, management of police call centres, building or managing a prison, providing inmates with clothes, food, healthcare, education, telephone calls to and from prison, and probation services and surveillance in the community are only a few potential avenues open to manipulation and corruption. In the USA alone (as of 2017) there are 4.65 million people under some sort of 'correctional control' (Eisen 2017) with 'correctional' institutions worth an estimated $80 billion. 'A set of bureaucratic, political and economic interests' (Schlosser 1998: 51–77) expanding the reach of criminal justice, regardless of need leads to a prison industrial complex. With this expansion, it is inevitable that some criminal justice services will encounter some form of corruption in state and private sectors.

This book expands on the corruption literature and helps broaden the discussion on why and how individuals, organizations and states commit corrupt acts in criminal justice systems and how they are captured (Dal Bo 2006) by vested state and/or private interests. Whilst political science and economics analyse the measurement of corruption, and/or how to prevent it, and legal research on corruption is concerned with breaches of rules and laws such disciplines rarely directly examine criminal justice systems. Instead they assess political corruption, which influences criminal justice rather than a detailed examination of a criminal justice agency. Sociology and criminology, however, have examined criminal justice corruption but mostly with a view to explaining, understanding and preventing police corruption. One explanation of corruption emphasizes that criminality is learned in interaction with others in a process of communication and from observations of what are referred to as definitions favourable to violation of law(s) (Sutherland 1939) which is relevant to corruption in law enforcement but could also refer to prison officers, state prosecutors and judges as a 'culture of corruption' is possible in all.

This book then reaches beyond the mostly police orientated literature on corruption and highlights how corruption can damage the credibility of a system of justice and legitimacy it needs to function. I consider criminal justice a flawed but necessary system in providing justice but offer a view that we should examine criminal justice as a business and the concomitant acts of corruption that this entails.

A Problem of Definition

As a discipline, criminology has a history of debating the usefulness and limitations of crime data and the problematic nature of recording crime and thus its measurement. The literature explains how crime is recorded and also why crime statistics substantially under-record crime. There is criticism of crime data but if we consider the data for what it is, an estimate of the level of crime, and are aware of the limitations, they serve a purpose and are of use to highlight the reach of crime and corruption in criminal justice systems. The problem here is that some types of corruption are not criminal, yet can damage the legitimacy of criminal justice, and some are criminal but difficult to unearth and expose. For all the limitations however, recorded crime is an antidote to wild inaccurate, sensational views of crime (Jones 2006), and instead highlights how a criminal justice system works.

Corruption, especially political corruption, is seen predominantly as a public sector issue. This, however, is slowly changing with recognition that the private sector is corrupt without any link to or involvement with the public sector (Hough 2015; Heywood 2015; Brooks 2016). The delivery of public services in criminal justice in some jurisdictions has also changed with services transferred to private sector. The transformation in the delivery of services, however, engenders new risks for corruption with vested interests between the public and private sectors. An emphasis on public sector corruption is now disingenuous and misses the reach and extent of corruption and by whom it is committed. As noted by Heywood (2015) there needs to be a recalibration of how we conceptualize corruption, study it empirically and analyse it before we know how best to combat it.

Attempts to classify corruption are compounded by trying to review the social, cultural and legal attitudes towards corruption and define corruption across jurisdictions. Even with a clear definition, which would be difficult, if not impossible, the measurement (Anderson and Heywood 2009; Foster et al. 2009; Brooks et al. 2013) and secretive nature of corruption is difficult to expose. Local variations on levels of corruption, attempts, if any, to reduce it, differ. This is more so at the cross-border international level as corruption is not anchored to a fixed abode and has no respect for international borders. The complex natures of the differences in social, cultural and political developments only 'muddy the waters' of what corruption is, and who has jurisdictional control. It is perhaps best to view corruption as a continuum (Brooks 2016): it can range from legal act(s) that are morally condemned to highly illegal and criminal acts that involve the public and private sector alone or in concert with one another. Traditional roles, particularly in the west where the public sector had a monopoly on providing services has passed, with the 'Balkanization' of state apparatuses as new public management reforms (NPM) have colonized much of public sector service delivery and promoted the separation of policy decisions from policy delivery (Heywood and Wright 1997: 91), which has affected and changed the delivery of some criminal justice services, particularly in neo-liberal jurisdictions.

These reforms have created new openings for corruption in 'western' jurisdictions and increased conflicts of interest as public service employees move between highly paid public and private sector positions (Eisen 2017) either after a few years employment or on retirement. The knowledge of the procedures and processes and contacts in a public sector body is invaluable to the private sector. These movements of people has raised some concern in different jurisdictions about the use of privileged information in the private sector, as one organization can secure privilege information and/or access, at the expense of others applying for public sector contracts (Heywood 2015). The net result of this is growing privatization of the state with an increase in abuse of office, lobbying ex-colleagues, inappropriate use of official information with kickbacks, bribes and embezzlement. The prospect of future corruption, perhaps beyond the reach of much of the criminal justice system is that it is committed by those *in* the criminal justice system or private sector working with it.

Therefore, because of these changes mentioned above, I prefer to avoid the oft-quoted Transparency International's (2012) well-worn phrase of 'the abuse of entrusted power for private gain', which has its limitations. Attempting to fit an all-encompassing definition for wide-ranging acts across criminal justice systems excludes acts of corruption rather than includes them; criminology and sociology offer a far more nuanced approach and help place acts of corruption onto a continuum of corruption and help highlight and analyse all acts on the continuum of corruption that range from deviant, non-criminal to criminal acts that can help analyse the reach, depth and breadth of corruption in criminal justice systems.

Outline of Book

Each chapter can be read chronologically or individually depending on the readers' interests.

Chapter 2—*What Is Criminal Justice Corruption?*—briefly assesses the problem of trying to define criminal justice corruption. I then examine the reach of state power (Foucault 1977) and criminal justice corruption and how this affects the legitimacy of justice (Beetham 1991; Coicaud 2002; Bottoms and Tankebe 2012). Furthermore, I highlight the reach of the privatization (Fitzgibbon 2016) of criminal justice services that also seek legitimacy similar to that of state criminal justice systems (Fitzgibbon and Lea 2017). Three themes—state power, legitimacy and privatization are reviewed here but surface to some extent in all the chapters as these are under threat or the cause of the threat to criminal justice, particularly in democratic nations.

Chapter 3—*Extent of Corruption in Criminal Justice Systems*—reviews the problem of measuring and assessing the extent of corruption in criminal justice systems. This chapter reviews the ongoing challenges in developing an accurate understanding of the extent of corruption (Brooks et al. 2013) in law enforcement/policing, the manipulation of scientific data to secure a conviction and the problem of measuring corruption behind prison walls. All of the above is difficult but some understanding of the level of corruption is important; if we have some estimate of corruption, we can potentially reduce its incidence and levels of victimization (Van Dijk 2015). Measurement, regardless of how rough, is therefore critical in providing some benchmark of corruption and identifying what factors are effective in preventing and reducing corruption in criminal justice.

Chapter 4—*Law Enforcement, Security and Corruption*—reflects on the substantial amount of literature on law enforcement and corruption. However, most of this is on national state law enforcement (Punch 2000, 2003; Tankebe 2010; Campbell and Campbell 2010; Kane and White 2013; Bacon 2014; Stanford 2015) bodies or specific police units (e.g. narcotics and/or vice) that have engaged in corruption. This chapter will build on this work but also consider the problem of trying to define law enforcement corruption and discuss the causes of corruption. This chapter then considers corruption in law enforcement rather than the 'police' as all of the above can corrupt national and international criminal justice systems, the problem of policing undercover and development of private security/policing and routes into corruption. I use the term police in this book to denote a national mostly uniformed service of officers on the streets unless indicated otherwise and 'policing' to indicate a method of action and hence one that is used by all involved in law enforcement. All of these law enforcement bodies, however, share one common need; the need for legitimacy (Bottoms and Tankebe 2012; Miller 2017). In addition, they also share a common threat to this legitimacy; internal and external corruption. This chapter then considers law enforcement reforms that have failed to prevent corruption.

Chapter 5—*The Jury: An Open Invitation to Corruption?*—considers a contemporary issue: and this is the corruption of the jury, and individual members use of the internet. Whilst members of the jury show bias and prejudicial behaviour (Daftary-Kapur et al. 2010) that will impact on the outcome of a case, I consider this more a corruption of the case rather than the jury system. Instead, I review the impact technology has already had on corrupting the jury system (Browning 2010; Kiernan and Colley 2012; Harvey 2014) and attempts to prevent and reduce this current and undoubted future problem.

Chapter 6—*Judicial Corruption: Magistrates, Judges and Prosecutors*—examines the corruption of the judiciary and state and private prosecutors. Due to the power often invested in such individuals and bodies investigation is often blocked (Chang and Liu 2007), or thwarted by political collusion (Braimah 2016), and/or an informal network of contacts that close ranks if corruption is suspected. This chapter reviews the types of judicial corruption that fall under political interference or administrative misconduct primarily but also considers how judicial independence can be a threat to 'justice' as well (Miller 2004). In addition, I consider how judges can extort and/or send signals that bribery is a possible route to a lenient, reduced and/or dismissed case. Finally I consider prosecutors power to stop an investigation into a case, direct law enforcement to find evidence (or lack of it) to discontinue the case, depending on the type of system—adversarial and prosecutorial—prevent witnesses being interviewed, and refuse to indict even if provided with overwhelming evidence of crime (Banks 2017). Judicial and prosecutorial power and the power to be corrupt is thus a core theme of this chapter.

Chapter 7—*An Archipelago of Profit: Custodial Institutions and Corruption*—will consider the definition and range and types of corruption in custodial institutions committed by inmates and officials e.g. bribery of 'correction/prison officers' to 'assist' an inmate by smuggling weapons, narcotics, mobile/cell phones in exchange for financial benefit, and/or sexual acts (Souryal 2009; Centre for the Advancement of Public Integrity 2016) and the consequences of these actions. In addition, I emphasize that some prison systems are under the control of inmates rather than prison officers, and this control of institutions reaches beyond a prison for some inmates in corrupt jurisdictions (Lessing 2016) and can corrupt criminal justice systems instead. The chapter then assesses the impact privatization has had on the prison system, particularly in the USA.

Chapter 8—*The Probation Service: Corruption in the Community*—highlights how a part of criminal justice system that is often seen as the most liberal part of the criminal justice system in democratic nations has the potential to be corrupt. This chapter offers a brief description of the types of corruption that can occur in probation services. This is followed by a reflection on the rise of shadow state (White 2013; Cracknell 2018), in both the form of the state and private sectors, and the reach and control of offenders in the community and the corruption of the rehabilitative ideal. This leads onto electronic monitoring (EM)

(Bartels and Martinovic 2017; Graham and McIvor 2017; Moss 2018) and the reach of corrupt practice in the private sector.

Chapter 9—*Vigilantes: The Corruption of the Justice System*—will highlight how some nations have lost control of the justice system, and conceded the role of punishment to terrorist and/or paramilitary groups and organized crime. This is particularly noticeable in Mexico (Ochoa and Tomas 2016), Nigeria (Harnischfeger 2003; Meagher 2007) and Northern Ireland (Monaghan 2004, 2008; Topping and Byrne 2012; Mullins and Wither 2016). This chapter therefore explores the need to contain victimization and maintain social order; however, such order is maintained outside the recognized legal order of justice. This chapter then is about extra-judicial punishment tacitly accepted by the police and committed by 'militias' outside the legal order and thus the contested notion of what criminal justice can and is able to do and the definition of 'justice'.

Chapter 10—*The Legal Profession: Professional Corruption*—chapter starts with a review of legal, professional ethics such as partisanship, neutrality, relationship with client(s), confidentiality and perjury (Banks 2017). I then briefly review types of crime committed by lawyers for personal benefit and then as a conduit of corruption (Middleton 2005; Middleton and Levi 2004, 2015) and risk to the legitimacy and credibility of criminal justice. The next section assesses this threat, if viewed as one, where defence lawyers employ every tactic—legal, breaching rules and illegal conduct—in defence of a client in a court of law. This is then placed into a theoretical framework of white-collar crime trying to explain why professionals engage in criminal acts alone or in concert with organized crime.

Chapter 11—*Conclusion: Equality in Criminal Justice—An Ideal We Are Still in Search Of?* In the final chapter, I will highlight the reach and problem of corruption in criminal justice and conclude that whilst corruption is impossible to stop completely, vested interests, which are sometimes the state criminal justice systems, and private sector need to take the matter of corruption seriously to secure the legitimacy and integrity if criminal justice is seen to be impartial and maintain at least enough credibility that its citizens in democratic nations value its existence.

References

Alpert, G. P., & Noble, J. J. (2009). Lies, True Lies and Conscious Deception: Police Officers and the Truth. *Police Quarterly, 12*, 237–254.

Anderson, S., & Heywood, P. M. (2009). The Politics of Perception Use and Abuse of Transparency International's Approach to Measuring Corruption. *Political Studies, 57*(4), 746–767.

Bacon, M. (2014). Police Culture and the New Policing Context. In J. Brown (Ed.), *The Future of Policing*. London: Routledge.

Banks, C. (2017). *Criminal Justice Ethics: Theory and Practice*. London: Sage.

Bartels, L., & Martinovic, M. (2017). Electronic Monitoring: The Experience in Australia. *European Journal of Probation, 9*(1), 80–102.

Beare, M. E. (2017). The Failures of Police Legitimacy: Attacks from Within. In V. Mitslegas, P. Alldridge, & L. Cheliotis (Eds.), *Globalisation, Criminal Law and Criminal Justice*. Oxford: Hart Publishing.

Beetham, D. (1991). *The Legitimation of Power*. London: Palgrave.

Bottoms, A., & Tankebe, J. (2012). Beyond Procedural Justice: A Dialogic Approach to Legitimacy in Criminal Justice. *Journal of Criminal Law and Criminology, 102*(1), 119–170.

Braimah, A. I. (2016). Are Judges Corrupt? An Empirical Analysis of the Ghana Judiciary. *Journal of Humanities and Social Science, 21*(8), 12–21.

Brooks, G. (2016). *Criminology of Corruption: Theoretical Approaches*. Basingstoke: Palgrave Macmillan.

Brooks, G., Lewis, C., Walsh, D., & Kim, H. (2013). *The Prevention of Corruption: Investigation, Enforcement and Governance*. Basingstoke: Palgrave Macmillan.

Brown, R., & Frank, J. (2006). Race and Officer Decision Making: Examining the Differences in Arrest Outcomes Between Black and White Officers. *Justice Quarterly, 23*(1), 86–126.

Browning, J. G. (2010). When All That Twitters Is Not Told. *Texas Bar Journal, 73*(3), 216–220.

Burkhardt, B. (2014). Private Prisons in Public Discourse: Measuring Moral Legitimacy. *Sociological Focus, 47*(4), 279–298.

Caldero, M. A., & Crank, J. P. (2011). *Police Ethics: The Corruption of Noble Cause*. Boston: Anderson.

Campbell, D. J., & Campbell, K. M. (2010). Soldiers as Police Officers/Police Officers as Soldiers: Role Evolution and Revolution in the United States. *Armed Forces and Society, 36*(92), 327–350.

Centre for the Advancement of Public Integrity. (2016). *Prison Corruption: The Problem and Some Potential Solutions*. Columbia Law School: Centre for the Advancement of Public Integrity.

Chang, J. J., & Liu, C. (2007). The Negligence Rule in the Presence of Judicial Corruption and Social Norms. *Atlantic Economic Journal, 35*, 203–215.

Coicaud, J. M. (2002). *Legitimacy and Politics: A Contribution to the Study of Political Right and Political Responsibility*. Cambridge: Cambridge University Press.

Cracknell, M. (2018). Post-release Reforms for Short Prison Sentences: Re-legitimising and Widening the Net of Punishment. *Probation Journal, 65*(3), 302–315.

Daftary-Kapur, T., Dumas, R., & Penrod, S. D. (2010). Jury Decision-Making Biases and How to Counter Them. *Legal and Criminological Psychology, 15*(1), 133–154.

Dal Bo, E. (2006). Regulatory Capture: A Review. *Oxford Review of Economic Policy, 22*(2), 203–225.

Del Pozo, B. (2005). One Dogma of Police Ethics: Gratuities and the 'Democratic Ethos' of Policing. *Criminal Justice Ethics, 24*(2), 25–46.

Diphoorn, T. (2016). Twilight Policing: Private Security Practices in South Africa. *British Journal of Criminology, 56*(2), 313–331.

Eisen, L. B. (2017). *Inside Private Prisons: An American Dilemma in the Age of Mass Incarceration*. New York: Columbia University Press.

Fitzgibbon, W. (2016). Innovation and Privatisation in the Probation Service in England and Wales. *British Journal of Community Justice, 14*(1), 71–76.

Fitzgibbon, W., & Lea, J. (2014). Defending Probation: Beyond Privatization and Security. *European Journal of Probation, 6*(1), 24–41.

Fitzgibbon, W., & Lea, J. (2017). Privatization and Coercion: The Question of Legitimacy. *Theoretical Criminology, 22*(4), 545–562.

Flake, D. F. (2015). When Any Sentence Is a Life Sentence: Employment Discrimination Against Ex-offenders. *Washington University Law Review, 93*(1), 45–102.

Foster, J. E., Horowitz, A. W., & Mendez, F. (2009). *An Axiomatic Approach to the Measurement of Corruption, Oxford Poverty & Human Development Initiative* (OPHI) (OPHI Working Paper No. 29). Oxford: Oxford Department of International Development and University of Oxford.

Foucault, M. (1977). *Discipline and Punish: The Birth of the Prison*. Harmondsworth: Penguin Books.

Gottschalk, M. (2015). *Caught: The Prison State and the Lockdown of American Politics*. Princeton, NJ: Princeton University Press.

Graham, H., & McIvor, G. (2017). Advancing Electronic Monitoring in Scotland: Understanding the Influences of Localism and Professional Ideologies. *European Journal of Probation, 9*(1), 62–79.
Graycar, A., & Prenzler, T. (2013). *Understanding and Preventing Corruption.* Basingstoke: Palgrave Macmillan.
Greitens, S. C. (2016). *Dictators and Their Secret Police: Coercive Institutions and State Violence.* Cambridge: Cambridge University Press.
Grillo, I. (2011). *El Narco: Inside Mexico's Criminal Insurgency.* New York: Bloomsbury.
Harnischfeger, J. (2003). The Bakassi Boys: Fighting Crime in Nigeria. *The Journal of Modern African Studies, 41*(1), 23–49.
Harvey, D. (2014). The Googling Juror: The Fate of the Jury Train in the Digital Paradigm. *New Zealand Law Review, 203,* 203–238.
Heywood, P. M. (2015). *Routledge Handbook of Political Corruption.* Abingdon: Routledge.
Heywood, P. M., & Wright, V. (1997). Executives, Bureaucracies and Decision-Making. In M. Rhodes, P. M. Heywood, & V. Wright (Eds.), *Development in West European Politics.* London: Macmillan.
Hough, D. (2015). *Corruption, Anti-corruption and Governance.* Basingstoke: Palgrave Macmillan.
Ivkovic, S. K. (2005). Police (Mis)behaviour: A Cross Cultural Study of Corruption Seriousness. *Policing: An International Journal of Police Strategies and Management, 28*(3), 546–566.
Johnston, M. (2005). *Syndromes of Corruption: Wealth, Power, Democracy.* Cambridge: Cambridge University Press.
Jones, S. (2006). *Criminology* (3rd ed.). Oxford: Oxford University Press.
Kane, R. J., & White, M. D. (2013). *Jammed Up: Bad Cops, Police Misconduct, and the New York City Police Department.* New York: New York University Press.
Kiernan, M. K., & Colley, E. (2012). Juror Misconduct in the Age of Social Networking. *Federation of Insurance and Corporate Counsel, Tampa, 62*(2) (Quarterly/Winter), 179–193.
Lessing, B. (2016). *Inside Out: The Challenge of Prison-Based Criminal Organizations* (Brookings Local Orders Papers Series 1–23).
Meagher, K. (2007). Hijacking Civil Society: The Inside Story of the Bakassi Boys Vigilante Group of South-Eastern Nigeria. *The Journal of Modern African Studies, 45*(1), 89–115.

Michelle, A. (2010). *The New Jim Crow: Mass Incarceration in the Age of Colorblindness*. New York: The New Press.
Middleton, D. J. (2005). The Legal and Regulatory Response to Solicitors Involved in Serious Fraud Is Regulatory Action More Effective Than Criminal Prosecution? *British Journal of Criminology, 45*, 810–836.
Middleton, D. J., & Levi, M. (2004). The Role of Solicitors in Facilitating 'Organized Crime': Situational Crime Opportunities and Their Regulation. *Crime, Law and Social Change, 42*, 123–161.
Middleton, D. J., & Levi, M. (2015). Let Sleeping Lawyers Lie: Organized Crime, Lawyers and the Regulation of Legal Services. *British Journal of Criminology, 55*, 647–668.
Miller, G. P. (2004). Bad Judges. *Texas Law Review, 83*(2), 431–487.
Miller, S. (2017). *Institutional Corruption: A Study in Applied Philosophy*. Cambridge: Cambridge University Press.
Monaghan, R. (2004). An Imperfect Peace: Paramilitary 'Punishments' in Northern Ireland. *Terrorism and Political Violence, 16*(3), 439–446.
Monaghan, R. (2008). Community-Based Justice in Northern Ireland and South Africa. *International Criminal Justice Review, 18*, 83–105.
Moss, B. (2018). Electronic Monitoring and Monitoring Probation: The Case of Ireland. *European Journal of Probation, 10*(2), 120–135.
Mullins, S., & Wither, J. K. (2016). Terrorism and Organized Crime. *Connections: The Quarterly Journal, 15*(3), 65–82.
Ochoa, J. A., & Tomas, C. L. (2016). Democracy and Vigilantism: The Case of Michoacán, Mexico. *International Journal for Crime, Justice and Social Democracy, 5*(4), 17–28.
Punch, M. (2000). Police Corruption and Its Prevention. *European Journal on Criminal Policy Research, 8*(3), 301–324.
Punch, M. (2003). Rotten Orchards: Pestilence, Police Misconduct and System Failure. *Policing and Society, 13*(2), 171–196.
Rodriguez, N. (2010). The Cumulative Effect of Race and Ethnicity in Juvenile Court Outcomes and Why Pre-adjudication Matters. *Journal of Research in Crime and Delinquency, 47*(3), 391–413.
Rose-Ackermann, S. (1978). *Corruption: A Study in Political Economy*. London: Academic Press.
Rothstein, B. (2011). *The Quality of Government: Corruption, Social Trust and Inequality in a Comparative Perspective*. Chicago: Chicago University Press.
Schlosser, E. (1998). The Prison Industrial Complex. *The Atlantic*, pp. 1–24.

Schmitt, J., & Warner, K. (2011). Ex-offenders and the Labor Market. *The Journal of Labor and Society, 14,* 87–109.
Skolnick, J. (2010). Enduring Issues of Police Culture and Demographics. *Policing and Society, 18*(1), 35–45.
Souryal, S. S. (2009). Deterring Corruption by Prison Personnel: A Principle-Based Perspective. *The Prison Journal, 89*(1), 21–45.
South, N. (1988). *Policing for Profit: The Private Security Sector.* London: Sage.
Spohn, C. (2015). Disadvantage and Sentencing of Black Defendants: Evolution of Sentencing Research. *Criminology and Public Policy, 14*(2), 1–8.
Standford, A. (2015). *Copping Out: The Consequences of Police Corruption and Misconduct.* Santa Barbara, CA: Praeger.
Sutherland, E. H. (1939). *Principles of Criminology* (3rd ed.). Philidelphia: Lippincott.
Tankebe, J. (2010). Public Confidence in the Police: Testing the Effects of Public Experiences of Police Corruption on Ghana. *British Journal of Criminology, 50,* 296–319.
Tonry, M. (2010). The Social, Psychological and Political Causes of Racial Disparities in the American Criminal Justice System. *Crime and Justice, 39*(1), 273–312.
Tonry, M. (2011). *Punishing Race: A Continuing American Dilemma.* New York: Oxford University Press.
Topping, J., & Byrne, J. (2012). Paramilitary Punishments in Belfast: Policing Beneath the Peace. *Journal of the Behavioural Sciences of Terrorism and Political Aggression, 4*(1), 41–45.
Transparency International. (2012). *Corruption Perception Index 2012.* London: Transparency International.
Tyler, J. C. (2014). Blind Injustice: The Supreme Court, Implicit Racial Bias and the Racial Disparity in the Criminal Justice System. *American Criminal Law Review, 51,* 689–713.
Van Dijk, J. (2015). The Case for Survey-Based Comparative Measures of Crime. *European Journal of Criminology, 12*(4), 437–456.
White, A. (2013, January 7). The Shadow State: Probation Chiefs Voice Doubts About Outsourcing. *New Statesman.*
White, A. (2014). Post-crisis Policing and Public–Private Partnerships: The Case of Lincolnshire Police and G4S. *British Journal of Criminology, 54*(6), 1002–1022.

White, A. (2015). The Politics of Police 'Privatization': A Multiple Streams Approach. *Criminology and Criminal Justice, 15*(3), 283–299.
Yadav, V., & Mukherjee, B. (2016). *The Politics of Corruption in Dictatorships*. Cambridge: Cambridge University Press.

2

What Is Criminal Justice Corruption?

Introduction

In this chapter, I emphasize the complex nature of what corruption is and how it is defined, and examine the reach of state power and criminal justice corruption that impacts on the legitimacy of justice. Furthermore, I highlight the reach of the privatization of criminal justice services that also seek legitimacy similar to the state to control and punish offenders.

In attempting to define any concept, act, or term and articulate it in such a way that it is understood, particularly beyond those familiar with the 'field of study', is a difficult task. This is particularly so with corruption (Heywood 2015). Any definition, as noted by Philp (2015) can have two elements; it can articulate the import and use of a word and also act as a tool to help construct an explanation; the social sciences are primarily concerned with the later as I am here. Understood as a tool, a definition aims to identify a set of criteria that suggests necessary and sufficient conditions for an act to occur. These, however,

G. Brooks, *Criminal Justice and Corruption*,
https://doi.org/10.1007/978-3-030-16038-8_2

differ depending on the theoretical approach, object of study and actual circumstances.

The object of study here is criminal justice and corruption and the key issues in this chapter are—state power, legitimacy and privatization. These are all historical and contemporary issues for criminal justice, and its ability to prevent and reduce corruption or inflame and encourage it. In some jurisdictions, the criminal justice system is little more than a crude vehicle of oppression that lacks both internal legitimacy from the majority or a substantial section of its own population (Greitens 2016; Yadav and Mukherjee 2016), and international legitimacy due to its application of state power. However, whilst criminal justice is often presented as 'blind' in democratic nations this also, at least, is questionable (Michelle 2010; Tyler 2014)? Keeping in mind that corruption can be viewed as unethical but legal to illegal and a civil and/or criminal breach of law(s) the role(s) criminal justice systems play in defining criminal acts of corruption, preventing it, punishing it and maintaining its own legitimacy often have a bearing on the type of criminal justice we encounter. This chapter is thus a brief review of state power, legitimacy and privatization of criminal justice systems and corruption; however, I start with a brief review of what corruption is and the problematic nature of its definition.

What Is Corruption?

The recurring problem we encounter in trying to construct a consistent and unambiguous definition of corruption is that political, social, and cultural factors undermine attempts to provide a definitive version of corruption. As a result, an identified unequivocal definition of corruption remains elusive. Corruption should therefore be viewed as a complex and multifaceted phenomena with a multiplicity of causes and effects, as it exhibits many different forms and functions in very diverse contexts, ranging from either a single act that transgresses a law(s) to a way of life for an individual, or people, and/or societal order, which is morally acceptable (Heywood 2015).

Exactly what counts as corruption is perhaps relative, but our understanding of it is rooted in social, political and cultural systems. Corruption is a product of its environment, history and social development as are criminal justice systems. We therefore fall into a trap whereby we try to define corruption as a technical problem that can be dealt with by changing processes and the incentive to act in a corrupt way must be blocked regardless of the often wide-ranging and diverse acts of corruption. It is also sometimes viewed as an illustration of moral decline: however, attention on morality alone is also flawed as it does little to assist those in the social sciences in explaining corruption with a focus instead on behavioural indicators and its potential manifestations.

The causes of corruption and subsequent solutions currently fall under three broad approaches; these are the rational economic, political science and legal approaches. I review each of these briefly in turn.

A rational-economic approach assumes that individuals, organizations and states simply act in self-interest. This view has dominated much of the debate about corruption and often proposes that the best way to reduce corruption is to reduce incentives to break rules by increasing the chances of apprehension and reducing avenues for corruption. However, there is little reference to criminal justice systems in the literature, and if we view people as self-interested why do police, prison, probation officers have such discretion to enforce the law? Discretion is needed to 'police' a population in the streets on in prison or on probation, and yet, here is the potential for corruption. Corrupt criminal justice officials do not always countenance the ultimate sanction, unless the acts are so egregious and criminal that a custodial sentence is the only option. Even then, this will not always materialize. If we view human behaviour in this self-interested way at the exclusion of other motivations our view of human conduct is that rules are followed or broken based on a cost–benefit analysis. But if an individual only acts in self-interest to secure maximum advantage it would be impossible to form working relationships, or at least only briefly, which are needed to be successful, and particularly in international law enforcement.

Local police can, however, simply build internal working relationships and claim to work for a community rather than with a community, and thus act in a corrupt way with little fear of potential sanctions (Beare 2017). In international law enforcement, however, individuals and organizations have to defer actions and sometimes abide by rules to achieve success. Lack of compliance with rules then is neither a statement that the individual or organization is, or is not corrupt. Such decision(s)—local, national or international—are conducted within a moral, legal, political framework and we are left with changes to the political and social structure or small adaptations in a stable context (Philp 2015) which fail to prevent corruption.

From a political science point of view the ultimate source of corruption, rent-seeking (this is where individuals/organizations seek to increase own wealth without producing new wealth) such as lobbying for state subsidies and/or imposing regulations on a competitor or a tax official seeking and accepting a bribe to reduce tax owed by the individual and/or organization (Warner 2015). In the criminal justice system, this rent-seeking could be demanding or accepting money or payment in kind not to arrest a person. Bribery, extortion and kickbacks could all be seen as rent-seeking in criminal justice systems as well. A reduction in incentives could range from a personal or official warning, temporary suspension and demotion, dismissed or charged for a criminal offence.

The solution often proposed is to introduce market competition into subsidized 'markets', which has happened with law enforcement, probation services and the prison sector in different jurisdictions (Eisen 2017; Fitzgibbon and Lea 2017). However, are the police a service to be purchased for those that can afford it or a public service for all citizens? In some cases, it appears that wealth and power, and race make a difference in how we are treated, depending on the jurisdiction (Michelle 2010; Tyler 2014). The police deliver a service to the affluent and powerful but seek rents from the poor and marginalized in some jurisdictions such as in the Philippines (Greitens 2016) where the police are seen as highly corrupt.

Criminal justice corruption can stem from political corruption. A tentative definition of political corruption then is: where a public official (A), violates the rules and/or norms of office, to the detriment of the interests of the public (B), (B) should benefit from this office but instead (A) benefits and a third party (C) who rewards or otherwise incentivizes them to secure access to products and/or services they would not otherwise obtain (Philp 2015: 22). This definition has some resonance regarding police corruption and links to organized crime. This definition does not assume that A, however, must break the law, and that corrupt acts do not need to always harm, or directly harm B (the public). The point here is that corruption is not defined solely by its consequences but more a combination of its intentions and distortion of process (Brooks 2016). Furthermore, if committing a corrupt act(s) to secure personal interests it is seen as corruption, but if rules are broken to secure wide public interest it can be seen as acceptable, depending on the acts e.g. a police officer(s) manufacture evidence to arrest a known criminal dealing in illegal narcotics. They have no personal financial reward, unless future promotion, but have stopped, perhaps temporarily the distribution of narcotics.

All political, bureaucratic and criminal justice systems can be corrupted by poor leadership—hence the refrain 'the fish rots from the head' but also from the body where it can undermine the process and be suborned by those in public office via bribes, lobbying and blackmail. These distinctions help recognize corruption as syndromes of corruption (Johnston 2005) where corruption is initiated from either A or C above. These economic and political views emphasize human agency and incentives, often with a focus on a corrupt bureaucracy and the existence of programmes that are vulnerable to corruption because of a lack of checks and balances to counter a monopoly, despite 'so-called' regulatory balances within the system (Philp 2015), as has often been exposed in law enforcement.

A legal approach suggests that the causes of corruption are mostly public sector vested interests ability to prevent, thwart enforcement of legal and/or regulatory rules, and laws where breaches occur. Yet again, this approach has some resonance for analysing criminal justice corruption. The problems with this approach are obvious when understanding how those in positions of power influence and shape the creation, and operation of the law, which can result in justifying inertia in the law when any changes in legislation would conflict with their own interests (Brooks 2016). In light of this legal definition, corrupt acts come to be viewed as an inappropriate yardstick; instead, they are more useful as measures of the influence of power than corruption (Brooks et al. 2013). In fact, it is often those that are supposed to uphold the law that are the most corrupt—unethical and/or criminal—and abuse the system and rule of law for personal benefit. Personal benefit, however, is often defended as a case of 'everybody was doing it' (which is also a technique of neutralization) (Sykes and Matza 1957) or actively seeking out corrupt avenues. Whilst an old example, the Knapp Commission's investigation into corruption in the New York Police Department in the 1970s described those that accepted bribes as part of the police culture as 'Grass-Eaters', whilst those that actively sought and demanded payments via threats and intimidation were referred to as 'Meat-Eaters'. Regardless of how these vegetarians and carnivores consumed, both were corrupt.

A lack of resources is often cited as the cause of regulatory lapses regardless of the sector but lack of oversight of organization and regulatory body and enforcement of sanctions are also significant. The key for this approach is to avoid any office having a monopoly in the distribution of a resource (Manzetti and Blake 1996; Andrews and Montinola 1998) but in the case of law enforcement, this is difficult to achieve even in democratic states. State law enforcement is the major and in some jurisdictions, only form of enforcement, unless we count the military in non-democratic states, but with the privatization in some 'western' jurisdictions such as England and Wales, USA and Australia, state law enforcement is now part of a 'policing family'.

This legal approach is also somewhat vague, particularly when trying to define and explain transnational corruption with the involvement of more than one jurisdiction. Using legal definitions, without an internationally established definition, simply increases the difficulty in undertaking operational measures and developing anti-corruption strategies (those that work anyway). A legal definition also requires, by its own very definition, that the corrupt behaviour should violate a principle of legality. However, not all-corrupt behaviour is illegal. It would be a misconception to confuse what is corrupt with what is illegal. Rules can be bent but not always broken or transgressed. Social norms are defined by values, as are laws, but not necessarily emerging from equivalent ideologies or foundations (Brooks et al. 2013). Furthermore, examining different cultural factors across the world, legal definitions are highly unsatisfactory.

All of these approaches, but mostly those that focus on the rational economic reason(s) for committing corruption use what is known as the principal–agent theory. Corruption is seen as a departure between the principal (those employing and/or directing) and the agent (such as a employee). Once the agent betrays the principal interest (public service) in pursuit of self-interest (Klitgaard 1988; Heywood 2015) corruption has occurred. This view of corruption then focuses on the conditions under which this corruption took place, this often entails a monopoly of resources, and lack of accountability, and thus looks for ways to design incentives (or disincentives) for the agent to act in the appropriate way to prevent corruption. This is a flawed approach in criminal justice, however, if the principal (high ranking police and prison officers and/or state prosecutors) directs agents (lower ranking officers/personnel) to behave in a corrupt manner, s/he can later deny any order was stated, and if the principal (high ranking police and prison officers and/or state prosecutors) directs agents (lower ranking officers/personnel) to uphold laws but the culture of lowest ranked officers is to discount them, corruption will occur. Discounting the laws and/or direction of them, however, by law enforcement if dealing with an egregious crime could help the public e.g. breach laws to prevent a serious crime(s). Such act(s) are at once corrupt (breached laws) yet beneficial to the public. These causal conditions, however, are limited. Probity in public office is explained by the absence of monopoly and high levels of accountability. This 'ideal' state of affairs is exactly that; 'ideal', but in reality much more complex. Therefore, these definitions of human behaviour, which is popular in the corruption literature, is limited, as so much depends on the structure and expectations that frame a relationship.

Whilst the above section considered rational economic, political and legal approaches to corruption I now draw predominantly on sociology and criminology and the disciplines explanatory power to understand state power, legitimacy and privatization of criminal justice and corruption.

State Power, Crime and Corruption

As noted in the introduction to this chapter corruption can range from legal but ethically questionable to illegal and criminal acts. Whilst we might disagree on what corruption is and how it can be defined, if at all, and if it should be criminal and punished accordingly, the exercise of power is not in doubt. How power is conceptualized and defined can vary depending on the discipline; definitions range from the capacity to direct and/or influence others or the course of events or resources; political and/or social power (Rothe and Kauzlarich 2016: 4); or in possessing power to order, control and act that has been delegated to individuals and organizations such as the police. For power to legitimately be used we expect, particularly with criminal justice, it to be exercised with care in protecting its citizens. This can, of course, depend on the political context—democratic or dictatorship.

As illustrated by Foucault (1977) power is exercised through legitimacy, by applying resources at its disposal, such as the power to control the discourse of a problem or event, reaffirming and reproducing itself. These mechanisms of power—the way in which it is dispersed—then produce 'knowledge' that reinforces the exercise of that power (Rothe and Kauzlarich 2016: 49). This is particularly noticeable regarding discourse; here the powerful can define the problem, or dismiss it as one. Once defined, rules, set parameters of how the 'problem' is/can be discussed, which in turn frames the 'truth' about the subject (Foucault 1980). An example here is that of the police in England and Wales' ability to define football fans at the Hillsborough Football stadium, along with high-profile figures and select newspapers as hooligans and animals (Scraton 2016), which persisted for many years after the event, but was eventually disclosed as mostly a manufactured, misleading account of what happened.

Power and those powerful enough to exercise it then can craft the conditions of supporting, enabling and managing unequal power relationships in either a brutal or subtle form. Brutal application of power lacks legitimacy but if framed as democratic and consensual it can appear to have legitimacy. As Gramsci (1971) noted hegemony can, if successful, lead to a situation where leadership is viewed as the natural state of affairs. Hegemony though is best understood as a process rather than end state, as an effort to naturalize and normalize a particular state of affairs rather than promise its achievement. 'Truth' or the discourse of truth is thus a construct of political and economic forces and of those that hold power. Truth thus becomes understood as common sense, or presented as such, and accepted as a way of thinking about a problem/issue, and what should be done about it. This is circular, however—the powerful can define a problem, then produce and sustain and extend it thus becoming a regime of truth (Foucault 1977: 2), which buttresses legitimate power.

Living under an absolute monarchy or a dictatorship power is perhaps more naked and brutal and seen only as legitimate by those with a vested interest in acquiring and maintaining power, but in democratic nations the maintenance of power is in constant negotiation to secure legitimacy and hold on to power. This negotiation for legitimacy is clearly seen in criminal justice systems in democratic nations but due to acts of corruption often falls short of its professed ideals and claims to legitimacy.

Whilst criminology is a discipline that has crime as its object of study, and there are many criminal acts of corruption, it has rarely been the focus of the voluminous literature in criminological research, unless of course the focus of attention is on law enforcement. This, however, is only one agency of state control and power and I suggest we need a systematic analysis of criminal justice systems as they can all sustain the regime of power beyond the police. Criminology often, but not always, uses the criminal law as its basis on which to define crime. In the case of corruption, the criminal law definition covers a substantial corpus of work but as stated above this definition fails to encapsulate the range of crimes that are part of the continuum of corruption (Brooks 2016) where lobbying and networking dilute, change laws and/or prevent them from reaching the statute book, as well as acts that might not be criminal but are a conduit to criminal corruption such as breaching environmental standards.

The majority of research so far, in criminology, has focused on policing and organized crime. This is due to the power invested in the police and the international reach of organized crime and its threats to the international legal economy (Gounev and Ruggiero 2012) where police collusion in some cases highlights criminal justice abuse of state power. In the case of corruption, differences in jurisdictions are made at political, enforcement and administrative level and that these links and types of behaviour between and within criminal justice, organized crime and legitimate business are sometimes similar. I do not claim that all criminal justice systems are corrupt, only that it sometimes is working with, and knowingly in collusion with organized crime, or because of poor internal regulation and compliance procedures that it commits a criminal act(s) or specifically individual officers or specialized units such as narcotics move beyond the parameters of legal state power.

The study of organized crime has stimulated attention on corruption but so far offered limited analysis of criminal justice, particularly as a whole, and instead made reference to corruption as if it is 'out there' in a country that is dismissed as corrupt (e.g. Russia) whilst ignoring democratic states or still presenting them as isolated incidents and acts of bad apples and rogue individuals (Punch 2003), which have been resoundingly dismissed (Brooks 2016). Even if overwhelming evidence of criminal justice corruption is available delay tactics, attempts to obfuscate the law and/or seek a civil remedy are employed. The same can be said of white-collar crime highlighted by Sutherland (1939) where the criminal law failed to cover all forms of white-collar crime which were, and still are, settled outside criminal justice by a civil law procedure or company disciplinary rules. One of the explanations for their exclusion from the definition of crime was and still is the social network. The social network refers to the culturally homogeneity of people such as judges where close personal relationships (see Chapter 6), and power relationships protect people from critical state definitions of crime(s) (Kramer et al. 2002) which are instead often presented as 'errors' and/or an individual mistake.

This concept of occupational white-collar passive corruption is also relevant in criminal justice systems. This is where an employee, in a public or private organization, has abused his position of power for personal benefit. Whilst it is the case that the offender(s), which could be law enforcement, magistrates, judges, probation employees and prison officers, all have some personal responsibility regarding passive corruption, the organizational and social context cannot be dismissed. Frequently, acts of corruption are a hybrid mixture of personal characteristics of the person(s) involved and the impact of organizational aspects such as organizational structure, culture, social cohesion and style of leadership and elements external to the organization such as the legal framework and law enforcement. Punch (2000, 2003) amply illustrated the complexity of occupational crime in his research on police corruption where he rejects the notion of a 'bad apple' and focuses more on bad orchards, and the institutional context where the organization, kind of work and the culture play a key-role (Huisman and Vande Walle 2010). In fact, a 'bad apple' can turn the whole barrel rancid. This is perhaps illustrated by the Macpherson Report (1999) of institutional racism in the Metropolitan Police in England, but prudence is still called for establishing a causal link (Punch 2000) between attitudes and acts of corruption and abuse of state power.

If systematic, however, rampant corruption in criminal justice systems is a state crime. Harmful behaviours committed by individuals and or organizations in some states, often employed in the criminal justice system as a tool of suppression upon its internal citizens (Chambliss 1989; Brooks 2016) are unquestionably corrupt. But it is 'below the radar corruption' in democratic nations that destabilize and undercut the legitimacy of criminal justice. The state is therefore also vulnerable in both democratic and non-democratic states to state capture, and particularly that of regulatory capture (Dal Bo 2006) where oversight is redirected, thwarted, and obfuscated for and by powerful public sector interests such as law enforcement and private vested interests (Brooks et al. 2013). State capture is and can be all or part of the infrastructure of the state and the services it delivers to its citizens, and the state is both a mechanism of control but also dependent upon criminal justice for order.

Explanations for acts of corruption then can be found on several levels: the level of individual social interactions, organizational level of structural and cultural characteristics of organizations and the institutional level of political economy and regulation (Kramer and Michalowski 2006). Vaughan (2002) has emphasized the importance of understanding these interconnections and the relationships between the environment, the organizational setting and the behaviour of individuals for acts of corruption, where on the macro-level, the criminogenic effect is attributed to the 'culture of competition' (Coleman 1995: 363). In this view, importance is placed on wealth and success, people are seen as autonomous individuals with powers of reason and free choice and therefore responsible for their own condition. The culture of competition defines the competitive struggle for personal achievement as positive, rather than negative or selfish. Competition is presented as producing maximum economic value, but this demand for success and the pursuit of wealth is seen by some as criminogenic in itself (Merton 1938; Punch 1996; Slapper and Tombs 1999) as law enforcement manufacture evidence to secure a conviction, judges extort and accept bribes (see Chapter 6), lawyers withhold key evidence to secure a conviction (see Chapter 10). Furthermore, the principle of calculated self-interest collides with the principles of sharing and reciprocal exchange, which is expected and necessary if transnational law enforcement is to be successful in dealing with international, cross border crimes.

The contribution to understanding and explaining corruption is wide and complex then, and focuses on individuals, organizations and the state, the motivation to act alone or in collusion, the concept of power and ability to define what is corrupt, our ability to think and act as 'free' rational individuals but also be constrained by the position we inhabit in our social structure, the ability to reject corruption as a choice and label 'others' as corrupt and justify acts of corruption. In this context then, how can criminal justice secure and maintain legitimacy? This is discussed in the next section.

Criminal Justice and Legitimacy

For any democratic criminal justice system to claim that its role is to protect people and punish offenders it needs legitimacy. But what is meant by legitimacy? In this section of the book, I clarify what is meant by legitimacy by drawing on work from political science, sociology, psychology and criminal justice. There are, of course, key elements to legitimacy regardless of the discipline and business that is under analysis, but for criminal justice, I will mainly focus on the dual and interactive character of legitimacy that considers those that hold and exercise power, the audiences and those subjected to it. There is evidence that highlights the importance of legitimacy in relation to the police (Tyler and Wakslak 2004), prison inmates (Useem and Kimball 1989; Sparks and Bottoms 2008) and the public (Tyler 1990, 2003) where people are treated by criminal justice professionals in either a 'fair' or disrespectful manner. Central to criminal justice legitimacy is that it is dialogic (Bottoms and Tankebe 2012) where claims to legitimacy by those that hold power are accepted or contested by those that are subjected it.

Before I progress though, a note of caution is needed here. I will refer to legitimacy which is focused on the present; concerned with recognition of the moral rightness of claims to exercise power here and now, rather than in the future. This is different from, and should not be confused with trust. Trust tends to be future orientated and can be defined as a positive expectation regarding individuals, and possibly institutional, future actions (Barbalet 2009).

The main theoretical approach to legitimacy is that of procedural justice (Tyler 1990) where we have instrumental and normative obedience to law(s); the normative obedience is then subdivided into personal morality (e.g. a set of principles on which we act) and legitimacy (our perception as to whether law enforcement officials rightly have authority and power to exercise). For Tyler people comply with the law not because they fear punishment but because they see law enforcement as legitimate. Here then, we see that normative compliance is considered more important than instrumental compliance if those that hold and wield power are to be seen as legitimate. If criminal justice is seen as procedurally fair it can lead to acceptance of the decision/outcome of a case and thus initial ascription of legitimacy. It follows that if the police, criminal justice process, and sentence passed are seen as legitimate, the public and those that are drawn into the criminal justice system are more willing to accept law enforcement orders and judicial sentences. This might be acceptable to those engaged with criminal justice before sentence but once imprisoned is legitimacy and power to punish maintained? Sparks et al. (1996) considered this to be a perennial problem in the prison system, as custodial institutions suffer occasional complete or near-complete breakdowns of order.

Research has also shown the importance of procedural justice in the prison system, but also beyond as officials have to consider their legitimacy in relation to more than one audience. These audiences have different issues that are significant to them (Liebling 2000, 2005, 2007; Eisen 2017). In the case of the prison system, this is obvious as mental health needs and acts of crime committed by inmates is diverse, but these are in contrast to the often punitive public view of how offenders should be treated. Procedural process, whilst important, is limited in scope since with competing definitions of legitimacy, particularly in law enforcement and criminal justice systems, it fails to really address what factors produce and sustain legitimacy, and how competing calls by different audiences with different interests are dealt with.

Since Weber (1978) is central to legitimacy, however, his work is a platform on which to base the debate regarding legitimacy. For Weber, the modern state, described as a compulsory organization with a territorial basis, the use of force is regarded as legitimate only so far as it is either permitted by the state or prescribed by it. Furthermore, it can explain the delegation of power of private policing and private prison sector developments, as they are under some kind of state regulation. If a state contracts out the running and management of a prison to the private sector it still continues to claim the right to determine under what circumstances the employees can use legitimate force. Some states, however, have passed power to international institutions such as the European Union, placing limitations on what individual states can do to its own citizens. Of course, such a position and accommodation is always open to withdrawal by the state. The examination of the legitimacy of the work of law enforcement officials is then of vital significance as law enforcement can and does reach beyond the daily exercise of power.

For Weber, there were pure types of legitimate domination: these are traditional, charismatic and legal-rational. Domination in this sense is the probability that a command in a specific context will be followed by some if not all. However, those in a position of power do not simply anticipate all citizens and those from particular groupings will always submit to commands regardless of whether obedience stems from (1) material motives (such as self-interest), (2) an emotional (affectual) affinity with the power-holder, or (3) ideal motives (such a philosophical or religious beliefs according to which citizens consider that it is their duty to obey) (Bottoms and Tankebe 2012: 128). We therefore could be motivated to 'follow the rules' by one or more of these motives; for Weber, though those that hold power will seek to secure obedience and attempt to establish and to cultivate the belief in legitimacy. Securing legitimacy then is an ongoing process and for legitimate domination it is not necessary that citizens accept the claim to legitimacy, nor any subsequent acts of obedience primarily (or even at all) oriented to legitimacy. As such we simply follow the law for a variety of non-normative reasons such as self-interest or weakness or that we are helpless. These 'reasons' are highly relevant to people that live under a dictatorship, or incarcerated in a prison, or simply an act of personal survival in a volatile environment.

Zelditch (2001) sees public legitimacy as a decision made and rules enacted by an individual or institution as 'right' and 'proper'. Such an approach centres on the reactions by citizens to judgments and rules made, a 'right to rule' assessed with reference to those that hold power and those that confer it upon them. Coicaud (2002) saw legitimacy as recognition of the right to rule where the normative character of legitimacy is emphasized where there is a positive recognition by citizens of someone to hold and exercise power and that any discussion on legitimacy must embrace those who exercise political power and those who are expected to conform. Here then legitimacy is seen as the recognition of the right to rule and if successfully established rationalizes the actions of those in a position of power—individuals and/or institution—and those that are obedient. By implication legitimacy within this definition is seen as conditional. For example, most citizens of a state might recognize a person of power or institution as having the right to rule, but if this power is corrupted the public recognition of a right to rule will be withdrawn and eventually challenged unless addressed (Bottoms and Tankebe 2012).

For Raz (2009) though, legitimate power is an intermingling of the notions of 'power' and 'right'. This approach distinguishes three kinds of individuals or institutions that hold effective power to command others: these are individuals or institutions that wield naked power; those with de facto power, and those with legitimate power. Those that wield naked power terrorize a population by dictatorship or on a small scale hostage situation, do not claim the right to rule, or suggest those under its control have a moral obligation to conform; it is hoped that orders are followed based on a combination of physical threats and fear, or a self-interested calculation of the consequences of resistance (Bottoms and Tankebe 2012).

De facto power is similar but differs in that they always claim legitimacy (in the sense of a right to rule). Here there is an attempt to legitimize power by claiming some element of the right to exercise it but such individuals/organizations are still only a de facto power and not a legitimate source of power because they have failed to secure a public audience in recognition of their right to rule. De facto power, however, can be divided into subtypes: (1) those in a position of power and effective command of a territory and claim authority such as a prison and (2) claims to legitimacy are accepted by the public as technically 'valid', yet acceptance is not 'recognition of the right to rule'. This second de facto power and acceptance might be secured by weakness and helplessness due to a lack of an alternative. This is seen in contexts such as the prison sector where there is a radical power differential between inmates and prison officers, depending on country and prison (Lessing 2016). In such situations, the powerless might have mixed emotions: it is accepted that someone has to hold power, but those that hold power hold effective de facto power and are therefore useful in providing a basic flow of essential services but powerless people have no way of challenging such de facto power and so 'respect' those in a position of power.

In this sense power-holders have minimal valid authority and this de facto power is simply dull compulsion/compliance rather than legitimate power. In the prison literature, it is well recognized that dull compulsion (Carrabine 2004) exists and the distinction between legitimacy and dull compulsion is, conceptually, of importance in criminal justice contexts, and it can also have significant practical consequences (Bottoms and Tankebe 2012). This dull compulsion though can be to prison officers or organized crime that 'runs' a prison (Lessing 2016).

This is a theoretical framework and as such in the real world the boundary between each of them will blur as individuals and criminal justice institutions are made to change because of some explicit act of corruption or bias.

Virtually all criminal justice systems, however, regardless of how brutal, claim to be legitimate as do corrupt organizations and law enforcement. The claim, no matter if viewed by some or many as bankrupt is an attempt at cultivation. Here, people with power attempt to communicate with audiences in an ongoing relationship since legitimacy must appear dialogic and relational in character (Bottoms and Tankebe 2012: 129). In power or seeking a claim to power to be legitimate is made by an individual and/or institution/organization, and then adjusted based on the public response. The response, however, can be brutal and violent or one of compromise. Legitimacy then is not a single transaction but an ongoing search for legitimacy. It therefore follows that it is possible for a criminal justice institution to be legitimate such as a prison, and yet also corrupt and prejudiced. If inmates accept the rules of confinement or a death penalty but public pressure challenges such a state of affairs the criminal justice system can be both legitimate and morally bankrupt at the same to different audiences.

However, what factors fashion and sustain and/or undermines criminal justice legitimacy? Both Beetham (1991) and Coicaud (2002) independently developed the same threefold conceptualization of the key factors of legitimacy. These are legal validity such as conformity to rules, shared values that justify these rules and consent. The opposite of these are illegitimacy (a breach of the established rules), a legitimacy deficit (a difference, a gap between rules and values or absence of shared values) and de-legitimation such as a withdrawal of consent.

This exercise of power, however, needs to be located within a respected legal framework. For Beetham (1991) power can be considered legitimate if it is acquired and exercised in accordance with established rules. These rules though can range from established laws or established unwritten conventions. In a law enforcement context, Dixon (1997: 1–2) emphasized that "a central tenet of the police claim to legitimacy is their subordination to law". This legitimacy is, however, challenged once criminal justice corruption is exposed.

Following established rules and laws is thus expected of law enforcement and criminal justice officials. Consent is and can be withdrawn and obedience declined if law enforcement and the criminal justice system have a blatant lack of obedience to law, or an absence of self-restraint. However, full enforcement of the law, or the prison rules, can sometimes fail to enhance legitimacy; indeed, it can even lead to a degree of de-legitimation. If the police set out to reduce street crime, such an approach can destabilize local, social order (Beare 2017). Full enforcement of the law then, can in some circumstances lead to disorder. Within a specific context, law enforcement might need to choose between law enforcement and the maintenance of public order.

Such an analysis is also valid in a prison context. Sykes (1958) highlighted how prison officers negotiate a series of 'understandings' with inmates in order to maintain a reasonable system of social order. Even though prison officers have substantial power strict enforcement of the rules is not always applied. Instead, the maintenance of order rather than strict adherence to rules and laws is followed. This was the case in the Maze prison in Northern Ireland where well-disciplined members of a paramilitary organization were able to organize concerted campaigns to obtain a reduction in the enforcement of rules.

These above examples might be extreme cases but the law functions, if it does, in a social context. This context is often presented as 'shared values' or at least prevailing values. Discussing values is problematic but for this book, I present them as a moral system of principles that appeal to action(s) by consensus.

Beetham (1991) suggested that those that hold power are only legitimate to the extent that the rules of power can be justified and shared by both prevailing and subordinate elements within a community/society/nation. To be legitimate then three 'tests' need to be passed: (1) to exercise power it must come from a valid source of legitimate power/authority (2) the power should be exercised in a manner that is considered justified in the context in which it is used and (3) the exercise of power must be seen to serve a recognizable public interest, rather than simply the interests of those that hold power. Shared values therefore set limits that define the conditions within which legitimate power may be exercised (negative effects), as well as providing those who govern with rules and resources within which they can seek to realize certain societal objectives (positive effects) (Bottoms and Tankebe 2012: 142).

How does this work in practice though? The law and law enforcement are not homogenous concepts; they are contested. All those in law enforcement, as acts of corruption show, do not work to a set of practices based on a single set of values. 'Rules' might be a set of principles influenced by the formal law, but often differ in practice (Punch 2000, 2003, 2009). Divergence from the rules is then hidden and/or covered by the police, who have developed 'presentational rules' that provide an acceptable appearance to the divergence from formal law to working to a 'local practice'. We therefore have two types of legitimacy; (1) legitimacy of the official legal system (the law in the books) and (2) legitimacy of the law in practice (local law officers' actual conduct and attempts to present such conduct as acceptable).

For Coicaud (2002), though consent is where the identification of power exists and continues only as long as normative consent exists. If consent is withdrawn, political, cultural, criminal justice legitimacy is undermined. If force is used instead of consent authority has already failed. However, many working in law enforcement and in custodial institutions sometimes use force. Once used, and if known rather than hidden, a debate follows on the acceptance of or criticism of excessive use of force (Beare 2017). The police in such a case will secure consent from specific sections of the public but criticism from others such as the use of force by police officers in the USA and black men (Tyler 2014). However, many police forces/services as they can be both, attempt to 'police by consent'. For whilst the state claims a monopoly in prescribing or permitting the legitimate use of force, which is often used by criminal justice officials, it insists, if at least a democratic nation, that such power is used sparingly, recognizing that where force is used, consensual authority has failed.

Raz (2009) claimed that consent, if willing, is preemptive. This is where the public agree in advance to treat laws and orders of that state as superseding and replacing personal judgment. Furthermore, an act of real consent changes the situation between those that hold power and those that are subjected to it. Preemptive and normative consent is not a 'one-off act of identification' (Bottoms and Tankebe 2012: 135). Rather it is an additional reason to respect authoritative directives and affects all encounters with individual and institutional 'power'. In the context of criminal justice some, not all, members of the public engage with law enforcement e.g. as witnesses or consultation on local policing and as such power is recognized and accepted as legitimate.

All of these types and notions of legitimacy, however, function on the understanding of 'shared' or as close as we can have 'shared values'. As previously noted, though, procedural justice encompasses different values: the quality of process by those in power, independence and neutrality, technical competence and consistency of decisions, particularly in similar cases, quality of treatment, and how the subject (the person) is treated; e.g. dignity, personal privacy, respect for moments of weakness. Research has shown that the absence of either quality of decision-making or quality of treatment can be powerfully de-legitimating (Bottoms and Tankebe 2012).

However, a note of caution is needed about the procedural justice approach. Secular changes in police legitimacy from one epoch to another could be different from explanations to individuals change(s), and that prior views, engagement with law enforcement, judiciary etc. are a powerful factor that can determine legitimacy or illegitimacy. This is perhaps hardly surprising in that our socialization and primary or secondary experience of law enforcement shape our views on legitimacy. How then is legitimacy maintained?

Beetham (1991) has argued, political legitimacy requires both a morally authoritative source and an ability to satisfy the ends which justify its enormous concentration of power. In the context of policing, attempting to manage legitimacy would therefore simply seek to demonstrate and appeal to its effectiveness. If this is the case effectiveness is a necessary but not a sufficient condition of legitimacy. Herbert (2006) suggested that no simple solution(s) are available to enhance police legitimacy. For Herbert legitimacy embraces elements of three different conditions for the police service: (1) the police must be subservient to public needs within an elective democracy; (2) a legitimate police service requires a degree of separation from the public, to uphold, if needed, the liberal values of the liberal-democratic state and to maintain police esprit de corps; and (3) the coordination of its nations citizens such as road traffic management. Although, as Herbert recognizes, sometimes a commitment to the norms of police culture can, in fact, override the commitment to liberal values it is suggested that to be fully legitimate, the police sometimes need to go beyond a reactive stance and become proactive, in generating (or constructively promoting) appropriate kinds of local social order (Bottoms and Tankebe 2012).

Those in a position of power though must convince themselves' that the exercise of power is acceptable and justified. Legitimacy may be important for the stability and effectiveness of power since unless those who exercise power are convinced that there is an adequate moral justification for continuation in office, it is doubtful they will be effective. A loss of 'internal legitimacy' can lead to disorganization of behaviour and an inability to perform as officers, judges etc. In addition, legitimacy can be regarded as a precondition for successful audience legitimacy; that is, it is necessary for those that hold power to cultivate credibility in the moral rightness of their own legitimacy prior to making claims to others to be legitimate. Furthermore, legitimacy within criminal justice contexts must contain an examination of the responses by those that hold power if seeking legitimacy. This dialogic framework highlights that legitimacy is constantly in flux and claims to legitimacy are contested and revised to justify a right to rule.

This complex dual role underscores the importance of ordinary officers' cultivation of appropriate (and not excessive) self-confidence in their moral right to exercise the enormous powers vested in them. However, such confidence can become outright corruption or noble cause corruption—the manufacture of evidence or testilying (Beare 2017) regarding a suspect and/or inflicting 'punishment' in the aftermath of a prison riot to inmates. In these actions, officers claim a normative validity beyond that which the state represents. In a criminal justice context, the development of legitimacy to rule and exercise power is best understood as the cultivation of self-confidence in the moral rightness of authority, within a framework of both official laws and regulations, and normative expectations (Bottoms and Tankebe 2012: 154).

Legitimacy then is important for consensual social order that can lead to legal compliance by citizens from either dull compulsion or willingness to engage with law enforcement, and subsequently a better flow of intelligence on local social order in a neighbourhood or within a prison. However, individual self-evaluation and institutional reflection can help lead to and/or increase legitimacy. Legitimacy should result in a critical self-awareness by police and prison officers, probation officers, lawyers, magistrates and judiciary and the ways in which power is exercised. This should in turn help to explain interactions that criminal justice employees and most of all police and prison officers with differential levels of self-legitimacy might have with citizens, including the use (deadly) force. The problem here is that conflict and coercion even in democratic nations are part of criminal justice systems work. It is impossible to avoid conflict, as this book will show, but it is how it is dealt with by individuals and institutions and if engagement with those ill-treated is considered, an honest and a candid attempt to resolve a matter of conflict.

Legitimacy in criminal justice is, in a democratic state an ongoing negotiation with some members of a country, blindly accepted by some, tacitly accepted by some, and selectively considered by some. Legitimacy is therefore elusive and multifaceted and in democratic nations needs to distinguish itself from an absolute monarch and dictatorship. Criminal justice corruption in democratic nations is far more damaging to its legitimacy than in a dictatorship where dull compulsion is paramount rather than public consent to exercise power, and many of the examples in this book disappointedly highlight the abuse of power in the name of criminal justice.

The Privatization of Criminal Justice

The privatization of criminal justice, particularly in some jurisdictions is a return to the past as criminal justice was primarily based on the power to purchase access to 'the law'. Once the major source of 'justice' where the ability to pay determined access, or in the case of prison, release, private involvement in criminal justice was promoted as customary and appropriate. Edged out with the development of the modern state, which had a virtual monopoly of state power, the private sector has returned to make profitable inroads into criminal justice once more. This part of the chapter then explores why this has happened, the changes in political and social thought on the use of the private sector to use 'legitimate coercion'. This has primarily been achieved by hollowing out (Rhodes 1994) the state and passing work from the police, probation, and prison system to the private sector. This 'extended police family' has developed systems of policing, in close cooperation with the state, on populations that they claim to help e.g. those in need of social housing. This is not a direct challenge to the state's ultimate monopoly of legitimate coercion, as it is still the inspector and custodian of the legal frameworks governing private sector contracts (Fitzgibbon and Lea 2017) to deliver a service(s), but this development is often downplayed and fails to consider the opportunity and power for the private sector to exercise day-to-day coercion and constraint of specific populations and/or geographical locations that were once public. In addition, private sector employees can and do lock inmates or suspects in cells, administer fixed penalty notices and sanction offenders for breaches of probation; these are profound issues of who has and who should have the legitimate power to punish.

In the United Kingdom 'modern' privatization started in the early 1990s, particularly the prison service. At this time privatization of criminal justice was limited and on the political margins. Such views have now changed, but still contested by prison reform organizations (Teague 2012; Hogg 2012; Fitzgibbon and Lea 2014, 2017). It needs to be noted though that to outsource is different from outright privatization. A crude distinction to outsource is to keep under contract and outright privatization is 'free' from contractual obligation with a state.

Developments occurred in policing in England and Wales as well: The Police Reform Act 2002 allowed Chief Constables (the highest rank of officers in England and Wales) to delegate specific police powers to non-police employees. In addition, the legislation created the Police Community Support Officer (PCSO are employed by the police but have limited powers). They can, however, issue Penalty Notices for Disorder (PNDs under the 2001 Criminal Justice Police Act) covering different types of anti-social behaviour and can search and detain a suspect for a short time pending the arrival of a police officer(s). The same legislation also provided for the delegation of similar powers to employees of private organizations/security patrolling public space.

The core change is a process of 'hollowing out' (Rhodes 2991) of state legitimacy without compromising the state as the ultimate repository of legitimate coercion. A distinction between the determination and allocation of punishment (Genders 2002) where the initial (legitimate) judgements by state officials—the police arresting a suspect or offender, initial probation assessment and court sentence—is used to justify subsequent acts by non-state employees if employed by a private company awarded a contract. This distinction is, of course, contested by reference to the fact that the management of sentenced populations will encompass independent potentially punitive judgements by prison officers and probation officers, which can and do result in variations in the harshness of prison and probation conditions, length of sentence and breach of license (Eisen 2017). The power to punish in this sense is not simply the allocation and management of the original sentence (South 1997; Moyle 1995, 2001) nor of course, restricted to the private sector because the public sector can also be sites of unchecked discretion exercised by individuals with personal interest.

However, a private company has to make a profit which can lead to a 'change' in the original sentence based on the search for profit and thus deployment of private sector resources. Illustrated by the recent privatization of the probation service in England, some organizations are tempted into all sorts of 'innovative' solutions that profoundly influence the actual conditions of the offenders' supervision (see Chapter 8) (Fitzgibbon and Lea 2014; Fitzgibbon 2016).

Policing private space such as a shopping centre raises equally complex questions of legitimacy. Private security firms (South 1988) now muddy the waters of what is the appropriate and legitimate use of power. The notion of policing in a democratic country is associated with the use of discretion and regulation (Reiner 2010; Bronitt and Stenning 2011; Beare 2017). The changing nature of policing public space though has changed with the rise of private security, police and citizens. The police can choose from a variety of sanctions available such as warning the offenders or arrest depending on the circumstances and 'attitude' and behaviour of the suspect. Discretion though is slowly displaced with a transactional process of enforcement in which a specific violation is dealt with by either police officers or private security with a fixed penalty notice depending on the location.

This is delegation of legitimacy: a private company secures its legitimacy via the state and/or local council and delegated subset of police powers. In reality, the use of discretion is limited to the decision to apply a penalty notice in a particular incident or pay no attention to it. The reality that private security personnel will engage with the 'offender' to prevent a crime in the manner of traditional police officers is problematic. This is hampered by the actual levels of a lack of status, authority and capacity to emit 'control signals' (Jackson et al. 2013; Rowland and Coupe 2014) or to participate in a 'legitimacy dialogue' (Bottoms and Tankebe 2012: 159) but state criminal justice systems, in neo-liberal jurisdictions, can construct a political climate where the private sector is an option, but at reduced cost.

The advance of delegated legitimacy in the penal systems and policing is attributed to social and political changes. Burkhardt (2014) claims, in the USA, that the private prison sector has secured acceptability by lobbying and arguing it is cost effective and flexible and beneficial and can supplement the state prison sector. Presenting itself in this way it has sidelined any debates regarding legitimacy. But this alone is insufficient to explain the rise of the private sector in criminal justice (Eisen 2017). A neo-liberal order that emboldened a focus on the individual and community as a source of resilience and self-reliance with a stress on crime control and prevention is conducive to public acceptance of security as a commodity to be bought and sold. This is part of the responsibilization strategy (Garland 1996) where the public are expected to become far more responsible for their own safety and blamed for their failure(s). Security is thus a commodity, if it can be afforded, but the question of legitimacy remains and how this is achieved, if at all, by the private sector.

The private sector has employed a number of techniques to secure legitimacy from the state and public in criminal justice. The work of Suchman (1995) is useful here. The most important form of legitimacy an organization can achieve is *cognitive* acceptance where the acceptance of an organization is seen as necessary and/or "inevitable part of a cultural account" (Suchman 1995: 582; Brinkerhoff 2005). Such a status is often beyond the reach of the private sector in criminal justice where the state is a repository of a monopoly of legitimate power (Jackson et al. 2012). The cognitive legitimacy of these state institutions is the retributive element in punishment and role of the police as symbolic of 'the state on the street' (Brogden and Ellison 2012) and state prison officers in custodial institutions. To complicate matters though there is also a hierarchy of legitimacy (McNeill and Robinson 2012) within criminal justice systems. For example, probation is often seen as a soft option to a prison sentence; this, however, can depend on the political climate, and/or offenders.

Suchman (1995) also noted that the private sector sought *pragmatic* legitimacy where it allegedly delivers cost-effective criminal justice services and still fulfil "the needs and interests of its stakeholders" (Brinkerhoff 2005: 4). Private sector legitimacy in criminal justice can be explained by private security closeness to the state and providing a service whilst hopefully sheltering in the shadow of the state's own legitimacy. In doing so the profile of competitive transnational organizations such as G4S or Serco emphasize its respect and concern for human rights to establish itself as a legitimate organization of criminal justice services in its own right. This competition is, however, now limited as private security and criminal justice services are in the hands of a few major organizations (Eisen 2017). Competition and 'payment by results' (Fitzgibbon 2016) perhaps offered some credible justification to employ the private sector, but with its expansion has come a reduction in competition, and potential for acts of corruption.

How though can the private sector achieve legitimacy in criminal justice? It has to secure approval from the state or some of it, and the public, or some of it. It appears possible if the private sector is under the regulatory control of the state. This is referred to as hiding behind the state but attempts to ensure private sector legitimacy is often through a regime of inspection and evaluation. There is little evidence to substantiate such a position, and I prefer the view that it is of little concern to the majority of the public unless we are involved in the criminal justice system as either employees or suspects or offenders. The criminal justice system is 'out there' to protect us without spending too much money on offenders. This is seen in the often punitive views of the public regarding sentencing and punishment of offenders. By nestling close to the state the private sector attempts to achieve some of its cognitive legitimacy but mostly achieves pragmatic legitimacy.

Private sector/security is thus engaged in 'legitimation work' to counter negative publicity that stems from acts of corruption (Thumala et al. 2011: 287). There have been attempts to professionalize private security with the development of the United Kingdom Security Authority in 2001 designed to distinguish between the professionals from the less competent and disreputable. This is a clear example of the private sectors search for pragmatic legitimacy (Genders 2002) but also cognitive legitimacy by working closely with the state (White 2010). This professionalization has also been referred to as 'symbolic borrowing' (e.g. a need to be seen as professional as the police) by recruiting ex-police officers onto boards of private sector organizations, having private security wear uniforms resembling the police, associating with the police, where possible, in part because to borrow its ethos of vocation and public service (Thumala et al. 2011: 297; see also White 2010). The private sector will copy and imitate state police to secure public legitimacy but as highlighted by Diphoorn (2016) and policing in Durban, South Africa it can lead to the public expecting private sector security to be called upon to deliver a full police service that is not possible nor legally acceptable. A legitimation strategy thus can backfire and the public come to view private security as a poor imitation of 'proper policing'. Such a dynamic is often absent with reference to prison and probation services as they rarely have direct interaction with the public in the way that police officers do. The private prison sector works closely with the state and much of what it is expected to do is behind closed doors in a security institution. This no doubt helped its rapid privatization in some jurisdictions.

The state still has cognitive legitimacy, but by delegating elements of this legitimacy it has enabled the private sector to achieve a degree of pragmatic legitimacy to the extent that it meets state needs. This context, however, should be seen as flexible as the private sector has withdrawn from managing criminal justice services before (Eisen 2017) and the situation is complex and nuanced. In fact, there are two issues to consider. The neo-liberal approach to criminal justice focuses on low-cost surveillance and monitoring of offenders at the expense of rehabilitation and social reintegration (Garland 2001; Wacquant 2009, 2010; Nellis 2014). Such surveillance and monitoring is often labour-intensive and leads to the deskilling of criminal justice practitioners; this, in turn, is part of the process by which the private sector enters into providing 'services' in criminal justice (Fitzgibbon 2007, 2008; Fitzgibbon and Lea 2014, 2017). The shift to surveillance reflects the transformation, particularly in the USA and elsewhere of the private prison sector and control of immigration centres (Eisen 2017). The prison system, in some jurisdictions has shifted from the management of offenders with a view to rehabilitation, to managing 'at risk' populations (Feeley and Simon 2006) to be kept under control. One such population is those seeking immigration to a country—legally and/or illegally—which the majority of the population need allegedly protecting from, and can thus be monitored by the private sector with little concern for treatment and legitimacy (Bosworth and Guild 2008; Eisen 2017).

Furthermore, the private sector has changed in size and scope. Whilst there are some small firms patrolling a shopping mall, these have been absorbed by international organizations leading to less competition, which is always a justification as to why privatization helps reduce cost. However, with little competition they can often be incompetent or corrupt and still keep hold of a contract (Menz 2011; White 2014; Ford 2015). In cases of suspected and/or alleged corruption conviction is difficult to achieve and extremely costly (Brooks 2016) but with a tendency to focus on individuals instead of an organization it allows them regardless of the service(s) it is providing to maximize profits at the expense and safety of those under its control, its employees and the public.

In 2016, G4S were under inquiry for serious abuse of young people in its Medway Secure Training Centre (STC). This inquiry highlighted concern about the "efficacy of monitoring" of inmates and "whether G4S staff had sufficient understanding and training in relation to the safeguarding of children" (Holden et al. 2016: 8) that culminated in the suspension and arrest of some employees for violent behaviour. By focusing on individuals an organization can claim it has continued commitment to high standards and that any transgression is an isolated incident and thus work with the state and blame criminal acts on its employees. In this way incompetent and/or wayward corrupt acts are presented as the acts of bad apples or rogue individuals (Punch 2003) similar to the state and an unexpected departure from standards insisted upon by the organization: it is the employees that violate such standards rather than the organization, which itself rigorously adheres to, or claims to. A refusal or lack of political will, to indict for breach of contract, failure to protect suspects and/or offenders and those simply detained in immigration centres is I suggest abdication of responsibility by the state.

This type of 'relationship', however, is known as a lock-in where a state increases the power of the private sector. The state loses capacity—in terms of personnel and expertise—to deliver the services it has outsourced. This, in turn, leads to further state cuts and deskilling in the interests of profitability in the private sector and it has become difficult, if not impossible, depending on the level of privatization and deskilling for the state to resume control of the outsourced services at a later date: hence the lock-in effect or 'state debilitation' (Leys 2006; Marquand 2004). With movement between the state such as civil service and private sector the culture of the private sector has slowly but steadily become part of criminal justice management. The private sector then can neutralize pragmatic legitimation and corruption with promises to address its conduct and blame individuals (House of Commons 2016; and see Eisen 2017 for private prison sector in USA).

Beyond pragmatic and cognitive legitimacy there is *normative* (*moral*) legitimacy, mostly only available to international known 'brand' named organizations. Normative legitimacy is a public relations exercise, often ongoing, to attempt to achieve public acceptance and legitimacy. It can achieve this by referring to its own standards even if under criminal investigation. The aim is to establish a type of legitimacy which 'reflects a pro-social logic that differs from narrow self-interest' (Suchman 1995:

579) and leads the company 'towards acceptable…standards, and values' (Brinkerhoff 2005: 4).

The more powerful the organization and reach it can launch its campaign for legitimacy. Depending on the size and power of the private criminal justice sector there is a marked dependence on it by the state via lock-in and as such state debilitation increases the independent power of the private sector without the need to hide behind the state. Normative legitimacy strategies attempt to deflect and/or downplay failures which would otherwise compromise pragmatic legitimacy by stressing 'company values'. Thus the rise of multinational organizations such as G4S and Serco are displacing pragmatic legitimacy and hiding behind the state with a new combination of lock-in and normative legitimacy. If part of its operation is under criticism or criminal investigation such a major company can withdraw from a contract and still make a profit because of its international reach. It can then at a later date reapply to manage the service(s) it was under investigation for. Furthermore, as mentioned above the private sector simply apes the state public sector. Mistakes are made—they are admitted in full or partially—lessons will be learned—and new procedures put in place. However, mistakes, acts of corruption still abound in both sectors. In some cases there might be a civil and/or criminal investigation, but not all individuals particularly in the state sector countenance punishment and resign (Fitzgibbon 2011). This approach or tactic has the effect of strengthening the cognitive legitimacy of an organization. Rather than 'hiding behind the state' the private sector can independently project an image of state procedures that suggest it can function in response to failure, in a similar way as the state to secure its legitimacy. The notion that company policy such as recruitment methods, instruction/education and internal workplace cultures provide a background conducive to periodic failure is thereby ruled out of public and political discourse. However, when an organization fails to stem incompetence and corruption around the world to what extent can this be blamed on individuals that commit similar acts in different places and different times rather than on company 'policy' and practice?

By drawing this section of the book to a close the conditions under which private sector might achieve a stable normative legitimacy is possible if, and this appears to have happened, there are only a few organizations that can deliver services in criminal justice on the scale required by the state; these can then lock-into national criminal justice systems and become new public–private 'assemblages' (Sassen 2008; Abrahamsen and Williams 2011); this in turn blurs state cognitive legitimacy and the normative legitimacy of private organizations that results from the progressive privatization of security and urban space and such transformation has provided new terrain for the development of the power to defend the privatization of criminal justice and thus its legitimacy.

Conclusion

This chapter started by highlighting the trouble in trying to define corruption and a brief review of rational-economic, political and legal theoretical explanations in the corruption literature as to why people are and/or commit corrupt acts. This was followed by the contribution sociology and criminology has made in helping us understand state power, legitimacy, the privatization of criminal justice and corruption. Whilst this chapter has highlighted the position and power criminal justice systems hold and can enforce there needs to be systematic rather than piecemeal and academic analysis of criminal justice corruption in both the public and private sector. Excellent work is produced but we need a corpus of work on more than law enforcement and corruption, which has been documented, and needs to be complemented by in-depth analysis—both theoretical and empirical—on magistrates, judiciary, lawyers, probation service, prison systems, the jury, legal representatives and vigilantism.

References

Abrahamsen, R., & Williams, M. C. (2011). *Security Beyond the State: Private Security in International Politics*. Cambridge: Cambridge University Press.

Andrews, J., & Montinola, G. R. (1998). *Corrupt Democratization: The Importance of Institutional Design in the Multidimensional Political*

Environments of Transition. Boston: Annual Meeting of the American Political Science Association.

Barbalet, J. (2009). A Characterization of Trust, and Its Consequences. *Theory and Society, 38*(4), 367–382.

Beare, M. E. (2017). The Failures of Police Legitimacy: Attacks from Within. In V. Mitslegas, P. Alldridge, & L. Cheliotis (Eds.), *Globalisation, Criminal Law and Criminal Justice*. Oxford: Hart Publishing.

Beetham, D. (1991). *The Legitimation of Power*. London: Palgrave.

Bosworth, M., & Guild, M. (2008). Governing Through Migration Control: Security and Citizenship in Britain. *British Journal of Criminology, 48*, 703–719.

Bottoms, A., & Tankebe, J. (2012). Beyond Procedural Justice: A Dialogic Approach to Legitimacy in Criminal Justice. *Journal of Criminal Law and Criminology, 102*(1), 119–170.

Brinkerhoff, D. (2005). *Organizational Legitimacy, Capacity, and Capacity Development*. Brussels: European Centre for Development Policy Management.

Brogden, M., & Ellison, G. (2012). *Policing in an Age of Austerity: A Postcolonial Perspective*. Abingdon: Routledge.

Bronitt, S., & Stenning, P. (2011). Understanding Discretion in Modern Policing. *Criminal Law Journal, 35*(6), 319–332.

Brooks, G. (2016). *Criminology of Corruption: Theoretical Approaches*. Basingstoke: Palgrave Macmillan.

Brooks, G., Lewis, C., Walsh, D., & Kim, H. (2013). *The Prevention of Corruption: Investigation, Enforcement and Governance*. Basingstoke: Palgrave Macmillan.

Burkhardt, B. (2014). Private Prisons in Public Discourse: Measuring Moral Legitimacy. *Sociological Focus, 47*(4), 279–298.

Carrabine, E. (2004). *Power, Discourse and Resistance: A Genealogy of the Strangeways Prison Riot*. Dartmouth: Ashgate.

Chambliss, W. (1989). State Organized Crime. *Criminology, 27*(2), 183–208.

Coicaud, J. M. (2002). *Legitimacy and Politics: A Contribution to the Study of Political Right and Political Responsibility*. Cambridge: Cambridge University Press.

Coleman, J. W. (1995). Motivation and Opportunity: Understanding the Causes of White Collar Crime. In G. Geis, R. Meier, & L. Salinger (Eds.), *White Collar Crime* (3rd ed.). New York: Free Press.

Dal Bo, E. (2006). Regulatory Capture: A Review. *Oxford Review of Economic Policy, 22*(2), 203–225.

Diphoorn, T. (2016). Twilight Policing: Private Security Practices in South Africa. *British Journal of Criminology, 56*(2), 313–331.
Dixon, D. (1997). *Law in Policing: Legal Regulation and Police Practices. Clarendon Studies in Criminology*. Oxford: Oxford University Press.
Eisen, L. B. (2017). *Inside Private Prisons: An American Dilemma in the Age of Mass Incarceration*. New York: Columbia University Press.
Feeley, M., & Simon, J. (2006). The New Penology: Notes on the Emerging Strategy of Corrections and Its Implications. *Criminology, 30*(4), 449–474.
Fitzgibbon, W. (2007). Risk Analysis and the New Practitioner: Myth or Reality? *Punishment and Society, 9*, 87–97.
Fitzgibbon, W. (2008). Deconstructing Probation: Risk and Developments in Practice. *Journal of Social Work Practice, 22*(1), 85–101.
Fitzgibbon, W. (2011). *Probation and Social Work on Trial: Violent Offenders and Child Abusers*. Basingstoke: Palgrave Macmillan.
Fitzgibbon, W. (2016). Innovation and Privatisation in the Probation Service in England and Wales. *British Journal of Community Justice, 14*(1), 71–76.
Fitzgibbon, W., & Lea, J. (2014). Defending Probation: Beyond Privatisation and Security. *European Journal of Probation, 6*(1), 24–41.
Fitzgibbon, W., & Lea, J. (2017). Privatization and Coercion: The Question of Legitimacy. *Theoretical Criminology, 22*(4), 545–562.
Ford, M. (2015). *The Ongoing Electronic Tagging Scandal: Centre for Crime and Justice Studies*. Available at www.crimeandjustice.org.uk/resources/ongoing-electronic-tagging-scandal. Accessed October 6, 2016.
Foucault, M. (1977). *Discipline and Punish: The Birth of the Prison*. Harmondsworth: Penguin Books.
Foucault, M. (1980). *Power/Knowledge: Selected Interviews and Other Writings 1972–1977* (C. Gordon, Ed.). New York: Pantheon Books.
Garland, D. (1996). The Limits of the Sovereign State: Strategies of Crime Control in Contemporary Society. *British Journal of Criminology, 36*(4), 445–471.
Garland, D. (2001). *The Culture of Control: Crime and Social Order in Contemporary Society*. Oxford: Oxford University Press.
Genders, E. (2002). Legitimacy, Accountability and Private Prisons. *Punishment & Society, 4*(3), 285–303.
Gounev, P., & Ruggerio, V. (2012). *Corruption and Organized Crime in Europe: Illegal Partnerships*. Abingdon: Routledge.
Gramsci, A. (1971). *Selections from the Prison Notebooks*. New York: International Publishers.

Greitens, S. C. (2016). *Dictators and their Secret Police: Coercive Institutions and State Violence*. Cambridge: Cambridge University Press.
Herbert, S. (2006). Tangled up in Blue: Conflicting Paths to Police Legitimacy. *Theorectical Criminology, 10*(4), 481–504.
Heywood, P. M. (2015). *Routledge Handbook of Political Corruption*. Abingdon: Routledge.
Hogg, A. (2012). The Privatisation of Non-Custodial Measures: An Uneasy Balance Between Legitimacy and Immediacy. *Oñati Socio-legal Series, 2*(4), 144–174.
Holden, G., Allen, B., Gray, S., & Thomas, E. (2016). *Medway Improvement Board: Final Report of the Board's Advice to Secretary of State for Justice*. London: Ministry of Justice.
House of Commons. (2016). *Committee of Public Accounts—Seventeenth Report Session 2016–17*. London: House of Commons.
Huisman, W., & Vande Walle, G. (2010). *The Criminology of Corruption: The Good Cause—Theoretical Perspectives on Corruption*. Opladen: Barbara Budrich.
Jackson, J., Bradford, B., Hough, M., & Murray, K. (2012). Compliance with the Law and Policing by Consent: Notes on Legal Legitimacy and Cynicism. In A. Crawford & A. Hucklesby (Eds.), *Legitimacy and Compliance in Criminal Justice*. London: Routledge.
Jackson, J., Huq, A., Bradford, B., & Tyler, T. R. (2013). Monopolizing Force? Police Legitimacy and Public Attitudes Towards the Acceptability of Violence. *Psychology, Public Policy and Law, 19*(4), 479–497.
Johnston, M. (2005). *Syndromes of Corruption: Wealth, Power and Democracy*. Cambridge: Cambridge University Press.
Klitgaard, R. (1988). *Controlling Corruption*. Berkeley: University of California Press.
Kramer, R. C., & Michalowski, R. J. (2006). *State-Corporate Crime: Wrongdoing at the Intersection of Business and Government*. New Brunswick, NJ: Rutgers University Press.
Kramer, R. C., Michalowski, R. J., & Kauzlarich, D. (2002). The Origins and Development of the Concept and Theory of State-Corporate Crime. *Crime and Delinquency, 48*(2), 263–282.
Lessing, B. (2016). *Inside Out: The Challenge of Prison-Based Criminal Organizations* (Brookings Local Orders Papers Series 1–23).
Leys, C. (2006). The Cynical State. In L. Panitch & C. Leys (Eds.), *Socialist Register 2006*. London: Merlin Press.
Liebling, A. (2000). Prison Officers, Policing and the Use of Discretion. *Theoretical Criminology, 4*(3), 333–357.

Liebling, A. (2005). The Late Modern Prison and the Question of Values. *Current Issues in Criminal Justice, 16*(2), 202–219.
Liebling, A. (2007). Why Prison Staff Culture Matters. In J. M. Byrne, D. Hummer, & F. S. Taxman (Eds.), *The Culture of Prison Violence*. New York: Pearson.
Macpherson, C. (1999). *The Stephen Lawrence Inquiry: Report of an Inquiry*. London: Home Office.
Manzetti, L., & Blake, C. (1996). Market Reforms and Corruption in Latin America. *Review of International Political Economy, 3*, 671–682.
Marquand, D. (2004). *The Decline of the Public: The Hollowing Out of Citizenship*. Cambridge: Polity Press.
McNeill, F., & Robinson, G. (2012). Liquid Legitimacy and Community Sanctions. In A. Crawford & A. Hucklesby (Eds.), *Legitimacy and Compliance in Criminal Justice*. Abingdon: Routledge.
Menz, G. (2011, March 16–19). *Outsourcing, Privatization and the Politics of Privatizing Migration.* Paper Prepared for Presentation at the International Studies Association Conference, Montreal, QC.
Merton, R. K. (1938). Social Structure and Anomie. *American Sociological Review, 3*, 672–682.
Michelle, A. (2010). *The New Jim Crow: Mass Incarceration in the Age of Colorblindness*. New York: The New Press.
Moyle, P. (1995). Private Prison Research in Queensland, Australia: A Case Study of Borallon Correctional Centre, 1991. *British Journal of Criminology, 35*(1), 34–62.
Moyle, P. (2001). Separating the Allocation of Punishment from Its Administration: Theoretical and Empirical Observations. *British Journal of Criminology, 41*(1), 77–100.
Nellis, M. (2014). Upgrading Electronic Monitoring, Downgrading Probation: Reconfiguring 'Offender Management' in England and Wales. *European Journal Probation, 6*(2), 169–191.
Philp, M. (2015). The Definition of Political Corruption. In P. M. Heywood (Ed.), *Routledge Handbook of Political Corruption*. London: Routledge.
Punch, M. (1996). *Dirty Business: Exploring Corporate Misconduct, Analysis and Cases*. London: Sage.
Punch, M. (2000). Suite Violence: Why Managers Murder and Corporations Kill. *Crime, Law and Social Change, 33*(3), 243–280.
Punch, M. (2003). Rotten Orchards: Pestilence, Police Misconduct and System Failure. *Policing and Society, 13*(2), 171–196.

Punch, M. (2009). *Police Corruption: Deviance, Accountability and Reform in Policing*. Cullompton: Willan Publishing.
Raz, J. (2009). *Between Authority and Interpretation: On the Theory of Law and Practical Reason*. Oxford: Oxford University Press.
Reiner, R. (2010). *The Politics of the Police*. Oxford: Oxford University Press.
Rhodes, R. A. W. (1994). The Hollowing Out of the State: The Changing Nature of Public Service in Britain. *The Political Quarterly, 65*(2), 138–151.
Rothe, D., & Kauzlarich, D. (2016). *Crimes of the Powerful: An Introduction*. Abingdon: Routledge.
Rowland, R., & Coupe, T. (2014). Patrol Officers and Public Reassurance: A Comparative Evaluation of Police Officers, PCSOs, ACSOs and Private Security Guards. *Policing and Society, 24*(3), 265–284.
Sassen, S. (2008). Neither Global Nor National: Novel Assemblages of Territory, Authority and Rights. *Ethics & Global Politics, 1*(1–2), 61–79.
Scraton, P. (2016). *Hillsborough—The Truth*. Edinburgh: Mainstream Publishing.
Slapper, G., & Tombs, S. (1999). *Corporate Crime*. Essex: Pearson.
South, N. (1988). *Policing for Profit: The Private Security Sector*. London: Sage.
South, N. (1997). Control, Crime and 'End of Century Criminology'. In P. Francis, P. Davies, & V. Jupp (Eds.), *Policing Futures: The Police, Law Enforcement and the Twenty-First Century*. London: Palgrave Macmillan.
Sparks, R., & Bottoms, A. E. (2008). Legitimacy and Imprisonment Revisited: Some Notes on the Problem of Order Ten Years After. In J. M. Byrne, D. Hummer, & F. S. Taxman (Eds.), *The Culture of Prison Violence*. Boston: Allyn & Bacon.
Sparks, R., Bottoms, A., & Hay, W. (1996). *Prisons and the Problem of Order*. Oxford: Clarendon Press.
Suchman, M. (1995). Managing Legitimacy: Strategic and Institutional Approaches. *The Academy of Management Review, 20*(3), 571–610.
Sutherland, E. H. (1939). *Principles of Criminology* (3rd ed.). Philadelphia: Lippincott.
Sykes, G. (1958). *The Society of Captives*. Princeton, NJ: Princeton University Press.
Sykes, G. M., & Matza, D. (1957). Techniques of Neutralization: A Theory of Delinquency. *American Sociological Review, 22*, 664–670.
Teague, M. (2012). Neoliberalism: Prisons and Probation in the United States and England and Wales. In P. Whitehead & P. Crawshaw (Eds.), *Organising Neoliberalism: Markets, Privatisation and Justice*. London: Anthem Press.

Thumala, A., Goold, B., & Loader, I. (2011). A Tainted Trade? Moral Ambivalence and Legitimation Work in the Private Security Industry. *British Journal of Sociology, 62*(2), 283–303.
Tyler, J. C. (2014). Blind Injustice: The Supreme Court, Implicit Racial Bias and the Racial Disparity in the Criminal Justice System. *American Criminal Law Review, 51*, 689–713.
Tyler, T. R. (1990). *Why People Obey the Law*. New Haven: Yale University.
Tyler, T. R. (2003). Procedural Justice, Legitimacy, and the Effective Rule of Law. *Crime and Justice, 30*, 283–357.
Tyler, T., & Wakslak, C. (2004). Profiling and Police Legitimacy: Procedural Justice, Attributions of Motive, and Acceptance of Police Authority. *Criminology, 42*(2), 253–282.
Useem, B., & Kimball, P. (1989). *States of Siege: U.S. Prison Riots, 1971–1986*. Oxford: Oxford University Press.
Vaughan, D. (2002). Criminology and the Sociology of Organizations: Analogy, Comparative Social Organization, and General Theory. *Crime, Law and Social Change, 37*(2), 117–136.
Wacquant, L. (2009). *Punishing the Poor: The Neoliberal Government of Social Insecurity*. Durham, NC: Duke University Press.
Wacquant, L. (2010). Crafting the Neoliberal State: Workfare, Prison Fare, and Social Insecurity. *Sociological Forum, 25*(2), 197–220.
Warner, C. M. (2015). Sources of Corruption in the European Union. In P. M. Heywood (Ed.), *Routledge Handbook of Political Corruption*. London: Routledge.
Weber, M. (1978). *Economy and Society* (Vol. 1). Berkeley: University of California Press.
White, A. (2010). *The Politics of Private Security: Regulation, Reform and Re-legitimation*. Houndmills: Palgrave Macmillan.
White, A. (2014). Post-crisis Policing and Public–Private Partnerships: The Case of Lincolnshire Police and G4S. *British Journal of Criminology, 54*(6), 1002–1022.
Yadav, V., & Mukherjee, B. (2016). *The Politics of Corruption in Dictatorships*. Cambridge: Cambridge University Press.
Zelditch, M. (2001). Processes of Legitimation: Recent Developments and New Directions. *Social Psychology Quarterly, 64*(1), 4–17.

3

Extent of Corruption in Criminal Justice Systems

Introduction

In Chapter 2 it was highlighted that no international consensus existed concerning a definition of corruption. This makes the subject difficult, if not impossible, to measure. Furthermore, there are often no witnesses and/or 'silent' witnesses with people sometimes unaware they are a victim of corruption. In criminal justice systems, however, this is perhaps different: people are both aware, but powerless, depending on the jurisdiction, and also unaware that they have been a victim of corruption. Individuals are a victim of corruption because of an encounter with corrupt law enforcement (Punch 2000, 2003, 2009; Gerber and Mendelson 2008; Caldero and Crank 2011; Kane and White 2013; Standford 2015; Diphoorn 2016; Miller 2017; Banks 2017), but fail to complain or report it, but can also be a victim of hidden corruption where law enforcement (Beare 2017) or state prosecutors fail to pass evidence across to a defence team (Gottschalk 2016) that indicates the suspects' innocence. Both types of corruption, blatant and hidden are thus hard to measure.

G. Brooks, *Criminal Justice and Corruption*,
https://doi.org/10.1007/978-3-030-16038-8_3

However, understanding the level of corruption is important; if we have some estimate of corruption and its causes we can potentially reduce its incidence. Measurement, regardless of how rough, is therefore critical in providing some benchmark of corruption and identifying what factors are effective in preventing and reducing it (Brooks et al. 2013; Heywood 2015; Hough 2015). There is ample criminal justice data available in democratic states on the police (IOPC 2018), deaths in police custody (Planty et al. 2015), arrest data and sentencing and prison numbers (Tyler 2014; Banks 2017) that can indicate potential and actual corruption, particularly in law enforcement, and to a limited extent judicial and prosecutorial practice. Since I am unable to consider all of the above I have chosen to consider corruption in law enforcement, which can be measured to some extent, the corruption of scientific practice and corruption in prison systems. The reason for this choice is that law enforcement corruption can, in combination with the manipulation of scientific data lead to a lengthy custodial sentence for an innocent man/woman that has become a victim of the criminal justice system rather than protected by it, and thus a victim of criminal justice corruption.

Measuring Crime and Corruption

There is literature available on the problem of how crime data is recorded and measured. Due to space, I offer a brief review of the main issues regarding crime data before progressing on to the equally complex and problematic recording and measurement of corruption. There are, as with all datasets issues of validity, but crime data, for all its criticism offers a better record of crime(s) that those that fall under the broad church of corruption.

As illustrated in Chapter 2, it is difficult to define corruption, if not impossible, and therefore difficult to measure. With crime data, even though flawed, we can record actual acts but these acts, e.g. a theft is a legal construct and placed in a offence category based on the interpretation of evidence by police officers. This is then potentially manipulated, twisted and contested in a court of law (see Chapters 6 and 9) by legal representatives. For corruption, which is on a continuum (Brooks 2016) from legal but unethical to highly illegal, all of the above issues are also present but due to the nature of criminal corruption (an act that has broken laws rather than normative 'standards') is often difficult to unearth, and in turn obtain relevant evidence to arrest and then convict, e.g. a corrupt act such as fraud can be presented as a crime, but also an administrative error, a mistake, unintentional and/or incorrect interpretation of evidence and data (Levi 1981, 1987, 2005, Gill 2005; Doig 2006; Brooks et al. 2013; Button and Brooks 2014; Button et al. 2015, 2017; Lewis et al. 2015; Brooks 2017) and as such is often contested.

Crime data, of which corruption is a part, is based on recorded police data, and court sentences. Police data and court sentences are useful to assess the extent of corruption, but are limited, e.g. what an individual was arrested for and then convicted for, which can be different based on level of evidence, case presented by the prosecution and/or defence, also based on limited evidence, witnesses that fail to present at court or commit perjury, plea bargaining to reduce possible sentence and/or blame a fellow criminal, and members of a jury that can be disinterested in the case, bias, prejudicial, and/or corrupt. In one criminal case, the potential for corruption—by design and intended or poor administration—can determine the outcome of a culpable or innocent individual's future.

Recording of crime data—surveys, self-reporting and experimental methods—has however, become increasingly sophisticated, particularly at the international level such as the International Classification of Crime for Statistical (ICCS) developed by the United Nations. Aware that factors impact on crime data of what is reported, how it is dealt with, and detected can differ and is thus reflected in national and international crime data. This is inescapable but still offers some measurement of crime. Developing far more sophisticated measures offers analytical insight into some crimes; whilst dependent on available data homicide can be analysed by understanding its *situational context* (was it part of a crime, individual or organized crime or hate crime), *relationship between victim(s) and offenders* (intimate partners, family member) and mechanism of act (firearm, knife, no object) (Bisogno et al. 2015). This is possible with homicide as there is a victim and crime committed (excluding euthanasia if legal in a state) but is far more complex with other types of crimes such as theft. But the whole process of trying to record and measure corruption is far more complex (Kaufmann et al. 2006).

Instead of simply relying on recorded crime a method of identifying the extent of corruption is to use victim surveys such as the National Crime Victimization Survey (NCVS) in the USA. A debate on the pitfalls of relying on official data as accurate reflections of crime rates is well-established in criminology and these victim surveys have repeatedly noted that crimes are not reported because of fear of repercussion from the offender(s), the police fail to take it (the crime) seriously; and lack of faith in the police. Official crime data is seen more as a measure of police operational action that reflects key policing issues at the time, or political expediency, whilst victimization surveys have increasingly become more sophisticated and are now considered to be a more reliable source for the calculation of crime levels.

This approach is a useful source of information on corruption in criminal justice with the International Crime Victim Survey (ICVS) producing estimates of corruption (Brooks et al. 2013). Developed by the United Nations Centre for International Crime Prevention it seeks to obtain details on the nature and seriousness of victimization and assess the level and impact of corruption based on victims' personal encounters with crime and corruption (Van Dijk 2015). Victimization data enables analysis of trends, as well as increasing the opportunity for the collection of detailed and as accurate information as possible via personal victimization caused by corruption. This approach also affords the possibility to measure the effects, if any, of anti-corruption approaches to tackle the problem. Victim surveys of corruption, however, are not exempt from the same issues that challenge the compilation of data and, indeed, all crime surveys. Furthermore, the EuroBarometer is a useful measure of public perception of corruption in the EU as it considers police corruption and judicial corruption in its members' states (see http://ec.europa.eu/COMMFrontOffice/publicopinion/index.cfm for a survey data since 1974).

However, to complicate matters there is often more than one victim with corruption. In addition victims of corruption are unaware of victimization, could be dispersed across the world and suffer the consequences of action(s) years after the act, e.g. Bhopal, India, and/or complicit but fail to acknowledge it. If this is the case what use is the corruption literature in helping understand criminal corruption?

The principal approaches to assess the extent of corruption are perception based, cross national surveys. These contain both objective and subjective elements: objective measures are quantifiable datasets that are considered verifiable such as the number of official complaints to the police (see below) (IOPC 2018), and actual numbers of convictions (Brooks et al. 2013). However, such datasets are more a reflection of corruption rather than its actual level in a particular country, and more an indication of the public's view of law enforcement and law enforcement resources and political attitude towards corruption. As a result, such official datasets are seen more as supplementary information to subjective approaches (but not wholly, as will be seen in this chapter).

Subjective approaches to understanding the extent of corruption are based on participant polls and surveys designed to 'measure' the level of perception of corruption. Transparency International's Corruption Perception Index and Global Corruption Barometer are well-known and seek to capture personal encounters and knowledge of corruption via 'ordinary' citizens; but such an approach is a limited predictor of corruption, as perceptions on corruption differ within a specific geographical region but also within and across nations.

To overcome the limitations of either subjective or objective approaches to measurement, preference is for aggregate indicators, a combination of both objective and subjective indicators. Aggregate indicators have become influential because they combine a wide array of individual indicators; sets of data that yield an average, reduce margins of error and bias that occur in individual measures, and calculate explicit margins of error and offer some data on the extent of corruption. There are a number of corruption tools used to measure corruption (see above) but others such as the World Governance Indicators (WGI) and the Business Environment and Enterprise Survey (BEEPS) developed by the World Bank are also available. The advantages and disadvantages of these have been dealt with elsewhere (see Brooks 2016) but one aspect of them needs some attention.

Urra (2007) identified three issues with aggregate data; these were the perception, error and a utility problem. For Urra the perception problem is the margin of error created when subjective indicators are used to produce complex statistical constructions that can produce an illusion of quantitative sophistication; the error problem is the internal margins of error already contained within the different sources of corruption data and errors relative to the concept itself, and corruption research encounters sampling errors (part of any social science research) and also that any proxy for corruption is imperfect; the utility problem is the space between measurement and solutions where broad measures of corruption are difficult if not impossible to turn into actual anti-corruption initiatives. This criticism, however, does not mean that we should abandon all attempts to measure corruption. It is imperfect, particularly with all types of crime, as those familiar with crime data are aware but those acts and crimes that are hidden add an extra dimension and complication to assessment.

The perception of corruption is often seen primarily as paying a bribe, which is mostly a hidden crime. This, however, fails to capture different types of corruption or the impact of corruption in commercial and criminal justice sectors. The perception of corruption is on those that accept a bribe rather than those that offer; the implicit suggestion is that bribes are only paid if and when needed rather than a pre-emptive way to secure contracts (Heywood 2015) and/or reduce the possibility of arrest with law enforcement or reduce the prospect of a sentence by a corrupt judge. This, however, is not always the case (see Chapter 7).

Such attempts to measure corruption are, however, useful; in *The Economist* (2018b: 48–49) it was noted that Brazilian citizens see law enforcement and the judiciary as highly corrupt. This is perhaps unsurprising in a country where its political leaders seem incredibly corrupt but this is a problem for Latin America (Cao and Zhao 2005; Seligson 2006; Macaulay 2007; Brinks 2008; Bailey and Taylor 2009; Corbacho et al. 2015) where political, law enforcement and judicial corruption are rich seams of profit for the corrupt.

Governance and control or lack of it, is often cited as a problem, particularly in neo-liberal circles that consider building democracy and economic development as a bulwark to corruption (see Freedom House at freedomhouse.org for a worldwide decline in a rule of law). The problem is that whilst such an approach to tackle corruption is inconclusive, and in some instances challenged, a view that corruption is 'out there' in Africa, Asia, Middle east, South America, etc. is little more than neo-colonialism via measurement. Such views are often underpinned with an attempt to foster 'western' interest and commercial contracts for the private security sector and criminal justice/security organizations such as G4S and Serco that work in both 'western' and developing jurisdictions. Governance for private sector criminal justice organizations though might mean low taxes and minimal regulation, or poor regulation that allows them to engage in corruption as a way of 'doing business' (Brooks 2016). As Heywood (2015: 144) suggests 'where perception, policy an action meets' it can 'act as a euphemism for free trade, an idealised role for civil society and a clear separation between bureaucracy and political influence', which can, however, aggravate the underlying causes of corruption that business might do everything—legal or illegal—to circumvent, thwart and change public policy. This public policy is often criminal justice policy and thwarted, and watered down and blocked in 'western' as well as developing jurisdictions for the benefit of private vested interests.

Small scale, local research, however, has started to offer a picture of corruption in a local context. It is important to understand the level of corruption and 'lived reality' of corruption (Heywood 2015). In an attempt to estimate the extent of corruption, Chaudhury et al. (2006), Banerjee et al. (2007), Bertrand et al. (2007), and Olken and Barron (2007) adopted observational small scale approaches to measure corruption in the public sector. None of these consider criminal justice with only some briefly touching on law enforcement matters but all highlight the need for small scale research.

The challenge that all these approaches in this part of the chapter encounter is that corruption is illicit in nature, thus its measurement seems quite intractable. For example, in terms of bribery, it would be difficult to establish with precision who was implicated in corrupt behaviour and exactly quantify how much was involved in a range of transactions. Measurement systems can also prompt responses that can undermine efforts to accurately pinpoint the extent of corruption. Once a monitoring system is in place, those determined to continue to engage in corruption adjust by developing ways to circumvent the new system and continue to act illicitly. As a result, efforts to monitor and measure corruption can continue to underestimate its prevalence. This will be illustrated in the next two sections.

Towards a Measurement of Law Enforcement Corruption

Roebuck and Baker (1973), Carter (1990), and Syed and Bruce (1998) identified eight types of police corruption, whilst Punch (1985) suggested nine. These, however, focused on the police rather than all law enforcement. Furthermore, much has changed since these types of corruption were suggested, and as I proposed earlier to examine the reach of corruption in criminal justice systems we need to move beyond the police and consider law enforcement and the privatization of 'policing' (White 2015) as a threat to corruption of the criminal justice system.

One way to assess the level of corruption is to draw on actual data produced by the police. This is possible in England and Wales because of the Independent Office for Police Conduct (IOPC) that records and analyses types and numbers of police complaints. Since the Police Reform Act 2002 (Home Office 2002), the police are responsible for recording complaints, with the IOPC dealing with the most serious and sensitive cases. Since 2012, however, changes to the police complaints system came into effect as a result of the Police (Complaints and Misconduct) Regulations 2012, the Police (Conduct) Regulations 2012 and the Police Reform and Social Responsibility Act 2011. The IOPC also replaced the Independent Police Complaints Commission (IPCC) in 2018 due to criticism of its failure to review deaths in police custody satisfactorily.

The IOPC now deals with cases that fall under 'official complaint' by a member of the public that refers to the conduct of a Senior Officer (Deputy or Assistant Chief Constable), a complaint which has been referred to the IOPC, a contravention of Article 2 (The Right to Life) and 3 (Torture) of the Human Rights Act, and a case that meets the threshold for misconduct. Misconduct is considered a breach of the Standards of Professional Behaviour whilst 'Gross misconduct' is seen as a breach of the Standards of Professional Behaviour that is so serious it could result in dismissal. The police must therefore record and investigate a complaint, which could lead to disciplinary or criminal proceedings. If dissatisfied with how a complaint is handled, of which there are twenty-seven different types (IOPC 2018: 10), it is possible for a member of the public to appeal. If a complaint is dealt with by local/regional police such a system might lead to a speedy result and feedback to the public/individual(s) that complained, but might not be seen as legitimate e.g. the police are investigating fellow police colleagues, which the public has complained about. As highlighted in Chapter 2 legitimacy is highly important if criminal justice as a whole is to function on a level that the public will consent to (Beetham 1991; Coicaud 2002; Bottoms and Tankebe 2012) and such a system needs public approval for it to be successful.

The police in England and Wales recorded a total of 31,671 cases in 2017/2018 (IOPC 2018: 5). A complaint, however, can include one or more claim of corruption and in 2017/2018 there were a total of 61,238 recorded for England and Wales. The most common was recorded under 'other neglect or failure in duty' category that accounted for 39% of all recorded data in 2017/2018. This category, however, fails to really explain what these individual complaints are about (IOPC 2018: 19). Neglect and failure in duty are vague and subjective rather than detailed and specific.

The total number of recorded acts under the category of 'corruption or malpractice' was 383. However, 108 of these were under some special requirement; a special requirement is where assessment on the level of seriousness of misconduct *must* be investigated, notices of investigation served on subjects of the complaint and formal procedure followed, and the investigation must consider if there is a case to answer at its conclusion (IOPC 2018: 49). In the context of policing malpractice, however, it could be seen as a negligent act or an omission to act whilst corruption is a 'plan to act' to personally benefit (Miller 2017).

These above data are still low numbers when we consider the potential for 'incidents' that could occur policing the public. But whilst a clear measurement of corruption and malpractice is recorded here there are other types of 'corrupt acts' recorded—these are unlawful/unnecessary arrest (total number 1475 investigated in 2017/2018) of which 208 were subject to special requirement(s), oppressive conduct/harassment (total number 1526 investigated in 2017/2018) of which 194 were subject to special requirement(s), sexual assault (total number 86 investigated in 2017/2018) of which 26 were subject to special requirement(s) (IOPC 2018: 10).

Are all these acts corrupt? Where is the line between acceptable and unacceptable conduct? Unlawful arrest is clear—it is unlawful, but this still needs to be proven. Furthermore, police can be subject to investigation but called as a witness regarding these 'incidents'. If called what will fellow law enforcement officers do? Defend a colleague or expose them as corrupt or guilty of sexual assault? To secure and then maintain legitimacy each case has to be treated with respect and caution. However, some cases will be malicious and unfounded and brought by members of the public out of malice. The problem here though is that a few inappropriate acts or serious criminal acts cause substantial harm both to victims and the reputation to law enforcement.

In this sense, some attempt to record and deal with corruption and all acts recorded by the IOPC should be commended. However, the contexts in which acts of corruption occur are important (Miller 2017). In the aftermath of the Knapp Commission (1972) that highlighted the extent of corruption in the New York Police Department (NYPD) it stated that 'except your pay check only' as a 'clean buck' was an illusion. The assumption then perhaps was that 'no matter how small a gift' it could be seen as an attempt to corrupt. But I suggest that corruption can occur without the recourse to 'gifts' or cash, and that sexual assault is both sexual assault and an act of corruption and oppressive conduct/harassment could also be seen as corruption. The problem here though is where the line of what is acceptable and unacceptable is in practice, particularly if seeking public consent? Are the police harassing a sex offender? Here I doubt the majority of the public would consider this unacceptable. However, if the act(s) were racially motivated harassment of a section or part of community it would no doubt be viewed as both unlawful/unnecessary and oppressive conduct/harassment (by some anyway). Public pronouncements to tackle such conduct, if seen as empty rhetoric, with limited reform, rarely addresses the problem of law enforcement corruption (Punch 2009) and drawing the line of police mis(conduct) might be seen as an administrative issue but is primarily an ethical one (Banks 2017) that impacts on criminal justice legitimacy. This problem is at the heart of policing. The boundary between acceptable practice and corruption is often blurred and difficult to measure (Miller 2017).

There is also the relationship between slight and major breaches of ethical conduct (Standford 2015; Beare 2017). There is often reference to the 'slippery slope' of corruption where small breaches can lead to major acts of corruption. For example, acceptance of a small benefit involves the same rationale as accepting a major benefit compromising professional impartiality, and engaging in one act leads to the justification and rationalization that a range of corrupt acts are acceptable. This process takes on a continuum of acts where law enforcement rationalizes each act redefining the self, employing techniques of neutralization (Sykes and Matza 1957) in an institutional context (Ashforth and Anand 2003).

Whilst a measure of corruption has been put forward here, is oppressive (which is perhaps personal and subjective) behaviour by the police still an act of corruption? It is impossible to establish a clear and definitive answer here let alone measurement, but recording and publishing data is welcomed. The context of the environment that the act occurs in is vitally important (Miller 2017), and with the rise in the use of the private sector in law enforcement corruption in policing could be about defrauding the state and/or the police (Fitzgibbon and Lea 2017) as much as the police mishandling property, discrimination, a failure of duty or some kind of 'irregularity'. Policing though is thought of as indivisible; it cannot be meaningfully divided between individuals or a collection of individuals and should be available for all, if policing in a democratic nation.

However, there has been a substantial move towards the use of private security/policing in the USA, European Union and United Kingdom (White 2015) and South Africa (Diphoorn 2016) and Russia (Gerber and Mendelson 2008). The impact of privatization is underestimated and has come to occupy a major position in the extended police family. A 'quiet revolution in policing' (Shearing 1981: 1) is now full volume where the reach of private security and the extent to which it shapes and 'complements' policing is radically different from the once 'modern' state coordinated policing. This is seen in the privatization of scientific work in policing.

There is an assumption that science is empirically robust, and that its 'results' presented in court, particularly by 'experts' are as close to objective fact in criminal justice as possible. In fact, the status to which DNA has been elevated in criminal justice is that 'if you put God on the stand', and His 'testimony conflicted with DNA evidence, everyone would say…why is God is lying..?' (De Fonzo 2005: 1). Faith in science and/or scientific methods, however, can be overstated, e.g. Sally Clark in England and Wales was accused and convicted (later overturned) for allegedly killing her two young sons based on partially flawed statistical data presented in court on cot deaths. A few years later the National Academy of Sciences in USA concluded that 'most forensic sciences… sacrifice appropriate methodology for the sake of expediency' (Giannelli 2010: 247). The power of 'scientific evidence', however, is often compelling, but it is in dealing with 'scientific evidence', and hidden relationships with law enforcement and scientists that can lead to blatant manipulation and corruption of 'evidence' to secure a conviction that corrupts the criminal justice system.

Whilst science used in criminal justice is sometimes flawed, it is the non-scientific aspects of a case such as perception and judgment by law enforcement that affect the outcome of 'scientific' methods. I avoid the contested debate regarding the lack of scientific rigor in some forensic science even though this can cause miscarriages of justice (Huff and Killias 2013; Gill 2014) but instead consider where law enforcement transmits views directly to scientific state or private colleagues.

'Evidence' is presented to technicians in a suggestive manner by law enforcement leading to a motivational bias. For example, Zain a forensic scientist in West Virginia, USA routinely reported results that favoured the police and prosecution but an investigation into his crime laboratory discovered that he falsified 134 cases (that we are aware of) in ten years (Giannelli 2007). As stated by the West Virginia Supreme Court these were 'shocking and…egregious violations and the corruption of our legal system' (1993: 508). This is a clear case of corruption but motivational bias is only one problem here; there is cognitive bias (role effects) where occupational settings and perception of role(s) can influence the presentation of results such as extraneous information which influences a decision where law enforcement claim to know who the guilty party is and only seek 'scientific' information to add to the armoury of evidence. Then there is confirmation bias where a hypothesis is tested (did this person commit the crime?) looking for instances/evidence to confirm this view, and reconstructive effects where we rely on memory to complete the information of what we think occurred. Such context bias is thought to have played an important part in the FBI's error in identifying Brandon Mayfield as the 'terrorist' that committed the Madrid train bombing in 2004 based on fingerprints. Brandon Mayfield was released after a couple of weeks in prison but many suspects spend years in prison based on context bias and flawed data (Gill 2014).

Whilst such a case above highlights the number of corrupt cases we will have limited knowledge of the real extent of the number of cases that have been fabricated. In addition, errors are made, rather than blatant corruption and these too impact on the legitimacy of scientific evidence and criminal justice procedure. Forensic science is thus not always 'scientific' even though it is supposed to be objective, scientific, accurate, factual and free from bias. Errors, bias or plain corruption are often compounded at later stages in criminal justice but with the status that science is afforded in criminal justice 'mistakes' can be difficult to correct and resolve, particularly if presented to a jury as accurate and statistically valid.

In the USA and Canada, it is the judge that decides if the individual is to be admitted as an 'expert' and which theoretical approach and underpinning methods of analysis are used in court as admissible evidence to determine scientific 'facts'. Federal standards were established in the USA in the Federal Rules of Evidence (1974) (see Frye v United States case) with the judge as the ultimate authority allowing evidence. In 1993, the Daubert case clarified that expert testimony must have evidentiary reliability and be both theoretical and methodological valid. However, the judge is still in the position of gatekeeper. The problem is that whilst demanding intellectual rigor in methodology and analysis of data it is assumed that judges are they are free from bias (see Chapter 6) and can make a judgement of on expert knowledge.

Some acts of corruption are simply mistakes, human error, some are flawed procedure(s), context and motivational bias, but fraud and fabrication of evidence in the sciences also appear in criminal justice (Giannelli 2010). This is particularly noticeable in a crime—state or private—forensic laboratory. There is a lack of independence with a state laboratory controlled by the police. Working closely law enforcement technicians can view them as colleagues, part of the same team, and thus have a pro-prosecution bias rather than objective assessment of data. There are advocates to privatize the analysis of data to make it independent as was done in the United Kingdom, but simply removing the laboratory from state law enforcement control to the private sector only shifts the problem rather than resolves it. For example, there is currently a mass review of 10,000 cases processed by a private laboratory in England that analysed data for cases on sex offences and violent cases that appear to be flawed. There were criticisms in 2010 to close the then state Forensic Science Service (FSS) in England and replace it with the private sector but perhaps based on political ideology rather than notions of justice an important part of criminal justice was outsourced. This is not a problem itself but once under contract, and a desire to keep it, the potential for corruption to occur increases as 'fast' results rather than 'sound' results are produced. The private sector, as seen in white-collar business crimes will find the results law enforcement need if it is dependent on it keeping the contract. It is it better to hope for independence, in those jurisdictions that it is possible in, but allow equal access to data regardless of whether the legal representation is prosecuting or defence, a league table of crime laboratory errors to be publically available, and most of all healthy but respectful cynicism regarding forensic science.

The extent of corruption here then is substantial: it can be police corruption, flawed science, a flaw in the process of analysis, human error, manufactured 'evidence', bias in the process to 'find' evidence of guilt, corrupted DNA/bloods samples (see Brants [2012] for the Netherlands and Gill [2014] for international issues) where probability is presented as unequivocal fact by 'experts' and prosecution. The extent of corruption, however, should not be presented as a miscarriage of justice; a miscarriage presents the case as flawed not the system. But if miscarriages keep occurring, which they do, how can this be put down to individual error? This is the equivalent of the bad apple (Punch 2003) proposition regarding the police or rogue traders in the financial sector (Brooks 2016), both of which have been discredited. The extent of corruption in criminal justice will be limited based on known acts, with estimates of potential corruption based on this knowledge; but with law enforcement, prosecutors, judges (see Chapter 6) with a vested interest in claiming the system is either mostly sound with individual mistakes and/or blatant with few egregious acts of corruption, the extent of criminal justice corruption will be the same as that of crime—a serious underestimation of the level and reach of the damage it causes.

Corruption in the Prison System

Law enforcement encounters and engagement with members of the public are often visible, and this alone can sometimes, depending on the jurisdiction, and attitudes affect how law enforcement behaves. This, however, is only partially correct. Deaths of suspects can occur 'in the field,' particularly in nations where all law enforcement is armed (I mean automatic weapons here rather than batons, Tasers, etc. even though these can lead to deaths). Deaths in public can occur, e.g. shooting, or vehicle collision death, or suicides committed in a law enforcement confrontation. There will, in some cases be footage of these encounters but deaths in police custody are similar to deaths in prison: difficult to detect what really happened. The problem here is that data is limited. Planty et al. (2015) have illustrated in the USA that such data is deficient due to a lack of standardized models of data collection, definition and scope, and police participation in providing data.

In a prison, behind closed walls this problem is exacerbated. Inmates are subjected to violence from both prison officers and fellow inmates, dependent on cultural and jurisdictional differences (Lessing 2016) and death can result in the hands of either. Corruption in prison is thus hard to measure and thus empirically difficult to deliver evidence as well as on the level and types of corruption. There are, however, types of corruption that are prevalent in prison systems such as smuggling contraband. The contraband can be mobile/cell phones, narcotics, part of a weapon, a knife, etc. and transferred in and out of prison by prison officers, or between inmates or visitors and inmates or administrative employees of a prison and inmates (Centre for the Advancement of Public Integrity 2016). These 'relationships' could be considered the conduit of corruption, the avenues down which contraband flows, but these have consequences beyond the smuggled object; smuggled weapons are used to harm both inmates and prison officers. Systemic corruption thus creates a dangerous and violent environment, particularly in a prison or prison system where the officers have lost control of part or all of the prison (see Chapter 7).

In addition smuggling phones and/or blades can lead to organized criminal gangs control of a prison, but also maintain and orchestrate crime from behind bars (Lessing 2016). Since this is the case how do we measure corruption in a prison or prison systems? In our calculations do we include crime committed on the outside by someone on the inside? Do we include the private sector's success in securing a contract via bribery to offer services in a prison or manage a prison or even build one? This is still corruption of the prison system. The best we can do, I suggest, is highlight the extent of corruption—this is not equal to or should mean the measurement of it—but an analysis of the avenues and reach of corruption.

I have highlighted above the conduits of corruption and the prevalence (or known prevalence) of smuggling physical objects such as phones but what is the kind of environment that fosters corruption in prison? Whilst some jurisdictions are politically corrupt dictatorships (Yadav and Mukherjee 2016) and under absolute monarchical rule where the system is corrupt, to understand what fosters corruption it is best to review the prison system in a democratic nation. Prison corruption is often put forward, as is most corruption, as the product of individual moral failure and opportunism or systemic failure. Poor pay and low employment standards seem to contribute to corruption: instruction and education of prison officers can range from a number of hours (e.g. approximately 200 hours in New York State) to a matter of weeks; pay is low so officers are no doubt tempted to 'earn' more from smuggling narcotics (anywhere between 400 and 800 dollars a shift) (Centre for the Advancement of Public Integrity 2016: 2).

However, as with all types of corruption, even criminal corruption the consequences, if caught, are often minimal. No prison will want an internal examination of corrupt practice(s), particularly if private, as it might lose a profitable contract (Burkhardt 2014), but a private or state prison will often blame corruption on individual officers if possible, poor education of officers or poor supervision of officers that will be addressed (Eisen 2017) by the state or private sector. These often fail to address corruption though.

Whilst aware that corruption in prison systems exist it is impossible to state if corruption in its many forms has diminished or how much of that reduction, if any, is attributable to anti-corruption measures or investigations. In 2006, the Metropolitan Police and Prison Services in England and Wales discovered that the smuggling of narcotics and weapons in the prison system were prevalent. This investigation contributed to the creation of an investigatory and anti-corruption unit sponsored by the Metropolitan Police and Prison Services to help combat corruption on a national level, providing protocols for a national corruption prevention programme, with clear definitions of corruption. In 2018, however, the same problem still existed. Ministry of Justice research (Ellison et al. 2018) illustrated that mobile/cell phones have become embedded in prison life with some 15,000 phones and sim cards discovered in the prison system in England and Wales. The phones were used to run criminal enterprises from prison cells and intimidate witnesses for upcoming court cases, whilst young offenders appear to use phones to intimidate and control partners on the outside and/or for phone sex.

Furthermore, an FBI investigation into the Georgia Deptartment of Corrections that took two years to complete unearthed evidence that prison officers were paid between $500 and $1000 per smuggled phone, and noted that in 2014–2015 more than 23,500 phones were seized in a state with an inmate population of approximately 50,000. The phones were used to commit a kidnapping, and narcotics offences and financial fraud(s) (Centre for the Advancement of Public Integrity 2016). This is only one example of a prison system, but the reach and extent of corruption is substantial. Whilst surveillance systems such as body scanners can help reduce some smuggling it is impossible to prevent all smuggling. Prison officers' sweeps for contraband help, but this is only successful depending on the culture of corruption in the prison, and in fact, who controls the prison—prison officers or organized crime (Lessing 2016).

To reduce smuggling clear procedures need to be implemented. However, changes to procedures are based on the assumption that closing down avenues for corruption will alter corrupt officers' behaviour (see economic, legal and political view on preventing corruption in Chapter 2). This is logical, but whilst it might alter behaviour it has limited use in preventing corruption as the above example illustrated. Everybody passing through the security system in a prison can be searched, metal detectors, random use of canine's to detect contraband, and prison management schemes and random prison officers' searches. The problem here, as elsewhere in this chapter is that corruption is a flexible beast, and those in a position of power that are meant to supervise officers could be the most corrupt. Since all of this is behind closed doors with perhaps annual inspections, the only interruption to the management of a prison, it is possible for systemic corruption to flourish.

Although penal codes can highlight corrupt acts such as accepting and/or demanding a bribe and accepting sexual favours, it is impossible, to offer a clear assessment of the reach of corruption in and outside of a prison. In addition corrupt transactions in a prison (especially by officers) are seldom reported for fear of potential retaliation by other officers and/or management. This is common in law enforcement, too. Criminal justice systems, however, are no different to commercial businesses, in protecting its institution. Due to the closed environment, it is possible to block access to a custodial institution for a period of time by claiming potential 'security breaches'. Therefore, there are no clear available statistics that can predict the number of corrupt acts committed in a prison or prison system. These reasons though do not render custodial institutions helpless or unable to gauge the extent of corruption, however.

We can count contraband recovered, and record all inappropriate relationships, if exposed and breaches on codes of conduct by officers and inmates (yet again, if recorded), but corrupt acts can still be estimated by a qualitative approach (Souryal 2009). Management can estimate the extent of corruption by monitoring several work indicators such as the numbers of formal and informal complaints of prison employees by inmates, written recordings of supervisors, and speaking to inmates. Whilst all are flawed to some extent, some data is still useful. Monitoring the progression of disciplinary actions of employees for violating rules and regulations can yield a statistical chart of increases or decreases by year, month, or week. Furthermore, watching for patterns of questionable behaviour by employees similar to businesses such as involvement in alcoholism, narcotics, and radical changes in lifestyle, sudden acquisition of wealth, unexpected requests for reassignment, and sudden resignations might indicate corruption inside the prison (Souryal 2009). This might be possible in a state prison system but the private sector will cite security but most of all commercial confidentiality as a way to prevent unwanted intrusion, and particularly so if breaching its contract.

For perhaps the best analysis of corruption in the prison system we must look beyond the prison walls. As illustrated inmates can reach beyond and commit crime on the outside whilst incarcerated (Lessing 2016), but with the expansion of the private sector in democratic nations it is important to consider how contracts to manage and/or build a prison are secured. Before a service is provided or brick laid corruption in the form of bribery, an inducement, offer of a lucrative move from the state to private sector employment can already corrupt the prison system. Whilst presented as 'doing business' if a contract is secured via corruption to what extent will this reach into the prison system and exploitation of inmates? (*The Economist* 2018a: 19). This is not a problem of the private sector but one that both private and public endure. This is relevant to criminal justice where vested interests seek to maintain relationships that are beneficial to them and thus corrupt criminal justice.

Conclusion

This chapter has highlighted how difficult it is to measure corruption in the criminal justice system. This criticism, however, does not mean that we should abandon all attempts to measure corruption. It is imperfect, particularly with all types of crime, as those familiar with crime data are aware but those acts and crimes that are hidden add that extra complication regarding assessment. It is, however, useful to consider and highlight the avenues of potential corruption in law enforcement, manipulation of scientific data and flaws underpinning some forensic approaches, and that corruption in the prison system reaches beyond prison walls. Furthermore, with substantial state funds in both democratic and non-democratic states spent on law enforcement and prison systems the opportunity for the private sector to be tempted to commit acts of corruption has to be part of our future calculations.

References

Ashforth, B. E., & Anand, V. (2003). The Normalization of Corruption in Organizations. *Research in Organizational Behavior, 25*, 1–52.

Bailey, J., & Taylor, M. J. (2009). Evade, Corrupt, or Confront? Organized Crime and the State in Brazil and Mexico. *Journal of Politics in Latin America, 2*, 3–29.

Banerjee, A., Duflo, E., & Glennerster, R. (2007). Putting a Band-Aid on a Corpse: Incentives for Nurses in the Indian Public Health Care System. *Journal of the European Economic Association, 6*(2–3), 487–500.

Banks, C. (2017). *Criminal Justice Ethics: Theory and Practice*. London: Sage.
Beare, M. E. (2017). The Failures of Police Legitimacy: Attacks from Within. In V. Mitslegas, P. Alldridge, & L. Cheliotis (Eds.), *Globalisation, Criminal Law and Criminal Justice*. Oxford: Hart Publishing.
Beetham, D. (1991). *The Legitimation of Power*. London: Palgrave.
Bertrand, M., Djankov, S., Hanna, R., & Mullainathan, S. (2007). Obtaining a Driver's License in India: An Experimental Approach to Studying Corruption. *Quarterly Journal of Economics, 122*(4), 1639–1676.
Bisogno, E., Dawson-Faber, J., & Jandl, M. (2015). The International Classification of Crime for Statistical Purposes: A New Instrument to Improve Comparative Criminological Research. *European Journal of Criminology, 12*(5), 535–550.
Bottoms, A., & Tankebe, J. (2012). Beyond Procedural Justice: A Dialogic Approach to Legitimacy in Criminal Justice. *Journal of Criminal Law and Criminology, 102*(1), 119–170.
Brants, C. (2012). Wrongful Convictions and Inquisitorial Process: The Case of The Netherlands. *University Cincinnati Law Review, 80*, 1069–1112.
Brinks, D. M. (2008). *The Judicial Response to Police Killings in Latin America: Inequality and the Rule of Law*. Cambridge: Cambridge University Press.
Brooks, G. (2016). *Criminology of Corruption: Theoretical Approaches*. Basingstoke: Palgrave Macmillan.
Brooks, G. (2017). Country Report: Fraud, Corruption and Waste in Health Sector in EU. In European Healthcare Fraud and Corruption Network (Ed.), *Healthcare Fraud, Corruption and Waste in Europe*. New York: Springer.
Brooks, G., Lewis, C., Walsh, D., & Kim, H. (2013). *The Prevention of Corruption: Investigation, Enforcement and Governance*. Basingstoke: Palgrave Macmillan.
Burkhardt, B. (2014). Private Prisons in Public Discourse: Measuring Moral Legitimacy. *Sociological Focus, 47*(4), 279–298.
Button, M., & Brooks, G. (2014). From 'Shallow' to 'Deep' Policing: 'Crash-for-Cash' Insurance Fraud Investigation in England and Wales and the Need for Greater Regulation. *Policing and Society: An International Journal of Research and Policy, 26*(2), 210–229.
Button, M., Brooks, G., Lewis, C., & Aleem, A. (2017). Just About Everybody Doing the Business? Explaining Cash-for-Crash Insurance Fraud in the United Kingdom. *Australian and New Zealand Journal of Criminology, 50*, 176–194.
Button, M., Wakefield, A., Brooks, G., Lewis, C., & Shepherd, D. (2015). Confronting the 'Fraud Bottleneck': Private Sanctions for Fraud and Their

Implications for Justice. *Journal of Criminological Research, Policy and Practice, 1*(3), 159–174.
Caldero, M. A., & Crank, J. P. (2011). *Police Ethics: The Corruption of Noble Cause*. Boston: Anderson.
Cao, L., & Zhao, J. S. (2005). Confidence in the Police in Latin America. *Journal of Criminal Justice, 33*(5), 403–412.
Carter, D. L. (1990). Drug-Related Corruption of Police Officers: A Contemporary Typology. *Journal of Criminal Justice, 18*(2), 85–98.
Centre for the Advancement of Public Integrity. (2016). *Prison Corruption: The Problem and Some Potential Solutions*. Columbia Law School: Centre for the Advancement of Public Integrity.
Chaudhury, N., Hammer, J., Kremer, M., Muralidharan, K., & Rogers, F. (2006). Missing in Action: Teacher and Health Worker Absence in Developing Countries. *Journal of Economic Perspectives, 20*(1), 91–116.
Coicaud, J. M. (2002). *Legitimacy and Politics: A Contribution to the Study of Political Right and Political Responsibility*. Cambridge: Cambridge University Press.
Corbacho, A., Philipp, J., & Ruiz-Vega, M. (2015). Crime and Erosion of Trust: Evidence for Latin America. *World Development, 70*, 400–415.
De Fonzo, J. H. (2005). The Crimes of Crime Labs. *Hofstra Law Review, 34*(1), 1–12.
Diphoorn, T. (2016). Twilight Policing: Private Security Practices in South Africa. *British Journal of Criminology, 56*(2), 313–331.
Doig, A. (2006). *Fraud*. Cullumpton: Willan Publishing.
Eisen, L. B. (2017). *Inside Private Prisons: An American Dilemma in the Age of Mass Incarceration*. New York: Columbia University Press.
Ellison, A., Coates, M., Pike, P. S., Smith-Yau, W., & Moore, R. (2018). *The Demand for and Use of Illicit Phones in Prison*. London: MOJ Analytical Series and HM Prison and Probation Service.
Fitzgibbon, W., & Lea, J. (2017). Privatization and Coercion: The Question of Legitimacy. *Theoretical Criminology, 22*(4), 545–562.
Gerber, T. P., & Mendelson, S. E. (2008). Public Experiences of Police Violence and Corruption in Contemporary Russia: A Case of Predatory Policing? *Law and Society Review, 42*(1), 1–44.
Giannelli, P. C. (2007). Wrongful Convictions and Forensic Science: The Need to Regulate Crime Labs. *North Carolina Law Review, 86*(1), 163–235.
Giannelli, P. C. (2010). *Independent Crime Laboratories: The Problem of Motivational and Cognitive Bias*. Cape Western Reserve University: CWRP Faculty Publication.
Gill, M. (2005). *Learning from Fraudsters*. Leicester: Perpetuity.

Gill, P. (2014). *Misleading DNA Evidence: Reasons for Miscarriages of Justice.* London: Academic Press.
Gottschalk, M. (2016). The Role of Lawyers as Defenders of White Collar Crime. In M. Edelbacher, P. Kratcoski, & B. Dobovsek (Eds.), *Corruption, Fraud, Organized Crime, and the Shadow Economy.* Boca Raton, FL: CRC Press.
Heywood, P. M. (2015). *Routledge Handbook of Political Corruption.* Abingdon: Routledge.
Home Office. (2002). *Police Reform Act 2002.* London: Home Office.
Hough, D. (2015). *Corruption, Anti-corruption and Governance.* Basingstoke: Palgrave Macmillan.
Huff, R., & Killias, M. (2013). *Wrongful Conviction: International Perspectives on Miscarriages of Justice.* London: Routledge.
Independent Office for Police Conduct. (2018). *Police Complaints: Statistics for England and Wales.* London: IOPC.
Kane, R. J., & White, M. D. (2013). *Jammed Up: Bad Cops, Police Misconduct, and the New York City Police Department.* New York: New York University Press.
Kaufmann, D. A., Kraay, A., & Mastruzzi, M. (2006). Measuring Corruption: Myths and Realities. *Development Outreach, 8*(2), 124–137.
Knapp Commission. (1972). *The Knapp Commission Report on Police Corruption.* New York: George Braziller.
Lessing, B. (2016). *Inside Out: The Challenge of Prison-Based Criminal Organizations* (Brookings Local Orders Papers Series 1–23).
Levi, M. (1981). *The Phantom Capitalists: The Organisation and Control of Long Firm Fraud.* London: Heinemann.
Levi, M. (1987). *Regulating Fraud: White Collar Crime and the Criminal Process.* London: Routledge.
Levi, M. (2005). International Fraud. In M. Natarjan (Ed.), *Introduction to International Criminal Justice.* Boston, MA: McGraw-Hill.
Lewis, C., Brooks, G., Button, M., Shepherd, D., & Wakefield, A. (2015). Evaluating the Case for Greater Use of Private Prosecutions in England and Wales for Fraud Offences. *International Journal of Law, Crime and Justice, 42*(1), 3–15.
Macaulay, F. (2007). Knowledge Production, Framing and Criminal Justice Reform in Latin America Author(s): Fiona Macaulay Source. *Journal of Latin American Studies, 39*(3), 627–651.
Miller, S. (2017). *Institutional Corruption: A Study in Applied Philosophy.* Cambridge: Cambridge University Press.
Olken, B. A., & Barron, P. (2007). The Simple Economics of Extortion: Evidence from Trucking in Aceh. *Journal of Political Economy, 117*(3), 1–57.

Planty, M., Burch, A., Banks, D., Couzens, L., Blanton, C., & Cribb, D. (2015). *Arrested Related Deaths Program: Data Quality Profile*. Washington, DC: Department of Justice, Office for Justice Programs and Bureau of Justice Statistics.

Punch, M. (1985). *Conduct Unbecoming: The Social Construction of Police Deviance and Control*. London: Tavistock.

Punch, M. (2000). Police Corruption and Its Prevention. *European Journal on Criminal Policy Research, 8*(3), 301–324.

Punch, M. (2003). Rotten Orchards: Pestilence, Police Misconduct and System Failure. *Policing and Society, 13*(2), 171–196.

Punch, M. (2009). *Police Corruption: Deviance, Accountability and Reform in Policing*. Cullompton: Willan Publishing.

Roebuck, J., & Barker, T. (1973). *An Empirical Typology of Police Corruption: A Study in Organizational Deviance*. Springfield, IL: Charles C. Thomas.

Seligson, M. A. (2006). The Measurement and Impact of Corruption Victimization: Survey Evidence from Latin America. *World Development, 34*(2), 381–404.

Shearing, C. (1981). *Organisational Police Deviance*. Toronto: Butterworths.

Souryal, S. S. (2009). Deterring Corruption by Prison Personnel: A Principle-Based Perspective. *The Prison Journal, 89*(1), 21–45.

Standford, A. (2015). *Copping Out: The Consequences of Police Corruption and Misconduct*. Santa Barbara, CA: Praeger.

Syed, T., & Bruce, D. (1998). Police Corruption: Towards a Working Definition. *African Security Review*, 7(1), 3–14.

Sykes, G. M., & Matza, D. (1957). Techniques of Neutralization: A Theory of Delinquency. *American Sociological Review, 22*, 664–670.

The Economist. (2018a, August 25). Dejected About Democracy. *The Economist*, p. 19.

The Economist. (2018b, November 10). The Stench of Failure. *The Economist*, pp. 48–49.

Tyler, J. C. (2014). Blind Injustice: The Supreme Court, Implicit Racial Bias and the Racial Disparity in the Criminal Justice System. *American Criminal Law Review, 51*, 689–713.

Urra, F. J. (2007). *Assessing Corruption an Analytical Review of Corruption Measurement and Its Problems: Perception, Error and Utility*. Georgetown: Georgetown University.

Van Dijk, J. (2015). The Case for Survey-Based Comparative Measures of Crime. *European Journal of Criminology, 12*(4), 437–456.

White, A. (2015). The Politics of Police 'Privatization': A Multiple Streams Approach. *Criminology and Criminal Justice, 15*(3), 283–299.
Yadav, V., & Mukherjee, B. (2016). *The Politics of Corruption in Dictatorships.* Cambridge: Cambridge University Press.

4

Law Enforcement, Security and Corruption

Introduction

There is a substantial amount of international literature on police corruption; however rather than reference the literature on England and Wales and USA which we always reference (see Sarre and Preznler 2005; Porter and Preznler 2016 for Australia), (Hinton 2006 for Argentina), (Steinberg 2008; Vigneswaran and Hornberger 2009; Newman and Faull 2011; Bradford et al. 2014; Ivokovic and Sauerman 2016 for South Africa), (Tanekebe 2009, 2010; Boateng 2018 for Ghana), (Boateng 2018 for Africa), (Ivokovic and Kang 2012 for South Korea), (Willis 2014 for Brazil), (Ivokvic 2009 for Croatia) and (Lobinar et al. 2016 for Solvenia and Jonathan-Zamir and Weisburd 2013 for Israel), (Gerber and Mendolson 2008; Rawlinson 2012 for Russia) is only a sample of the international literature available of which only a fraction of this is on law enforcement corruption. I make this distinction here (as I did in Chapter 2) between law enforcement and police because

G. Brooks, *Criminal Justice and Corruption*,
https://doi.org/10.1007/978-3-030-16038-8_4

referring only to the police is a somewhat understated reach of a states' law enforcement capacity. Border and immigration and revenue, customs and excise also 'police' both its borders and citizens (Gounev and Bezlov 2012). This chapter then considers corruption in law enforcement rather than the 'police' as all of the above can corrupt national and international criminal justice systems.

There is a contemporary body of literature on policing and legitimacy (Bradford et al. 2017; Gottschalk 2017; Griffiths and Clark 2017; Kochel 2017; McCluskey and Reisig 2017; Miller 2017; Roche and Roux 2017; Skinns et al. 2017) and whilst some characteristics of law enforcement have changed, corrupt acts continue to remain a constant companion no matter what reforms are invoked. Aware that demands on law enforcement increase, often without the personnel and/or funds to deliver a 'service' in some democratic states public approval of some law enforcement is still positive, in some jurisdictions such as the United Kingdom and Royal Mounted Canadian Police (Beare 2017) but even here the reputation of law enforcement has declined from its high water mark in the 1950s.

Self-inflicted corruption scandals have contributed to significant pockets of disapproval. The existence of an 'enacted environment' (Manning 1979) with the ability of law enforcement to define—or at least influence—its working environment can lead to both internal and external breaches of conduct and outright corruption. Whilst corruption fails to change law enforcement in a police state, corruption scandals in democratic states harm law enforcement, its credibility and public legitimacy to act, and ultimately to work *for* the public rather than *for* the benefit of law enforcement. Furthermore, the police are sometimes engaged in symbolic policing (Innes 2004, 2014; Coomber et al. 2017) rather than corruption but this type of policing also fails to benefit the public.

I touch on these issues above but emphasize the causes of corruption, undercover work, the development and problem of private policing/security and conclude with a review of law enforcement reform.

Causes of Law Enforcement Corruption

In the previous chapter, I briefly reviewed the extent of corruption in law enforcement, and prison sector: here however, I discuss some of the reasons put forward to explain the causes of corruption. These are a combination of constant and variable factors that often blur and should be seen as complementing and competing factors that are potential routes into corruption. Roebuck and Barker (1973) listed a range of acts decades ago but are worth mentioning here: dishonest and criminal recruits (Lewis and Blum 1964); 'faulty' training and supervision (Tappan 1960), lack of professional standards (Skolnick 1967)—much has changed with standards now though, but these are dependent on country, historical development of police, geography, political will and independence from the state, societal appetite and demands for illegal services and socialisation of new recruits into corrupt practices.

Law enforcement often profess that corruption is that of an individual or at most a corrupt unit of officers rather than institutional. These 'bad apples' or rogue individuals is popular with all organizations—law enforcement and financial sector (Brooks 2016) as an explanation of corruption. However, repeated exposure of corrupt national and international law enforcement bodies and specialised units attests otherwise with systems of internal corruption highly organized, protected and reinforced by a tolerance of or selective blindness to acts of corruption.

The individual explanation for corruption is criticized but the subculture or canteen culture (Punch 2000, 2003, 2009), especially in the police, is still of explanatory value. This culture is said to contain high internal solidarity and secrecy, protecting corrupt colleagues. To protect colleagues and secure convictions lying was, and still is for some acceptable and necessary practice (Beare 2017). The police break the law, and whilst under some notion of noble cause corruption—the manipulation of evidence—to secure the conviction of a known offender is contested, the manipulation of evidence to simply convict someone, even though the police are aware the individual is possibly innocent, is corruption. There is a distinction between those that break the law and those that abide by it; it is not a personal matter of moral fibre (or lack of it) but the culture and content and particularly in the context of what is learnt in the course of 'working practice'.

This 'working practice' is perhaps explained by differential association (Sutherland 1940) where a person(s) of respectability and social status—law enforcement, judges and prosecutors—commit corrupt acts in the course of his/her occupation and cultural environment (Lilly et al. 1989, 2015). Once inducted and seduced into a corrupt system of behaviour individuals, at the interactional level learn that criminal behaviour is acceptable and justified in association with colleagues. This, however, is only if, the 'weight of the favourable definitions exceeds the weight of unfavourable definitions' (Sutherland 1949: 234). Coleman (1992: 57) stressed that justifications for acts were not ex post facto excuses to rationalize an action already completed but were psychologically present before crime was committed and a major part of the motivation to act. Sykes and Matza (1957) also referred to these rationalizations as 'techniques of neutralization' which allowed individuals to engage in corruption and yet maintain a positive self-concept.

This is perhaps reflected in one of the most corrupting influences on criminal justice with what is known as testilying (Beare 2017). This is where law enforcement personnel knowingly commit perjury to secure a conviction in a court of law. Testilying appears pervasive in law enforcement regardless of the jurisdiction, particularly where the law enforcement both arrest and take a case(s) to court, are presented as witnesses in case(s) and institutional pressure to conform to a corrupt system where law enforcement needs a positive self-concept of itself.

For Ashforth and Anand (2003) a positive self-concept is a combination of institutionalization, rationalization and socialization. The combination of these elements are that institutionalization is where an initial corrupt act becomes embedded in structures and processes such as testilying (Beare 2017), rationalization is justification(s) put forward to commit a corrupt act, and socialization is where new employees are induced or seduced to view corruption as permissible. It is possible to see how law enforcement can be 'seduced' into a positive self-concept dealing with 'criminals' and justifying bending rules and/or breaking them to secure a conviction.

In the absence of institutionalization, and interaction, however, it is doubtful that acts of corruption become embedded in organizational structures and processes and thereby part of a routine and way of 'policing' and thus the rationalization and subsequent socialization of such acts will be absent too; corruption might exist, however, in a small part or section such as a vice squad rather than all of an organization.

Corruption is said to be institutionalized when it is stable, resists change and is transmitted via peers (Oliver 1992; Zucker 1977) and endures because individuals involved are not prompted by a cognitive dissonance to challenge established corrupt practices. The social cocoon of organizational socialization is a powerful 'force' that seduces individuals into acceptance of corruption or to mute moral awareness. Further, socialization practices can themselves become institutionalized and strongly influence new employees that encounter 'indoctrination' of set practices and views of 'how we do it here' by established members of an organization.

The boundary between acceptable practice and corruption is often blurred, however, and difficult to measure (Klockars 1985: 56). If and under what circumstances is it justifiable (Gerber and Jackson 2017) to use illegitimate methods to achieve set ends? The problem is that moral cynicism could lead law enforcement to regard corruption as ends in itself particularly if the criminal justice system is seen as highly inefficient (e.g. offenders released from prison after brief period of time for a serious crime).

Institutionalized socialization increases new employees' acceptance of organizational practices and leads to common interpretations and less questioning of policing practice(s). Corruption is therefore more likely to be accepted precisely because it is packaged in a way that prevents dissent and renders systems of practice into seemingly objective accounts of reality (Brooks 2016). Socialization and rationalization reinforce one another and serve as an explanatory sedative and justification for acts of corruption. The social cocoon of socialization can provide a protective environment for actions that new employees might reject, unless inducted into the culture of the organization. Corruption, if left unchallenged—internally and externally—has the potential to seep into the fibre of an organization and its practices through the process of institutionalization, and effect the conduct and actions of individuals (Ashforth and Anand 2003). These are constant factors, regardless of the jurisdiction, which contribute to the potential for corruption in law enforcement.

In addition law enforcement also has the power to exercise the freedom to enforce or discount an offence. There is opportunity here for such decisions to be influenced by material benefit rather than professional judgement. It is not only the variability in the use of discretion that is crucial here, it is also types of law enforcement that increase the chances of corruption, e.g. narcotics, where the nature of the violation(s) can seduce and 'capture' (Dal Bo 2006) law enforcement personnel. Discretion is, however, necessary for law enforcement to act and function, but also a problem for law enforcement.

Discretion, inherent in much law enforcement is difficult to control. Even under the best circumstances (Goldstein 1990: 6), officers are out 'in the field', even in a prosecutorial system, and not subject to direct surveillance and supervision. To state the obvious, this allows law enforcement to resist direct control, management, legislation and disciplinary actions. In such situations, rules will be violated. Before we condemn law enforcement, however, most of us want the discretion to interpret our working conditions free from management oversight but are unable to perhaps change the entire course of an individual's life by an act of corruption. The relative invisibility of law enforcement, can therefore be exploited, particularly the most secretive undercover aspects of law enforcement. This low visibility has changed for the majority of police work, though, with the number of mobile/cell phones in use by the public. But to this problem, we can add management support—tacitly mostly—for breaching set rules. As Punch (2009) highlighted senior officers constantly reiterate the need to stick to formal rules but then display an emphasis on success even where the rules have been bent.

This discretion and low management control or implicit support to break the rules is backed by a culture of peer pressure and secrecy and informal rules. Rules, particularly in law enforcement serve two purposes: one, minimize the chances of external control and oversight, and two, keep corruption under control. These rules are maintained because of perhaps the most powerful informal rule: the rule of silence (Lobinar et al. 2016; Porter and Preznler 2016).

A combination of discretion, management corruption and the rule of silence or deniability is illustrated in the Hillsborough disaster in the United Kingdom where the power to label and define an individual(s) as hooligans, and as offenders rather than victims is an example of law enforcement, combined with political expediency and bias journalism of the power of law enforcement institutions' capacity to thwart 'justice'. The disaster at Hillsborough football stadium in the United Kingdom, in 1989 where 96 people—men, women and children—were killed in a fatal crush (Scraton 1999) with approximately 766 injured is an old case but one that has continued as 'justice' is sought by those affected by the disaster. As such it is an old but contemporary example of the power of vested interests to label and manipulate and reconstruct the 'truth' by rejecting claims of police corruption of the truth, where statements were amended, legal progress blocked where possible, and silence. There are ample accounts of the disaster at Hillsborough by those that seek the 'truth' and 'justice' (Scraton 1999, 2000, 2004, 2016; Williams 2014) and it is therefore not my intention to replicate this body of knowledge here.

Truth, however, is an enigmatic concept as seen in many cases of corruption; its definition, identification and verification involve intellectual, political and legal processes seemingly straightforward, yet inherently complex. Establishing precisely and contextually 'what really happened' at any moment in time, in specific circumstances, is complicated. Underpinning legal processes and the administration of justice in democratic states is supposedly a consensus on the weighing and weighting of personal truths, and the examination of what happened based on our ability to recall events. In principle, at least, justice should offer procedures through which the truth can be aggregated rather than manufactured. Criminal and civil investigations, official and unofficial reviews and inquests and court and tribunals examinations are bound by evidence. However, such official bodies reproduce structural inequality (Brooks 2016).

Such structural inequality often deflects attention away from the power and strength to determine the context and 'truth' of an event. Whilst power is derived from the material conditions of production and reproduction, it is realized in the state, its institutions and its interventions. The state, in this case, claims legitimacy to establish the truth. As Foucault (1980: 131) states, 'Each society has its régime of truth… the types of disclosure which it accepts…the mechanisms and instances which enable one to distinguish…the techniques and procedures accorded value in the acquisition of truth'. It is simply that those with power define the truth, and that knowledge of the truth and right to be heard are not equally distributed, particularly in dictatorships (Greitens 2016). Institutional power affords its holders the capacity to determine versions of 'truth' and/or denial. A case in Russia illustrates institutional power: in 2004 local police were joined by members of a special police (OMON) unit in a region in Russia where a predominantly Muslim population resides. They arrested, for what appears no reason, young men in cafes, restaurants and public places and beat them in public and then illegally held them in custody for several days. A subsequent investigation and institutional denial, of course, failed to unearth anything illegal and/or corrupt (Gerber and Mendolson 2008).

Discourses of denial, however, can take different forms; the 'classic' discourse of official denial; the strategy of spinning a defensive position into an attack on the critic; (also seen as condemning those that condemn you) and partial acknowledgement of different points of view (Cohen 1996). Within these denials, there are different positions. For example, in 'classic' discourse there is literal denial (nothing happened); interpretive denial (what happened is really something else); implicatory denial (what happened is justified) (Brooks 2016). These denials and manipulation of the truth are regularly part of corruption discourse by individuals and organizations and often, and disappointingly so, supported by official state discourse or passive acceptance that law enforcement is 'right'. The problem with those seeking justice from a criminal justice system and corrupt organizations, however, is the positions of power of those representing law and order, which is bolstered by the 'language of legalism' (Cohen 1996) where states, law enforcement, corrupt organizations, harness its processes and procedures to conduct a sophisticated 'legal defence' and obfuscation of the 'truth'. The criminal justice system needs to at least be seen as impartial. If, however, used as a tool to obfuscate, and manufacture an official or partial 'truth' amount to little more than a show of concern and fabricated sympathy, it harms the legitimacy of criminal justice, once exposed.

By combining all the 'causes' of corruption mentioned so far with discretion, limited management control or involvement, and a code of secrecy, the opportunity to succumb to temptation is perhaps to be human. This is a potential danger of those engaged in undercover work, and illegal markets that are popular—narcotics, gambling and prostitution. This 'invitational edge of corruption' (Manning and Redlinger 1977: 354; Botelo and Rivera 2000; Beck and Lee 2002) are understandably acute. The consequence of this context, depending on the jurisdiction, is that non-enforcement is relatively common, and the opportunity to negotiate a 'sign of appreciation' to exercise discretion can become frequent and regular. This context explaining law enforcement corruption is thus highly important. Small breaches can potentially lead to major acts of corruption. For example, acceptance of a small benefit involves the same rationale as accepting a major benefit compromising professional impartiality, and engaging in one acts leads to the justification and rationalization that a range of corrupt acts are acceptable. The problem here though is what is acceptable and unacceptable in practice (Miller 2017).

In order to understand organizational corruption and how it occurs, a distinction needs to be drawn between crime committed in the course of an occupation and collective, systemic corruption. An organization, however, is unable to think and act as a conscious body aware of its own acts and though organizations are run by a collection of individuals, it is this collection of roles and functions that individuals occupy and shape the conduct of an employee's behaviour. As such, individual's morality is of less importance that the structure in which s/he works (Boisjoly 1995). It is not the moral standards and virtues of the individuals that determine the conduct of the organization; it is the structure and culture of the organization that directs human action and interaction in the course of a structured law enforcement environment, e.g. the notion of canteen culture. Most organizations, however, are structured in such a way where they can be manipulated to behave in a legal or illegal manner. The structure is only part of the problem. It is the role and attitude of senior management that can turn a legitimate organization into one that is inherently 'criminogenic'. All of these 'causes' are relevant to law enforcement.

Policing Undercover

If corruption 'on the streets' by the police is a potential avenue of corruption then undercover law enforcement is even more problematic (Ross 2004; Mitchell et al. 2005; Ross 2007, 2008; Joh 2009; Kruisbergen et al. 2011; Tinto 2012; Nathan 2017). Undercover work allows law enforcement to act without public knowledge. To do so, however, law enforcement needs public legitimacy to act in its interests (Gerber and Jackson 2017), and sometimes where appropriate use its power; but the problem here is that lack of and/or reduced accountability that can be invoked in the name of national security and undercover work. Law enforcement can invoke the threat of security/public disturbance and employ policing tactics beyond 'normal' policing such as 'kettling' or containment tactics. Furthermore, it can define a community as dangerous and in need of surveillance (Kochel 2017) and thus police undercover. In such a context policing then needs little justification if aimed at organized crime and/or organizations seen as a threat to the state but such tactics can be used in an urban environment/community if a threat is established—be it real or manufactured. These potential avenues for corruption are dealt with in turn below.

Law enforcement can directly control a neighbourhood without a national and/or serious criminal threat. The police can police 'poor neighbourhoods' by 'lying' or exaggerating the state of a community. In many situations such as dealing with organized crime, the police are able to define a situation and successfully justify any action, and even break the law to achieve it and what is claimed a public aim. This is understandable but should an estate, a community presented as a major problem, e.g. potential 'youth crime', encounter such intrusive practice? The problem here is that, for some residents it will be acceptable, and for some, not only those engaged in crime, as unacceptable. Law enforcement has to manage diverse needs and its legitimacy. But if working unchecked and in what are referred to as 'free zones' (Beare 2017), local residents might consider policing tactics as intrusive and brutal, particularly if innocent people are constantly stopped and searched. The police can claim, however, that the community is a problem, often in need of a law enforcement rather than social solution. By claiming that some urban parts of a city are 'out-of-control' and defined as a problem zone the police can present an elite armed unit as a necessity and often work with near impunity in that 'community'. This policing is not undercover nor in disguise but is unseen in the sense that the targeted population is without a voice and can often lead to increased surveillance. An example of this type of 'policing strategy' is the Toronto Anti-Violence Intervention Strategy (TAVIS) units and Neighbourhood TAVIS Initiative (NTI). This intervention failed to increase the safety on the streets (Beare 2017) but increased police power. Without public consent the police lack the legitimacy needed to be ultimately successful, and policing in this way has the potential to be counter-productive leading to future distrust of law enforcement.

Undercover work can differ; it can be to obtain intelligence to disrupt a criminal organization or known or seeming threat to the state. Such a method is used to secure 'intelligence' but also induce a confession and/or entrap 'criminals'. Furthermore, law enforcement, particularly undercover, can undermine a criminal investigation or proceedings by mislaying key information (this, however, can be both as visible police and/or undercover). A long-term aim of undercover work though is about more than intelligence. It could be to put individuals 'in-debt' to law enforcement that can be called in later to prevent major crime(s) and thus benefit the public. This is possible where law enforcement sometimes overlook illegal acts such as personal narcotic consumption, prostitution and pornography. This can be for a variety of reasons: processing offenders in possession of a small amount of narcotics leads to an increase in paperwork, law enforcement accept/demand sex from 'sex workers' so they can continue to 'trade' and some pornography is seen as adult behaviour but only problematic if children are involved.

Protecting illegal acts law enforcement can thus engage in a failure to act (protect suspects) where law enforcement withhold evidence (as can prosecutors), which clearly indicate innocence. This evidence can be withheld because of complete faith in the victim (or supposed victim). There is also a failure to act (protect victims) but undercover, and as with much of crime, the offenders can be victims and the victims are offenders. For law enforcement then such situations are a legal but moral minefield (Miller 2017) and some sympathy should I suggest be forthcoming for trying to unearth and uncover sufficient evidence to secure a conviction, particularly if working undercover with organized crime.

The police, particularly if working in a democratic state (Johnston 2013) with a diverse population (Murphy and Cherney 2012) are under immense pressure to secure evidence to secure a conviction. The desire for a conviction, however, is not the sole province of the police. It is the police though that is undercover, and uses the protection(s) the state affords them. This can end in a violation of legal process, depending on the country, with an emphasis on 'police justice' rather than legal, rule of law justice.

This result can also be seen where law enforcement is found encouraging vigilantism. In some jurisdictions vigilantism is seen as acceptable by both the public and law enforcement (see Chapter 9). Vigilantism is sometimes tacitly accepted by law enforcement because they are either unable to prevent crime and/or arrest suspects due to a lack of community acceptance (see Northern Ireland), or the law restricts the acts law enforcement can legitimately conduct, e.g. abuse of suspects, or the state is ineffectual in policing its country (see Mexico) as it is so corrupt. In some nations the criminal justice system is seen as so corrupt that vigilantism is the only viable option to protect politically disenfranchised, marginalized citizens.

For undercover work though what is acceptable conduct is sometimes blurred. By its very nature undercover law enforcement has no option but to sometimes engage in criminal acts—to think otherwise I suggest is foolish. To be accepted by organized crime undercover law enforcement needs to sometimes break the law. This is perhaps justified with organized crime and/or a terrorist threat but can be seen as an unwanted extension of state power in a local community that is defined as problematic where faith and trust in the law enforcement could rapidly decline, and hence its legitimacy to act, in a democratic state.

There is also an issue of 'trust' (Jackson et al. 2012; Boateng 2018; Kochel 2017) or lack of it, within and between national and international law enforcement bodies to consider as well. There are 'circles of trust' (Sztompka 1999; Zucker 1985) which are characteristics based, process based and institutional. By characteristics based I mean belonging to a similar policing community and shared cultural values; process based is interaction with others from which trust will follow, and institutional-based trust stems from rules, ethics and professional standards. A law enforcement 'relationship' might rely on one of more of the circles of trust above, but also informal contacts, working with individuals and/or specific units of law enforcement. However, a lack of trust, and this can be at the international level, could hamper both policing and judicial transnational cooperation particularly in a covert undercover manner (Cocq and Galli 2017). Relationships in the state police can be potentially corrupt, e.g. break laws policing a community and/or undercover, a lack of trust within and across specialized law enforcement units, and national and international law enforcement bodies. Lack of trust, however, can lead to corruption—withhold evidence, lose evidence, block investigation in crime at local, national and international levels. These relationships though are the results of historical and cultural differences and this potential problem in policing has become more complex with the move towards the use of private security/policing in the USA, European Union and United Kingdom. The impact of privatization has come to occupy a major position in the extended police family and this commercial market has slowly expanded. This private sector policing, however, needs to secure trust and legitimacy from state law enforcement to which I now turn.

Private Policing

Private security is not on the margins providing services to the state in the name of policing and security; it is an important part of the criminal justice system, and particularly policing (Prenzler 2006; Sarre 2005,

2008, 2010). This expansion into policing has allowed private security to challenge the sovereignty of neo-liberal nation states and the traditional centralized methods of regulating society and increase its share of the policing market (White 2010). Commercialized or paid security is the most pervasive type of policing but it has to be noted that 'security' is not, if it ever was, the sole monopoly of the constitutional state. The development of private property in some jurisdictions, particularly in urban settings, has eroded the power of the state to 'steer' all types of 'policing' with the development of private enclaves policed by private security. This process of pluralization (more specifically, privatization) of policing is a unique challenge to policing a modern diverse population in some states, and the maintenance of order, I suggest, is ripe for corruption. The potential for corruption is similar to that of state law enforcement, e.g. abuse of power particularly towards non-residents of private enclaves, payment for preferential services/security of property, targeting people based on race and specific characteristics, but also breach of private security contracts. This potential for corruption is international rather than national with multinationals such as G4S, Chubb and Serco (Johnston 2006; Wood and Kempa 2005; White 2015) employed around the world and involved in private security work and typical criminal justice roles.

Unable to protect the public, at least at the level which it expects in 'western' jurisdictions, law enforcement has attempted to 'responsibilize' civil society for its own risk management (Garland 2001). The financial weakness of some states has contributed to the shift where spending on the police and public services leads to a security vacuum filled by the private sector (Button and Park 2009; Button 2012, 2016). In the context of liquid modernity (Bauman 2000) people collectively yearn for safety and protection, which leads to the optimal circumstances for private security to flourish. As such with the need to sell 'security' the private sector will pursue a client's objectives (Joh 2004: 61) rather than public objectives, and make profitable business deals (South 1988) where those that pay (or more explicitly can pay) are protected from a real or seeming threat.

A note of caution is required here though; private policing can and does offer and complement public policing and security. The problem is often the lack of accountability; a company commits a crime, mostly a white collar crime, but as with fraud and acts of corruption the punishment is financial, which the company can afford (Brooks 2016). It is also often hidden and as such the level of criminal justice corruption, particularly by the private sector, becomes even more opaque and impossible to measure. This will fail to deter those that are corrupt and can even embolden others to behave the same way. Furthermore, acts of corruption often breach and compromise rights and freedoms in some states and private sector security corruption is in addition to state law enforcement corruption, which weakens the integrity of criminal justice as criminal acts can and are downgraded as civil breaches. Private security and privatized criminal justice roles can thus extend the reach of corruption.

This is particularly noticeable where 'excessive use of force' has been used by the private sector with offenders in prison. This use of force, however, is not a direct challenge to the state's ultimate monopoly of legitimate coercion, as it is still the inspector and custodian of the legal frameworks that oversee private sector contracts to deliver a service(s). But this development is often downplayed and fails to consider the opportunity and power for the private sector to exercise day-to-day coercion and constraint of specific populations and/or geographical locations that were once public, and the lack of oversight and management of private sector contracts (e.g. disorder at HMP Oakwood, mismanagement of HMP Thameside and accusations of sexual impropriety at an immigration removal centre) (NAO 2013; Nellis 2014) in England. Private sector employees can and do also lock inmates or suspects in cells, administer penalty notices and sanction offenders for breaches of probation (for the latter example, see USA and Chapter 8).

These are profound issues regarding the legitimate power to punish. The major change in criminal justice legitimacy has been the 'hollowing out' (Rhodes 1994) of the state. Here, legitimacy is still possible without compromising the state as the ultimate repository of legitimate coercion but this is contested. The distinction between the determination and allocation of punishment (Genders 2002) where the initial (legitimate) judgements by state officials—the police arresting a suspect or offender, initial probation assessment and court sentence—is now used to justify subsequent acts by non-state employees. A state contract bestows on the private sector some credibility to run criminal justice services such as sentenced populations where potentially punitive judgements by private prison officers are exercised, e.g. extend sentence for breach of conditions (Eisen 2017). The issue is not, of course, restricted to the private sector because a public sector prison can be a site of unchecked punitive behaviour exercised by individuals with personal interest.

Policing private space such as a shopping centre also raises complex questions of legitimacy. The notion of policing in a democratic country is associated with the use of legitimate discretion (Beare 2017). However, the changing nature of policing public spaces has changed the relationship between the police and citizens. The police can choose from a variety of sanctions available such as warning offenders or arrest depending on the circumstances and 'attitude' and behaviour of the suspect. But this discretion is being slowly displaced with a transactional process of enforcement in which a specific violation is dealt with by either police officers or private security depending on the location. A private company secures its legitimacy via the state delegated subset of police powers but private security still lacks status, authority and capacity to emit 'control signals' (Jackson et al. 2013; Rowland and Coupe 2014) or to participate in a 'legitimacy dialogue' (Bottoms and Tankebe 2012: 159) with some members of the public.

Private policing and security though has secured political acceptability by lobbying and arguing it is cost effective and flexible. The private sector (see Chapter 2) has employed a number of techniques to secure legitimacy (Suchman 1995), but the expansion of private sector policing and security has not reduced state law enforcement corruption. Instead it has opened new avenues for corruption, particularly in the form of kickbacks. This is where law enforcement—public or private or a combination of both—receive products, services or cash for disregarding a criminal infraction. This can be both active and passive though some law enforcement will actively seek payment of some kind and some will accept if offered.

Furthermore, the privatization of law enforcement has the potential to corrupt criminal justice contracts to run 'services' secured via bribery/kickbacks. Services are corrupted as private sector organizations breach rules/break contracts/put in claims for work and/or supervision of offenders that are frauds (White 2015). The private sector can secure a contract to 'run' state police services by bribery or kickbacks, and therefore before a 'public service' has been provided corruption of the criminal justice system has already occurred. Often blamed on an 'accountancy error' and poor administration, which the private sector promises to address, the criminal justice system is still corrupted. Much of the literature has understandably examined state police corruption at the expense of private police. This now, however, is an important development and one that the literature on law enforcement is still limited regarding the issue of corruption at individual, unit and organizational level.

Private personnel have become an integral part of policing and offer a kaleidoscope of professional services and variety of products such as guarding (both in-house and via contract), security equipment production and installation, investigation of white-collar crime and advice on risk management. The silent rise of private security, no matter how it attempts to present itself as professional is the same as state law enforcement, potentially, and sometimes, corrupt.

Preventing and Reducing Law Enforcement Corruption

In the final section of this chapter, I consider the attempts employed to prevent and reduce corruption. There is not the space here to be exhaustive. However, a problem with law enforcement, as with any employment, can start at the recruitment stage. 'Proper' assessment of candidates appears a straightforward task, e.g. check for criminal records, membership of political party, depending on jurisdiction, and candidates qualifications. There is an immediate problem here; if law enforcement is corrupt it will do its best to hire candidates that suit its ethos. This is not the sole province of law enforcement as initial tests are used in a variety of commercial businesses to exclude people with the 'incorrect attitude', as defined by the business.

Once accepted new recruits undergo 'instruction' into what is expected of them (depending on the type of law enforcement) and this, also depending on the fellow officers, exercises completed (in class and/or in the field) and law enforcement potential for institutionalization and socialization and hence corruption. However, the impact of potential corruption is limited as a recruit, it is 'on the street' that socialization into the agency that will establish networks of loyalty within the police and often undermine internal and external control.

Much has been made of ethics and values (Banks 2017) in developing current and future police officers, particularly in supervisory roles, but a code of ethics itself will not, if ever, alter a culture of corruption, or prevent a specialized unit from corruption (Miller 2017). It can, however, offer direction and assistance. If coupled with deterrence—in this sense fear of exposure and discipline and/or conviction—it could have an effect on potentially corrupt officers. There is, however, little sign that threats deter. Long-term compliance needs more that a threat of exposure to have any major impact since it is clear that systemic corruption only exists if tolerated, in collusion or controlled by management. Yet again, this can be said of every business. Punch (2009) suggested that 'positive symbolic leadership' is useful in reducing potential corruption. Whilst it is possible to design and adopt a code of ethics and/or conduct, there is still the problem of implementation. If imposed by management on officers, it will not succeed; a policy will have been produced but old practice maintained 'on the streets'. There will be a structure of rules because of the nature of policing but these will not suppress discretion, only advance its exercise (Newman 1999).

Internal control of an organization might use a twin-track approach, and this might include preventive and punitive control. These approaches attempt to prevent the commission of corruption, and punish corrupt officers. But law enforcement (as well as other businesses) is often reluctant to hold people to account within an organization unless under external pressure from a regulatory body or public condemnation. The recent collapse of the Independent Police Complaints Commission (IPCC) in England and Wales is a perfect example. The IPCC was replaced by the Independent Office for Police Conduct (IOPC) in 2018 because of public anger and mistrust regarding investigations into the deaths of several men in police custody. This is not to claim that all law enforcement personnel are corrupt and obstructive, but it is possible that organizational inertia or calculated obstruction could thwart a suitable investigation into police misconduct. This is to simply recognize that 'punishment' of law enforcement is difficult.

There are, however, primary sources of information on which law enforcement corruption is potentially exposed. The public can complain about corrupt police officers but this can depend on the member of the public that is complaining and how law enforcement define and discredit them, e.g. a young male with a conviction (see above about power to define and control the discourse). If the corruption is systemic, complaining will fail to prevent the internal problem of corruption. However, 'public exposure'—via internal or external routes—could affect law enforcement in (1) if law enforcement is exposed as corrupt they will/can lose legitimacy with some members of the public and (2) in addition public exposure highlights how difficult it is to determine the 'truth' regarding corruption, and the number of complaints decrease, and corruption continues unaffected. The problem here though is that law enforcement rarely exposes corrupt law enforcement. Law enforcement, however, is not monolithic and the culture of policing appears to have been overstated. This is only relevant to jurisdictions that have shown a willingness to change, be it pushed on to them or accepted.

Preventing or reducing corruption is also possible using internal units. They can record conversations or access emails, observe locations known for the 'invitational edge' of corruption and use 'integrity tests' where artificial situations are manufactured to test officers' probity. These tests though test if s/he is corruptible rather than actually corrupt (Marx 1992). There a raft of ethical issues (Banks 2017; Miller 2017) here to consider around entrapment, but these can apply to all that work in the criminal justice system. Depending on the circumstances individuals that might refuse a temptation succumb, and such 'tests' should perhaps only be used if there is sufficient evidence of corruption. This, however, raises the question as to what is sufficient and what is/are the sources of this evidence? The investigation has to also consider if a suspect is interviewed early in an investigation if this will alert other corrupt officers, which leads to the destruction of evidence needed for the case.

External changes to policing can be made as seen above but for real change reform has to happen from within. This, yet again, is relevant to all businesses regardless of the line of work. Corruption is still predominantly defined as an individual problem, a rogue trader, and that if discovered an internal procedure will resolve the matter. This, however, is often not the case, and can be partly explained by businesses preventing the corruption reaching its own control and compliance systems, and the capacity to thwart and block external investigation. This can be done by claiming that the information presented to an internal control system was considered false and/or it failed to reach the standard of proof required. There are also few effective avenues of punishment. During corruption scandals there is always a tussle over the definition of if corruption is an individual or organizational problem. Both internal and external transformation needs to occur to reduce corruption in the future, but this has to be as transparent as possible otherwise, and particularly with law enforcement the legitimacy of policing will be damaged by the corruption itself but also how it is dealt with.

Conclusion

From the evidence presented in this chapter, law enforcement corruption can be in any jurisdiction regardless if it is democratic or of a non-democratic status. There are also illegal acts that need policing that are on the 'invitational edge' of corruption; these are characterized by a degree of secrecy, invisibility from management, administrative or democratic oversight. However, it must be noted that there will always be some type of corruption in law enforcement, particularly in non-democratic states that rarely seek legitimacy but instead display naked power. The problem for law enforcement in democratic states is that corruption by individuals, units or an organization, harm the credibility and legitimacy of its own institution and tarnish the reputation of *all* law enforcement. No environment is completely free from corruption, and corrupt acts are on a continuum of corruption (Brooks 2016) ranging from legal but unethical to highly illegal and criminal acts. It is, however, perhaps the position of power that law enforcement has that if abused is far more damaging to its legitimacy 'to police' than commercial businesses that engage in corruption and driven by profit.

References

Ashforth, B. E., & Anand, V. (2003). The Normalization of Corruption in Organizations. *Research in Organizational Behavior, 25*, 1–52.

Banks, C. (2017). *Criminal Justice Ethics: Theory and Practice*. London: Sage.

Bauman, Z. (2000). *Liquid Modernity*. Cambridge: Polity Press.

Beare, M. E. (2017). The Failures of Police Legitimacy: Attacks from Within. In V. Mitslegas, P. Alldridge, & L. Cheliotis (Eds.), *Globalisation, Criminal Law and Criminal Justice*. Oxford: Hart Publishing.

Beck, A., & Lee, R. (2002). Attitudes to Corruption Amongst Russian Police Officers and Trainees. *Crime, Law and Social Change, 38*, 357–372.

Boateng, F. D. (2018). Institutional Trust and Performance: A Study of the Police in Ghana. *Australian & New Zealand Journal of Criminology, 5*(2), 164–182.

Boateng, J. (2018). Police Legitimacy in Africa: A Multi-level Multinational Analysis. *Policing and Society, 28*(9), 1105–1120.

Boisjoly, R. M. (1995). Commentary on 'Technology and Civil Disobedience: Why Engineers Have a Special Duty to Obey the Law'. *Science and Engineering Ethics, 1*(2), 169–171.

Botelo, N. A., & Rivera, A. L. (2000). Everything in the Job Is Money: Inside the Mexican Police. *World Policy, 17*, 61–70.

Bottoms, A., & Tankebe, J. (2012). Beyond Procedural Justice: A Dialogic Approach to Legitimacy in Criminal Justice. *Journal of Criminal Law and Criminology, 102*(1), 119–170.

Bradford, B., Huq, A., Jackson, J., & Roberts, B. (2014). What Price Fairness When Security Is at Stake? Police Legitimacy in South Africa. *Regulation and Governance, 8*(2), 246–268.

Bradford, B., Milani, J., & Jackson, J. (2017). Identity, Legitimacy and 'Making Sense' of Police Use of Force. *Policing: An International Journal, 40*(3), 614–627.

Brooks, G. (2016). *Criminology of Corruption: Theoretical Approaches*. Basingstoke: Palgrave Macmillan.

Button, M. (2012). *Private Policing*. London: Willan Publishing.
Button, M. (2016). *Security Officers and Policing: Powers, Culture and Control in the Governance of Private Space*. Aldershot: Ashgate.
Button, M., & Park, H. (2009). Security Officers and the Policing of Private Space in South Korea: Profile, Powers and Occupational Hazards. *Policing and Society, 19*(3), 247–262.
Cocq, C., & Galli, F. (2017). The Evolving Role of Europol in the Fight Against Serious Crime: Current Challenges and Future Prospects. In S. Hufnagel & C. Mccartney (Eds.), *Trust in International Police and Justice Cooperation*. Oxford: Hart Publishing.
Cohen, S. (1996). Government Responses to Human Rights Reports: Claims, Denials, and Counterclaims. *Human Rights Quarterly, 18*(3), 517–543.
Coleman, J. W. (1992). The Theory of White-Collar Crime: From Sutherland to the 1990s. In K. Schlegal & D. Weisburd (Eds.), *White Collar Crime Reconsidered*. York, PA: Maple Press.
Coomber, R., Moyle, L., & Mahoney, M. (2017). Symbolic Policing: Situating Target Police Operations/'Crackdowns' on Street Level Drug Markets. *Policing and Society: An International Journal of Research and Policy, 29*(1) 1–17.
Dal Bo, E. (2006). Regulatory Capture: A Review. *Oxford Review of Economic Policy, 22*(2), 203–225.
Eisen, L. B. (2017). *Inside Private Prisons: An American Dilemma in the Age of Mass Incarceration*. New York: Columbia University Press.
Foucault, M. (1980). *Power/Knowledge: Selected Interviews and Other Writings 1972–1977* (C. Gordon, Ed.). New York: Pantheon Books.
Garland, D. (2001). *The Culture of Control: Crime and Social Order in Contemporary Society*. Oxford: Oxford University Press.
Genders, E. (2002). Legitimacy, Accountability and Private Prisons. *Punishment & Society, 4*(3), 285–303.
Gerber, M. M., & Jackson, J. (2017). Justifying Violence: Legitimacy, Ideology and Public Support for Police Use of Force. *Psychology, Crime and Law, 23*(1), 79–95.
Gerber, T. P., & Mendolson, S. E. (2008). Public Experiences of Police Violence in Contemporary Russia: A Case of Predatory Policing? *Law and Society Review, 42*(1), 1–44.
Goldstein, H. (1990). *Problem Oriented Policing*. New York: McGraw-Hill.
Gottschalk, P. (2017). Private Police Legitimacy: The Case of Internal Investigations by Fraud Examiners. *Policing: An International Journal, 40*(3), 628–640.

Gounev, P., & Bezlov, T. (2012). Corruption and Criminal Markets. In P. Gounev & V. Ruggerio (Eds.), *Corruption and Organized Crime in Europe*. Abingdon: Routledge.

Greitens, S. C. (2016). *Dictators and Their Secret Police: Coercive Institutions and State Violence*. Cambridge: Cambridge University Press.

Griffiths, C. T., & Clark, P. (2017). Building Police Legitimacy in a High Demand Environment: The Case of Yukon, Canada. *Policing: An International Journal, 40*(3), 560–573.

Hinton, M. (2006). *The State on the Streets: Police and Politics in Argentina and Brazil*. Boulder: Lynne Rienner.

Innes, M. (2004). Signal Crimes and Signal Disorders: Notes on Deviance as Communicative Action. *British Journal of Sociology, 55*(3), 335–355.

Innes, M. (2014). *Signal Crimes, Social Reactions to Crime, Disorder and Control*. Oxford: Oxford University Press.

Ivokvic, S. K. (2009). The Croation Police, Police Integrity, and Transition Toward Democratic Policing. *Policing and International Journal, 32*(3), 459–488.

Ivokovic, S. K., & Kang, W. (2012). Police Integrity in South Korea. *Policing: An International Journal of Police Strategies & Management, 35*(1), 76–103.

Ivokovic, S. K., & Sauerman, A. (2016). Police Integrity in South Africa: A Tale of Three Police Agencies. *Policing: An International Journal, 39*(2), 268–283.

Jackson, J., Bradford, B., Stanko, E. A., & Hohl, K. (2012). *Just Authority? Trust in the Police in England and Wales*. London: Routledge.

Jackson, J., Huq, A., Bradford, B., & Tyler, T. R. (2013). Monopolizing Force? Police Legitimacy and Public Attitudes Towards the Acceptability of Violence. *Psychology, Public Policy and Law, 19*(4), 479–497.

Joh, E. (2004). The Paradox of Private Policing. *The Journal of Criminal Law and Criminology, 95*(1), 49–131.

Joh, E. E. (2009). Breaking the Law to Enforce It: Undercover Police Participation in Crime. *Stanford Law Review, 62*, 155–199.

Johnston, L. (2006). Transnational Security Governance. In J. Wood & B. Dupont (Eds.), *Democracy, Society and the Governance of Security*. Cambridge: Cambridge University Press.

Johnston, M. (2013). *Corruption, Contention and Reform: The Power of Deep Democratization*. Cambridge: Cambridge University Press.

Jonathan-Zamir, T., & Weisburd, D. (2013). The Effects of Security Threats on Antecedents of Police Legitimacy: Findings from a Quasi-Experiment in Israel. *Journal of Research in Crime and Delinquency, 50*(1), 3–32.

Klockars, C. B. (1985). The Dirty Harry Problem. In F. A. Elliston & M. Feldberg (Eds.), *Moral Issues in Police Work*. Totowa, NJ: Rowan and Allanheld.

Kochel, T. R. (2017). Legitimacy Judgments in Neighbourhood Context: Antecedents in 'Good' Versus 'Bad' Neighbourhoods. *Policing: An International Journal, 40*(3), 529–523.

Kruisbergen, E. W., de Jong, D., & Kleemans, E. (2011). Undercover Policing: Assumptions and Empirical Evidence. *The British Journal of Criminology, 51*(2), 394–412.

Lewis, E., & Blum, R. (1964). Selection Standards: A Critical Approach. In R. H. Blum (Ed.), *Police Selection*. Springfield, IL: Charles C. Thomas.

Lilly, R. J., Cullen, F. T., & Ball, R. A. (1989). *Criminological Theory: Context and Consequences*. Thousand Oaks, CA: Sage.

Lilly, R. J., Cullen, F. T., & Ball, R. A. (2015). *Criminological Theory: Context and Consequences*. Thousand Oaks, CA: Sage.

Lobinar, B., Pristan, K., Cuvan, B., & Mesko, G. (2016). The Code of Silence and Female Officers in Slovenia: Gender Differences in Willingness to Report Police Misconduct. *Policing: An International Journal, 39*(2), 387–400.

Manning, P. K. (1979). The Social Control of Police Work. In S. Holdaway (Ed.), *The British Police*. London: Edward Arnold.

Manning, P. K., & Redlinger, L. J. (1977). Invitational Edges. In C. B. Klockars (Ed.), *Thinking About Police*. New York: McGraw-Hill.

Marx, G. T. (1992). When the Guards Guard Themselves: Undercover Tactics Turned Inward. *Policing and Society, 2,* 151–172.

McCluskey, J. D., & Reisig, M. (2017). Explaining Procedural Justice During Police-Suspect Encounters: A Systematic Social Observation Study. *Policing: An International Journal, 40*(3), 574–586.

Miller, S. (2017). *Institutional Corruption: A Study in Applied Philosophy*. Cambridge: Cambridge University Press.

Mitchell, K. J., Wolak, J., & Finkelhor, D. (2005). Police Posing as Juveniles Online to Catch Sex Offenders: Is It Working? *Sexual Abuse a Journal of Research and Treatment, 17,* 241–267.

Murphy, K., & Cherney, A. (2012). Understanding Cooperation with Police in a Diverse Society. *British Journal of Criminology, 52,* 181–201.

Nathan, C. (2017). Liability to Deception and Manipulation: The Ethics of Undercover Policing. *Journal of Applied Philosophy, 34*(3), 370–388.

National Audit Office. (2013). *The Ministry of Justice's Electronic Monitoring Contracts* (HC 737 Session 2013–2014). London: The Stationary Office.

Nellis, M. (2014). Understanding the Electronic Monitoring of Offenders in Europe: Expansion, Regulation and Prospects. *Crime, Law and Social Change, 62,* 489–510.
Newman, T. (1999). *Understanding and Preventing Police Corruption: Lessons from the Literature* (Police Research Series Paper 110). London: Home Office.
Newman, G., & Faull, A. (2011). *Protector of Predator? Tackling Police Corruption in South Africa* (ISS Monograph Number 182). South Africa: Open Society Foundation.
Oliver, C. (1992). The Antecedents of Deinstitutionalization. *Organization Studies, 13*(4), 563–588.
Porter, L., & Preznler, T. (2016). The Code of Silence and Ethical Perceptions: Exploring Police Office Unwillingness to Report Misconduct. *Policing: An International Journal, 39*(2), 370–386.
Prenzler, T. (2005). Mapping the Australian Security Industry. *Security Journal, 18*(4), 51–64.
Prenzler, T. (2006). Private Investigators. In M. Gill (Ed.), *Handbook of Security*. Houndmills and Hampshire: Palgrave Macmillan.
Punch, M. (2000). Police Corruption and Its Prevention. *European Journal on Criminal Policy Research, 8*(3), 301–324.
Punch, M. (2003). Rotten Orchards: Pestilence, Police Misconduct and System Failure. *Policing and Society, 13*(2), 171–196.
Punch, M. (2009). *Police Corruption: Deviance, Accountability and Reform in Policing*. Cullompton: Willan Publishing.
Rawlinson, P. (2012). Corruption, Organised Crime and the Free Market in Russia. In P. Gounev & V. Ruggiero (Eds.), *Corruption and Organised Crime in Europe*. Abingdon: Routledge.
Rhodes, R. A. W. (1994). The Hollowing Out of the State: The Changing Nature of Public Service in Britain. *The Political Quarterly, 65*(2), 138–151.
Roche, S., & Roux, G. (2017). The 'Silver Bullet' to Good Policing: A Mirage—An Analysis of the Effects of Political Ideology and Ethnic Identity on Procedural Justice. *Policing: An International Journal, 40*(3), 514–528.
Roebuck, J., & Barker, T. (1973). *An Empirical Typology of Police Corruption: A Study in Organizational Deviance*. Springfield, IL: Charles C. Thomas.
Ross, J. E. (2004). Impediments to Transnational Cooperation in Undercover Policing: A Comparative Study of the United States and Italy. *The American Journal of Comparative Law, 52,* 569–623.

Ross, J. E. (2007). The Place of Covert Surveillance in Democratic Societies: A Comparative Study of the United States and Germany. *The American Journal of Comparative Law, 55*, 493–579.

Ross, J. E. (2008). Undercover Policing and the Shifting Terms of Scholarly Debate: The United States and Europe in Counterpoint. *Annual Review of Law and Social Science, 4*, 239–273.

Rowland, R., & Coupe, T. (2014). Patrol Officers and Public Reassurance: A Comparative Evaluation of Police Officers, PCSOs, ACSOs and Private Security Guards. *Policing and Society, 24*(3), 265–284.

Sarre, R. (2005). Researching Private Policing: Challenges and Agendas for Researchers. *Security Journal, 18*(3), 57–70.

Sarre, R. (2008). The Legal Powers of Private Security Personnel: Some Policy Considerations and Legislative Options. *QUT Law and Justice Journal, 8*(2), 301–313.

Sarre, R. (2010). The Law in Australia on Citizen's Arrest. *Australasian Policing: A Journal of Professional Practice and Research, 1*(2), 9–10.

Sarre, R., & Preznler, T. (2005). Policing Corruption: An Australian Perspective. In R. D. K. Das & H. J. Albrecth (Eds.), *Policing Corruption: International Perspectives*. Lanham, MD: Lexington Books.

Scraton, P. (1999). Policing with Contempt: The Degrading of Truth and Denial of Justice in the Aftermath of the Hillsborough Disaster. *Journal of Law and Society, 26*(3), 273–297.

Scraton, P. (2000). *Hillsborough: The Truth*. Edinburgh: Mainstream.

Scraton, P. (2004). Death on the Terraces: The Contexts and Injustices of the 1989 Hillsborough Disaster. *Soccer & Society, 5*(2), 183–200.

Scraton, P. (2016). *Hillsborough: The Truth*. Edinburgh: Mainstream.

Skinns, L., Rice, L., Sprawson, A., & Wooff, A. (2017). Police Legitimacy in Context: An Exploration of 'Soft Power' in Police Custody in England. *Policing: An International Journal, 40*(3), 601–613.

Skolnick, J. (1967). *Justice Without Trial: Law Enforcement in Democratic Society*. New York: Wiley.

Steinberg, J. (2008). *Thin Blue: The Unwritten Rules of Policing South Africa*. Johannesburg: Jonathan Ball.

South, N. (1988). *Policing for Profit: The Private Security Sector*. London: Sage.

Suchman, M. (1995). Managing Legitimacy: Strategic and Institutional Approaches. *The Academy of Management Review, 20*(3), 571–610.

Sutherland, E. H. (1940). White Collar Criminality. *American Sociological Review, 5*, 1–12.

Sutherland, E. H. (1949). *White Collar Crime*. New York: Dryden Press.
Sykes, G. M., & Matza, D. (1957). Techniques of Neutralization: A Theory of Delinquency. *American Sociological Review, 22*, 664–670.
Sztompka, P. (1999). *Trust: A Sociological Theory*. Cambridge: Cambridge University Press.
Tappan, P. W. (1960). *Crime, Justice and Correction*. New York: McGraw-Hill.
Tanekebe, J. (2009). Self-help, Policing, and Procedural Justice: Ghanian Vigilantism and the Rule of Law. *Law and Society Review, 43*, 245–268.
Tanekebe, J. (2010). Public Confidence in the Police Testing the Effects of Public Experiences of Police Corruption in Ghana. *British Journal Criminology, 50*(2), 296–319.
Tinto, E. K. (2012). Undercover Policing: Overstated Culpability. *New York University Public Law and Legal Theory Working Papers, 34*, 1401–1454.
Vigneswaran, D., & Hornberger, J. (2009). *Beyond 'Good Cop'/'Bad Cop': Understanding Informality and Police Corruption in South Africa*. Johannesburg: University of the Witwatersrand.
White, A. (2010). *The Politics of Private Security: Regulation, Reform and Re-legitimation*. Houndmills: Palgrave Macmillan.
White, A. (2015). The Politics of Police 'Privatization': A Multiple Streams Approach. *Criminology and Criminal Justice, 15*(3), 283–299.
Williams, J. (2014). Justice for the 96? Hillsborough, Politics and English Football. In M. Hopkins & J. Treadwelll (Eds.), *Football Hooliganism, Fan Behaviour and Crime: Contemporary Issues*. Basingstoke: Palgrave Macmillan.
Willis, G. D. (2014). Antagonistic Authorities and the Civil Police in Sau Paulo, Brazil. *Latin American Research Review, 49*(1), 3–22.
Wood, J., & Kempa, M. (2005). Understanding Global Trends in Policing: Explanatory and Normative Dimensions. In J. Sheptycki & A. Wardak (Eds.), *Transnational and Comparative Criminology*. London: Glasshouse.
Zucker, L. G. (1977). Where Do Institutional Patterns Come from? Organizations as Actors in Social Systems. In L. G. Zucker (Ed.), *Institutional Patterns and Organizations: Culture and Environment*. Cambridge, MA: Ballinger.
Zucker, L. (1985). *Production of Trust: Institutional Sources of Economic Structure 1840–1920* (Working Paper Series No. 82). Los Angeles: University of California.

5
The Jury and Potential for Corruption

Introduction

There is a wealth of literature available on the historical development of the jury system in common law systems referred to as a bulwark of justice. This, however, is best read elsewhere as I am far more concerned with a contemporary issue: and this is the corruption of the jury, and individual members' use of the internet. There is psychological literature on bias and prejudice (Brewer and Williams 2005; Levett et al. 2005; Daftary-Kapur et al. 2010; Bornstein and Greene 2011; Leiberman and Krauss 2016) that can affect the outcome of cases and for organized crime (Campbell 2013: 111–157) where bribery, blackmail, threats and intimidation, etc. can all occur. All of these can occur face-to-face, however, but also via the internet, particularly threats and intimidation.

With the development of the internet and social sites, threats, intimidation and insults, and cases and characters in the court room reach into public discourse on social sites. This is a problem, as I highlight in this chapter, but independent research by members of a jury is not new; it is an old problem but the internet allows individual research from a variety of locations, and communication with jury members, lawyers,

G. Brooks, *Criminal Justice and Corruption*,
https://doi.org/10.1007/978-3-030-16038-8_5

witnesses and offenders whilst a case is in progress. Research though, causes potentially prejudicial, irrelevant and inaccurate information on which to assess a case instead of responding to the evidence under consideration. A note of caution has to be raised here, though: in the literature on the jury, there is little reflection on 'evidence' that is withheld by the police or prosecutors to secure a conviction. The jury is expected to assess an individual's culpability on limited and sometimes bias and prejudicial information presented by law enforcement and/or state prosecutors and/or scientific specialists rather than *all* available 'evidence'. Epitomized by a member of a jury suggesting 'the legal system is not designed to discover the truth' (Morrison 2011: 4) and subjected to testilying (see Chapter 4), it is logical to ask 'what is the role of the jury if it is expected to come to a conclusion on incomplete, and sometimes prejudicial data?'

This is a threat to the legitimacy of criminal justice (Brooks 2016) but is now combined with access to the internet (Harvey 2014) where inappropriate sources of information are ubiquitous, and personal threats and intimidation are posted online. However, some definition of what is meant by social media is and can be useful, that shows the ubiquity of electronic devices that can be used to engage in independent research and send and post messages online about a criminal case. Social media can be defined as web-based services that allow individuals to (1) construct a public or semi-public profile within a bounded system (2) articulate a list of others with whom they share a connection and (3) view and traverse their list of connections and those made by others within the system (Boyd and Ellison 2007). These platforms enable people to instantly share information including postings, photographs and personal and/or posted links to film/video footage as well as view communication by others (Bartels and Lee 2013). There is a 'diverse ecology of social media sites' for the public, such as Facebook, or status updates such as Twitter or specific sites that foster hate, which can expose us to prejudicial information (Kim et al. 2013).

This chapter reviews the need for a contemporary understanding of how the jury is subverted and corrupted. Whilst corruption is external—bribery, threats, etc.—to a jury or individual members—I examine the internal—individual jury members searching for information on the internet which is populated with bias, prejudicial, sham 'news' and articles and the extent to which this can corrupt criminal justice.

What Is the Problem with Independent Research?

It is claimed that the jury has the power to: (1) reject the law that criminalizes the wrong for which the defendant is accused (2) reject not the criminalization of the act but the level of sanction attached to it or (3) accept the law and concomitant sanction but have no wish to see them applied to the defendant on trial. However, this jury nullification suggests that a jury consciously acts to undermine the law, which is naïve (Matravers 2004). Instead the jury (or some members of it) are perhaps basing judgement on non-legal 'facts' on the case such as race, age, and 'character' of the person on trial.

Independent research by a member of a jury is problematic as under the current procedural and evidentiary landscape it undercuts the adversarial system. In the 'ideal' adversarial process, each party advocates its position before an impartial judge and jury that *should* then render judgement after weighing the information presented (Crosby 2012; Manhas 2014; Braun 2017). This, however, is a model and ideal. Independent research potentially exposes all of the jury to prejudicial, irrelevant or inaccurate information, if presented in the jury room without the knowledge of the police, prosecutors, defence and judge. As a result, some evidence is not subjected to adversarial review, such as cross-examination or rebuttal, and as such both sides lose the opportunity to respond to all the information that could influence the outcome of the case. But if the police (see Chapters 3 and 4), prosecutors (see Chapters 6 and 10) and judge (see Chapter 6) all exclude or withhold 'evidence', this opportunity is lost anyway. The jury then works on limited rather than all available information; evidence has been filtered and excluded by the police and prosecutors as irrelevant and/or damaging to secure a conviction, with judges excluding information as inadmissible. However, as noted by Bankowski (1988: 9) law enforcement and the jury reach conclusions via different rationalities, or 'truth certifying procedures', which will sometimes, at least, fail to correspond and connect in the same case.

Investigative research has occurred prior to the development and expansion of the Internet, e.g. Saperito v. State (1986) (a jury member visited an apartment where an assault occurred to measure the width of the doors), or (People v. Phillips, 1981) (where a member of a jury conducted an experiment to determine if baking soda dissolved in water overnight, in a murder case) (Morrison 2011: 4). Now, though much of this can be done via the internet, at home, in a coffee shop, on public transport or in a court of law.

However, filtered criminal justice information, and particularly relevant evidence, that is knowingly 'lost' or hidden by law enforcement and/or state prosecutors is also a corruption of the criminal process. Therefore, is independent research negative? This is dependent on what an individual will search for, how it is obtained (such as disreputable internet site) and how it is used in its final assessment. If individual members of the jury discover information hidden by the police and/or prosecutors, is this not a contribution to the available evidence? This might be rare but as cases come to light that information and particularly relevant evidence was withheld, people will seek access to the internet. Rather than simply focus on the jury then, it has to be noted that adversarial criminal justice systems limit access to relevant information.

With the ubiquity of the internet and personal electronic devices, independent research has increased with access to the internet. In 'western' democratic nations such as Australia with a population of approximately 24.4 million as of 2017; it is estimated 16 million people have/use Facebook, 14.8 million access YouTube, 5 million use Instagram and 2.8 million Twitter (Braun 2017: 1638). It is inevitable that some members of the jury will access these sites before, at or after a trial.

This access is a current and future problem (Bell 2010) that criminal justice systems have yet to address relying almost exclusively on traditional inhibitory rules, such as mistrials and sequestration with a view that a jury is an irrational body of citizens capable of injecting 'lay acid' into the system (Crosby 2012) that is in need of control. This control restricts what a jury can see and hear drawing on laws of evidence (e.g. dismissing hearsay), and that a jury must act in a legally acceptable manner: both are communicated via a judge. There is some merit here regarding the control of a jury as independent internet research has created lengthy, costly litigation (Manhas 2014). The typical current judicial response to independent research (if known or discovered) is before-the-fact protection—jury instructions prohibiting outside research—and after-the-fact protection—declaring a mistrial and ordering a new trial. A before-the-fact safeguard is prohibiting the use of electronic devices in the courthouse, sequestering the jury, whilst after the facts is a fine for the member of the jury and/or holding them in contempt of court or ultimately a prison sentence for breeching court rules.

All these protections are predominately negative, in that they punish or exclude members of a jury from access to sources of information, and seem to inhibit involvement in criminal justice. Aptly described by Manhas (2014: 7) such negative sanctions suffocate interest and investment in the trial and 'reduce the jury to that of a machine, mechanically crunching the carefully screened evidence that is funnelled into it, producing a verdict'. These sanctions could be considered a punishment for engaging in the trial, and indeed can exceed those on police officers and prosecutors that withhold evidence. Engagement in itself is not the problem; it is how members of a jury engage. But if members of the criminal justice system—law enforcement (see Chapters 3 and 4), prosecutors and judges (see Chapter 6)—withhold and/or mislead the jury and little, if any sanction is employed on the police, judicial, legal regulatory body what signal has it sent to members of a current and future jury? It appears that the jury is there to blindly accept the information put forward. Its role then is to assess limited information on which to decide an individual's immediate and current future. Furthermore, a jury with sometimes limited evidence has to decide if a defendant acted dishonestly, by reference to contemporary standards, or acted in reasonable self-defence (Crosby 2012). Legal instruction is available but standards change, reasonable is subjective and so is competent and whilst instruction will be communicated via a judge regarding the law and its interpretation of standards and 'events' limited evidence is still part of the problem.

This system, I suggest works well only, and only if all relevant information is put forward. How can a jury be actively involved if it is the repository of bias, prejudicial, limited information? As Morrison in (Manhas 2014: 7) has pointed out, some of the constraints on members of a jury 'reflect the modern conception of impartiality, which is frequently, confused with …passivity'. The internet, however, has radically changed the landscape.

But why do members of a jury seek out 'extra' information? There seems to be four key reasons. These are (1) investigating facts, (2) double-checking the law, (3) publicizing experiences, and (4) contacting a third party or a combination of these. Each is dealt with in-turn but should be read as an overlapping problem as is illustrated below.

In a case in Florida, USA (Morrison 2011) regarding the illegal running of an Internet pharmacy it was discovered by the judge that, seven weeks into the trial, the majority of the jury had conducted Internet research regarding the case. They searched for definitions of medical terms, whilst one enterprising member of the jury discovered that one of the defendants had once been implicated for prescribing medicine that was used in a double suicide. The judge, unsurprisingly, declared a mistrial. A few more examples from USA help illuminate the reach and breadth of independent research: in one case a member of a jury looked up the MySpace profile of a young victim in a sexual abuse case (Browning 2010), in another case one attempted to access an offender's prior criminal record on a police department website, and one went as far as researching the effect on blood alcohol levels of Narcan in a vehicular homicide case, and yet another attempted to establish whether a particular type of firearm could have damaged a bulletproof vest (Morrison 2010: 5). It appears then that members of the jury distrust legal counsel, law enforcement and 'expert' witness if prepared to conduct such research.

Why is this happening? One plausible explanation is that a jury is barred from considering all available evidence. It appears that the jury is not to be trusted (Crobsy 2012). This, however, is an old problem. Even Bentham (in 1827) cited in Morrison (2011: 6) suggested that the jury should be allowed to hear all the evidence and decide if credible, and claimed if not 'fit to be trusted with this, not even with the benefit of the judge's assistance and advice, what is it they are fit to be trusted with?' Furthermore, knowledge of the extent of independent research is limited (as is hiding and the manufacture of evidence by law enforcement and prosecutors).

Despite the fact that courts will state, it is the duty of the court to instruct the jury as to the law, and the jury to follow the law as it is laid down by a court, independent research on legal terminology is also conducted. This is perhaps most noticeable in sentencing; whilst criminal justice systems are to be commended publishing sentence ranges including mandatory minimum and maximum sentences, jury members can access these, as we can, but armed with such knowledge will members of a jury soften personal judgement or seek to secure the maximum penalty if a defendant is guilty? In a case in North Carolina in 2010 a jury foreman searched and brought sentencing statues on narcotics violations to court: the judge declared a mistrial (Morrison 2010); and in England a young 21 year old posted on Facebook in 2013 that he was on jury service and could now send an accused sex offender to prison before trial commenced (Braun 2017) for which he was jailed for two months. In the above example it appears that either the judge failed to explain the rules a jury is subject to in a court of law or this person failed to listen or simply dismissed the rules as irrelevant or became excited at punishing a 'sex offender' and putting people in prison.

We are not supposed to know how or why a jury reached a verdict, but due to blogging and tweeting, we can have a 'running commentary' of the characters of the jury, the judge, defendants, prosecutors, etc. Some are harmless postings but some will damage the legitimacy of a trial and case. For example, in a burglary case in San Diego, USA in 2007 a jury foreman failed to disclose he was a lawyer before being empanelled on a jury, and then provided details by blogging about the case and jury deliberations; a jury foreman in a murder case in California in 2008 was held in contempt of court for posting a photograph of the murder weapon online and hosting a chat room that discussed the trial (Morrison 2010). Posting personal views on members of a jury or judge or offender(s) are one example of publicizing experiences, but if under threat of some sanction, an affluent and adept person can utilize the internet to wage a propaganda campaign planting favourable information in 'cyber-space' that we, and that of a jury, can stumble upon if engaged in independent research. This also can lead to a prejudicial outcome in a court case questioning the legitimacy of criminal trials: however, a high profile campaign can backfire as much as mitigate accusations levelled at a specific offender(s).

There are a few issues here to address. Postings, status updates and tweets could chill robust discussion and inhibit participating in a jury for fear they become the subject of personal posting. In addition the Internet has been used by some to solicit outside opinions on a case; e.g. in England, in Burnley Crown Court, Lancashire in 2008 a woman on a sex abuse case was unable to decide on a verdict; unable to come to a verdict she posted salient facts of the case on Facebook and held a poll to reach a conclusion. She was dismissed and the trial continued. In Tucson, Arizona, USA (Morrison 2010) a witness repeatedly texted another witness and advised him how to testify (Greene and Spaeth 2010). In Western Australia in 2016 in a member of jury on a murder case posted on Facebook that the defendant was 'guilty' before the trial had started (Braun 2017: 1642) and was subsequently dismissed. These dispatches from the 'black box' of the jury room subvert the gravity of the process and as such, with social media exposure, the authority of jury verdicts could decline. If the linchpin of the jury's legitimacy is that its verdicts are opaque, and its mistakes are hidden, exposing the deliberative process, (even in real time), personal views, and independent research, and improper 'relationships' effects criminal justice credibility. This is exacerbated with encounters between members of a jury. These are not a new problem, but requesting friendship online is. Whilst the majority are online private communications, possible prejudicial views between fellow jury members and/or judge/lawyers and even defendants can and do occur.

Reponses to this problem typically take two forms: (1) negative rules/ or court rules to reduce independent research and by blocking access to outside sources or punishment of the use of such sources, and (2) outside mechanisms, to remove or lessen the impact of independent research. For example a negative or court rule is to forbid the use of electronic devices in the courthouse and an outside mechanism is for prosecutors and defence to block access to the jury. In addition to negative rules and outside mechanisms, there is a potential third response, one which has been neglected: positive rules, or court rules that channel jury activity, as well as independent research, into something productive in an adversarial system (Manhas 2014). These are broken down into negative rules and outside influences below.

Negative Rules

Negative rules, as stated above are court rules that attempt to reduce independent research; court rules, as with all rules fail to prevent all breaches of codes, laws and rules. The best we can hope for is to reduce sources of independent research such as the internet and electronic devices or by punishing or otherwise members of a jury that attempt to access such sources. These rules are considered essential to a 'fair' jury trial—but only relevant to the jury as a corruption of criminal justice has potentially already occurred prior to a case(s) reaching court. These rules are an attempt to prevent individual members of a jury from a more flexible, informed role, because of fears of prejudicial or otherwise inappropriate sources. This I understand, but negative rules alone fail to block access to the internet. These rules are briefly examined in turn.

Forbidding electronic devices help prevent independent research and also use of social media sites, particularly at the trial stage or deliberation, where courts forbid the use of electronic devices in the courthouse (Bell 2010). This makes sense as some members of a jury or only one, could search for 'evidence' on the defendant and/or tweet thoughts on the case, the judge and/or prosecutors and defence counsel. This though is an incomplete solution. It should, but not always, prevent the use of electronic devices in the courthouse, but in some jurisdictions, such as

Michigan, USA can be used outside the court for personal communication rather than information on the case. Furthermore, the court is unable to prevent the use of electronic devices outside its control. Major criminal trials, however, last for days, weeks and can sometimes fall into months, and the expectation that members of a jury will abstain from independent research is, I suggest, naive. For this reason, banning electronic devices can be seen as a less effective (and less burdensome) version of sequestration (Manhas 2014).

Sequestration is the ultimate negative rule, in that exposure to outside information and use of electronics are closely monitored and access to the internet is effectively blocked. This is hardly a practical or desirable option in most criminal cases but is perhaps useful in high-profile cases (Braun 2017). This option is expensive and also places members of a jury under immense stress and effectively under a form of 'house' arrest for the duration of the trial. Most importantly, while sequestration is unquestionably effective, relying on this reveals the myopia of a system of negative rules (Manhas 2014). Sequestration only addresses access to information, not the bias or prejudicial attitude of members of a jury. If a jury is considered a bulwark of adversarial criminal justice systems it needs a jury, or at least some of the jury to be engaged. Sequestration, however, still fails to completely block access to the internet and electronic devices, and whilst the best option to block access to unwanted searches, the value of this effectiveness is undercut by its harshness and cost.

Aside from perhaps rare cases that are not the main diet of criminal justice systems, blocking access to the internet is not completely possible. Sequestration, however, offers no solution to low-profile cases and in Australia is considered economically untenable (Braun 2017). Manhas (2014) claims that sequestration is undeniably effective, which is impossible to counteract, but I disagree with the view that efforts should be made to expand its reach, even if the court system can effectuate such an expansion in a palatable manner. How this is to be achieved needs developing, but regardless of the palatable manner, which will be different to different members of the jury, it is still a restriction on the liberty of members of the jury that affects them, family and employers.

Jury instructions via a judge and clerks of the court is a potential way forward to respond to internet use by adopting more detailed, explicit instructions and potential sanctions. These instructions should highlight how it can prejudice a trial and lead to a costly mistrial. Simply warning members of a jury, however, that it is unacceptable and prohibited will, and has, had little impact. No number of admonishments can prevent independent research. Regardless of the level of independent research, which is hard to assess, it is an issue that needs to be addressed since in some jurisdictions access is so prevalent. The impact of jury instruction on independent research is currently unclear (Mckimme et al. 2014; Baguley et al. 2017) and is in need of in-depth research.

There is the potential for members of a jury to report other members' internet use. This, however, is still a negative rule and is 'after the event' and is remedial, not pre-emptive. It can emphasize the damage of independent research and harm it causes (Manhas 2014) but fails to prevent all independent research. The problem here is that reporting can be both useful and malicious. In Arizona, USA, in a murder case one member of the jury informed the judge that the rest of the jury (eleven members) were pressuring him to change his guilty verdict. He also claimed that another member of the jury had accessed the internet via cell phone at the deliberation stage to discover the outcome of the jury verdict if a unanimous vote was not reached. Consequently the jury members were interviewed but it became clear that none of the jury had used the internet. Instead this one disaffected jury member was trying to block all discussion and deliberation on the case and manipulate the system, which caused a mistrial (Greene and Spaeth 2010).

The problem that arises, of course, is what to do once a violation is reported. One option is to admonish, but not actually discipline, in the hopes of securing cooperation (Kiernan and Colley 2012), or exclude the individual from participating in deliberations and replaced with an alternate; or punish them—a fine—if violating the prohibition on independent jury research. This later approach, however, could deter people from willingly serving on a jury. I emphasize once more that whilst understandable that members of any jury are subject to rules by the time case(s) reach court, police, and prosecutors and judges and 'experts' could have withheld and/or overstated 'evidence', and yet still expect the jury to assess the case. Some evidence withheld is justifiable but some is withheld on purpose to secure a conviction, and so miscarriages occur. This is particularly noticeable relying on scientific data and presentation of 'facts' in jury trials. Even if we have complete faith in science as flawless, there is always the human element to consider. For Page et al. (2011: 15) this faith in science in uniqueness is cultural ideology—it is accepted as 'scientific' via the social transmission of cultural forces rather than robust scientific process. This is not to dismiss science in criminal justice but to raise caution. The evidentiary value of an item is subject to the interpretation of that evidence by those individuals responsible for presenting it to a judge and jury. Testimony provided by an individual to a court of law, depending on the person, has the potential to be damaging to either offender or victim.

There are, however, types of witness testimony, material, fact and expert. Eyewitnesses and character witnesses are primarily members of the public and seen as material witnesses; law enforcement and others involved in the processing of crime scenes and evidence are considered witnesses of 'fact', and expert witnesses have a particular field of knowledge. Material and 'fact' witness statements are based on direct knowledge or observation of an event, whilst expert statements is, or should, be based on observation and knowledge of science. Experts can thus be seen as the most objective—removed from the crime—and offer rational assessment of evidence provided.

All of this can still lead to a mistrial. Declaring a mistrial is more than a remedy for a violation of the prohibition on independent research, it should also deter research. As a remedy, however, it is a rule of last resort; it is the nuclear option. A new trial is expensive, it is after the event, and is unable to ensure that members of a new jury will follow court rules. These examples of prohibition are all 'after the event' and corruption of the case, if discovered, has already potentially occurred. Since courts are ultimately unable either to completely block access to research or to inhibit the inclination to research, it appears that the most appropriate method is to disregard potential offenders at *voir dire* stage (picking the jury), but this is not part of all common law systems. No Australian jurisdiction has a *voir dire* comparable to the USA even though based on a common law system. This is because Australia is a federalized nation same as the USA but individual states approach legal procedure in slightly ways (Braun 2017).

Finally if we dismiss a member of the jury because s/he has a strong social media profile and a high rate of internet and electronics use, we will exclude mostly young people, and have an 'old' jury; but this is only now. In the future all will have some kind of internet and electronics use. Furthermore, there is no indication that a person with high internet use will use it for improper ends.

The internet though is also used by lawyers to examine potential individuals and search for digital or internet 'footprints'—e.g. running Google searches on social networking sites and databases. This practice is approved and encouraged in USA by courts and state bar associations (Manhas 2014: 824). Putting aside the concern for personal privacy here, even the best vetting process will miss some jury members that conduct independent research, but internet usage could also be an advantage in a court case. This ultimately comes down to the context of the specific case at hand, and in some instances, it may be impossible to adequately immunize a trial and its outcome from damaging information available on the internet (such as if the client has an extensive criminal record). This process, though still fails to address why some people break the rules.

The corrupting dynamic between independent research and the adversarial system is a function of the particular procedural and evidentiary rules. Such a system is loathed to implement reforms that allow a jury to become more active, and has mostly established rules that attempt to deal with the problem of independent research, and this could be viewed as an attempt to reassert state power. This reactionary instinct has produced negative rules and outside mechanisms such as searching for an individuals' digital footprint but fails to recognize that corruption has already occurred, and that this 'tinkering at the edges' is unviable and is perhaps misguided in the internet age. This is because it is trying to block access—the availability of means—rather than the root cause—the intent—to research. Unfortunately, access is increasingly easy to satisfy, despite courts' efforts to block access. Although inhibitory steps are useful, they are ultimately insufficient: the internet's ease-of-access to information and ease-of-access to the internet is impossible to prevent by anything short of prohibitively expensive and draconian measures such as sequestration of the jury (Manhas 2014).

In this contemporary context then it appears that trust in the jury system is under strain. It is possible though to consider special verdict systems and 'route to verdict's' directions to ensure a jury will comply with the requirements of court legality. The 'special verdict' approach consists of replacing the jury's 'guilty' or 'not guilty' verdict with a series of answers to a set of factual questions. 'Route to verdict' directions address the problem of jury disobedience leaving to the jury the final determination of innocence or guilt, but like the special verdict system involve giving the jury a logical sequence of questions, couched in words which address the essential legal issues, to be answered by the jury in order to arrive at their verdict (Crosby 2012). All of the above measures are limited; how then should we, if at all, prevent independent research?

Preventing Independent Research

Since it is clear that members of the jury will research laws, scientific claims, people and places, and it is impossible to prevent all research what can be done now and in the future to prevent this? I start by suggesting that there has to be recognition that in democratic states that faith in the integrity of law enforcement has fallen (see example of Royal Canadian Mounted Police in Canada in Chapter 4) (Beare 2017). Whilst law enforcement still has a highly respected profile in some jurisdictions, it is seen as bias and prejudicial elsewhere. This is perhaps by sections of a population rather than all, but will a loss of credibility, even if only temporary, affect members of a jury that potentially distrust law enforcement and state prosecutor's version of events and evidence? To simply expect the jury to accept what information is presented as sufficient under these conditions and with access to the internet is unrealistic.

In addition independent research could be solved by a framework of positive rules, negative rules and outside mechanisms. Manhas (2014) has suggested that members of the jury should be allowed to question witnesses and offenders (but here via a judge), and also allow access to an online record. This could quell the desire to search for information, but this can depend on the type and range of issues a jury can raise? This approach though fails to address the already bias and prejudicial attitudes in a jury. If a member of the jury holds prejudicial attitudes and his/her question is rejected, this could confirm such attitudes rather than address them. Good intentions can harvest poor outcomes, and the management of expectations here is paramount.

This is not to dismiss what are positive contributions and suggestions to deal with this intractable problem as one reform in civil courts in Florida, USA, is to allow members of jury to ask questions (Morrison 2011). This has some academic basis for positive reinforcement and engagement by members of a jury (Frankel 1990; Dann 1993; DeBarba 2002), yet resistance is still in place, particularly for criminal trials. However, as suggested by Manhas (2014: 827–831) such an approach could counter the desire for independent research, and even suggests that members of a jury should be able to raise questions during the course of a trial. This addresses what was previously an activity that would have been thwarted by the adversarial process (independent research) is transformed into an act that strengthens it (by adding to the completeness of the record on which the jury makes its decision).

Such an approach can help expose corruption; it could expose poor collection of data by law enforcement and state prosecutors, attempts to hide or withhold key information, and so acts as a buttress preventing corruption of a criminal trial; it will also expose members of a jury that have conducted 'outside' research, depending on the issues raised, and thus courts can investigate and respond accordingly before having to demand an expensive retrial. Such a system could also reduce objections, particularly if a question is posed via a jury as legal counsel could fear animosity should a party object.

Furthermore, Manhas (2014) has suggested that all members of a jury should be allowed access to a centralized, court maintained electronic record. Whilst I am supportive of the main thrust of this proposal issues beyond what type of information should be in the record need to be addressed. For example, if written in legalese will all (or any) members of the jury understand the documentation? If only a few understand, they can control the outcomes of cases by providing a personal interpretation of laws/events rather than what is in the documentation. In addition such documentation could lead members of the jury to seek clarification of terminology, etc., and thus slow criminal cases down, resulting in increased costs. Levels of education of the jury, pointless questions to the judge, defence counsel protesting about the information in the documentation, etc., are all possible in such an approach. None of this, however, will stop s/he that is determined to conduct independent research.

Finally, with attempts to cut the costs of criminal justice in some jurisdictions (see England and Wales) (The Secret Barrister 2018) video trials in which all testimony is pre-recorded is a potential way forward. However, the judge has the power to edit the footage before seen by the jury. Whilst this approach economizes time and eliminates the possibility of a mistrial (as the judge can edit out inadmissible comments, questions and answers), it can still be corrupted. As seen in chapter six, judges commit corrupt acts too. This approach could perhaps prevent effective but exorbitant sequestration but still fails to address lack of information for the jury, and most of all allows a judge editorial control of cases. This approach, I suggest, is open to abuse.

However, it is possible to conduct cases in 'real time'. Canada and Australia has systems in place for civil issues and England and Wales is experimenting with low level motor car offences and others. In England and Wales all cases start in the magistrate's court but pass on the most serious cases to the crown court. To increase the speed of justice (not necessarily its quality), a video link is established between the court and a police station or prison and court and the case is conducted online. The results are inconclusive but this seems popular with low-level offenders that represent themselves. Lawyers are keen to digitize paper systems but are concerned that defendants struggle to understand the civil/criminal procedure without a lawyer present. This view could be based on the fact that lawyers have a vested financial interest in representing 'offenders', but if a video link is via a police station or prison, it is possible that individuals are tainted by association and seen as guilty based on a physical location (*Economist* 2018: 28–29) rather than the case. No system is flawless but as it stands, is the jury fit for purpose in criminal trials in the 'internet age'?

Conclusion

This chapter has highlighted the intractable problem of the use and application of technology and its reach and use by members of a jury. It has reviewed the rules currently in place to prevent and/or punish 'wayward' members of a jury. These were criticized as expensive such as sequestration and mistrial. Accepting that the internet and electronic devices are prevalent and jury members will use them to research names, places, legal terminology, scientific procedures, suggestions were made as how to counteract this independent research. These need revision but at least recognize that the current system is limited in preventing the use of the internet and the proliferation of misleading, incorrect, bias and prejudicial information online; this though is tempered with recognition that the information the jury hears is often limited and/or incomplete. What is absent from most of the literature though is that, in a criminal trial, the jury has to decide the outcome of a case, but this can and is based on prior corruption by an individual or criminal justice agency. By the time a case reaches the jury, a number of egregious corrupt acts could have occurred; and on this basis the jury, on limited, withheld and/or corrupt information and scientific data is expected to decide innocence or guilt?

References

Baguley, C., McKimme, B., & Masser, B. (2017). Deconstructing the Simplification of the Jury: How Simplifying the Complexities Affects Jurors. *Law and Human Behaviour, 41*(3), 284–304.

Bankowski, Z. (1988). The Jury and Reality. In M. Findlay & P. Duff (Eds.), *The Jury Under Attack*. London: Butterworths.

Bartels, L., & Lee, J. (2013). Jurors Using Social Media in Our Courts: Challenges and Responses. *Journal of Judicial Administration, 23*, 35–57.

Beare, M. E. (2017). The Failures of Police Legitimacy: Attacks from Within. In V. Mitslegas, P. Alldridge, & L. Cheliotis (Eds.), *Globalisation, Criminal Law and Criminal Justice*. Oxford: Hart Publishing.

Bell, D. W. (2010). Juror Misconduct and the Internet. *American Journal of Criminal Law, 38*(1), 81–99.

Bornstein, B. H., & Greene, E. (2011). Jury Decision Making: Implications for and from Psychology. *Current Directions in Psychological Science, 20*(1), 63–67.

Boyd, D. M., & Ellison, N. B. (2007). Social Network Sites: Definition, History and Scholarship. *Journal of Computer-Mediated Communication, 13*(1), 210–230.

Braun, K. (2017). Yesterday is History, Tommorrow is a Mystery—the Fate of the Australian Jury System in the Age of Social Media Dependency. *University of New South Wales Law Journal, 40*(4), 1642–1662.

Brewer, N., & Williams, K. (2005). *Psychology and the Law: An Empirical Perspective*. London: Guildford Press.

Brooks, G. (2016). *Criminology of Corruption: Theoretical Approaches*. Basingstoke: Palgrave Macmillan.

Browning, J. G. (2010). When All That Twitters Is Not Told. *Texas Bar Journal, 73*(3), 216–220.

Campbell, L. (2013). *Organised Crime and the Law: A Comparative Analysis*. Oxford: Hart Publishing.

Crosby, K. (2012). Controlling Devlin's Jury: What the Jury Thinks and What the Jury Sees Online. *Criminal Law Review, 1*, 15–29.

Daftary-Kapur, T., Dumas, R., & Penrod, S. D. (2010). Jury Decision-Making Biases and How to Counter Them. *Legal and Criminological Psychology, 15*(1), 133–154.

Dann, M. B. (1993). "Learning Lessons" and "Speaking Rights": Creating Educated and Democratic Juries. *Indiana Law Journal, 68*(4), 1229–1261.

DeBarba, K. (2002). Maintaining the Adversarial System: The Practice of Allowing Jurors to Question Witnesses During Trial. *Vanderbilt Law Review, 55*(5), 1521–1548.

Frankel, M. A. (1990). A Trial Judge's Perspective on Providing Tools for Rational Jury Decision-Making. *Northwestern University Law Review, 85*(1), 221–224.

Greene, R. R., & Spaeth, J. M. (2010, February 1–10). Are Tweeters or Googlers in Your Jury Box? *Arizona Attorney, 46*, 38–45.

Harvey, D. (2014). The Googling Juror: The Fate of the Jury Train in the Digital Paradigm. *New Zealand Law Review, 203,* 203–238.
Kiernan, M. K., & Colley, E. (2012). Juror Misconduct in the Age of Social Networking. *Federation of Insurance and Corporate Counsel, Tampa, 62*(2) (Quarterly/Winter), 179–193.
Kim, Y., Chen, H. T., & de Zuniga, H. G. (2013). Stumbling Upon News on the Internet: Effects of Incidental News Exposure and Relative Entertainment Use on Political Engagement. *Computers in Human Behaviour, 29*(6), 2607–2614.
Leiberman, J. D., & Krauss, D. A. (2016). *Jury Psychology: Social Aspects of Trial Processes: Psychology in the Courtroom* (Vol. 1). Abingdon: Routledge.
Levett, L. M., Danielsen, E. M., Bull Kovera, M., & Cutler, B. L. (2005). The Psychology and Jury and Juror Decision Making. In N. Brewer & K. Williams (Eds.), *Psychology and The Law: An Empirical Perspective* (pp. 365–406). London: Guildford Press.
Manhas, R. (2014). Responding to Independent Juror Research in the Internet Age: Positive Rules, Negative Rules, and Outside Mechanisms. *Michigan Law Review, 112*(5), 809–831.
Matravers, M. (2004). 'More Than Just Illogical': Truth and Jury Nullification. In A. Duff, L. Farmer, S. Marshall, & V. Tadros (Eds.), *The Trial on Trial: Truth and Due Process* (Vol. 1, pp. 71–83). Oxford: Hart Publishing.
Mckimme, B., Antrobus, E., & Baguley, C. (2014). Objective and Subjective Comprehensions of Jury Instructions in Criminal Trials. *New Criminal Law Review, 17*(2), 163–183.
Morrison, C. M. (2010). Jury 2.0. *Hasting Law Journal, 62*(6), 1579–1632.
Morrison, C. M. (2011). Can the Jury Trial Survive Google. *Criminal Justice, 25*(4) (Winter), 4–15.
Page, M., Taylor, J., & Blenkin, M. (2011). Uniqueness in the Forensic Identification Sciences—Fact or Fiction? *Forensic Science International, 206*(1–3), 12–18.
The Economist. (2018, October 27–November 2). Trial by Media, pp. 28–29.
The Secret Barrister. (2018). *The Secret Barrister: Stories of the Law and How It's Broken.* London: Macmillan.

6

Judicial Corruption: Magistrates, Judges and Prosecutors

Introduction

Much has been written about the corruption in and of law enforcement with a little on corruption of the judiciary and prosecutors. This is due to the political collusion and power invested in such individuals and bodies that can thwart investigation. Political collusion, however, can be simply political e.g. a corrupt state is uncovered but judges fail to accept the threshold of evidence as sufficient for prosecution. This type of outcome is seen in Italy (Della Porta and Pizzorno 1996; Della Porta and Vannucci 1997), and Mexico (Nagle 2010), Poland (Plywaczewsky 2004) and Lithuania (Gutauskas et al. 2004) with elements of organized crime but mostly political corruption discovered in Africa (VonDoepp 2005), USA (Alt and Lassen 2008), Ukraine (Darden 2008), India (Raj 2017) and China (Wang 2017; Li 2018). These are only a few examples of the literature available on judicial corruption, informal networks of contacts and political collusion.

This chapter offers a broad review of the types of judicial corruption that primarily fall under political interference or administrative misconduct but also considers how judicial independence can be a threat to

G. Brooks, *Criminal Justice and Corruption*,
https://doi.org/10.1007/978-3-030-16038-8_6

'justice' as well. I use judge and magistrate as representatives of the legal system here to indicate individuals with power to pass judgement on others, but were relevant make a distinction between them. Judges tend to have different and far more extensive sentencing powers than magistrates as a rule, and thus deal with serious criminal cases. This is not to diminish the role of magistrates but I am concerned here with corruption at the highest level of the judiciary where political collusion thwarts criminal justice and harms its legitimacy in particular. With judicial/prosecutorial corruption defined as the use of public power "for the private benefit of court personnel" (Bascaglia 2001 in Braimah 2016: 13) which leads, if not already entrenched, to organized crime, and corruption of the criminal justice system and decline in notions of justice and legitimacy this chapter highlights the reach and potential consequences of judicial and prosecutorial corruption.

I start with 'what is judicial corruption' before moving onto consider the potential for corruption in 'independent' judicial systems. This is followed by the judicial capacity for extortion and penchant for bribery in some jurisdictions. I then consider attempts to prevent judicial corruption before a review of prosecutorial corruption (Banks 2017) where administrative corruption e.g. hiding information relevant to a case(s), and personal and political collusion and relationships with law enforcement also threatens our notion of 'justice'.

What Is Judicial Corruption?

Judicial corruption often falls under either political interference or administrative misconduct. Whilst political interference can lead to administrative corruption the judiciary can also act independently, and commit corrupt acts without political interference or pressure. This can, of course, depend on the type of political system—dictatorship or democratic—but while corruption is perhaps expected in a politically corrupt system it is less so in a democratic one. However, the rule of law can and is used as a political weapon in democratic states (Maravall and Przeworski 2001). Trying to define judicial corruption, the same as any type of corruption is complex verging on impossible. However, it is possible to detect some types of political and judicial collusion that leads to a corruption of 'justice'. Defined under petty or administrative and operational or major types of corruption judicial corruption can manifest itself as petty corruption by extortion of resources from the public, charging illegal fees to locate or dislocate files to expedite or delay a court case. Grand or major corruption is politically motivated court rulings. A useful example here, but still has resonance elsewhere, is a nation that is seen as democratic and yet has periodic judicial scandals; Italy. Pizzorno (1992: 62–63 in Della Porta 2001: 3) has classified political-judicial corruption as:

1. *Class collusion*: where magistrates/judges hold ideological views that are reflected in judgments on cases. Facts are downplayed or dismissed to accommodate personal, class-biased views. For example, many magistrates/judges in the 1950s in Italy had previously been recruited under the political yoke of fascism, and implemented what were seen by some as repressive labour laws (Della Porta 2001).
2. *Interest collusion*: where 'the conduct of the magistrates/judges (particularly in the highest ranks of judiciary) is influenced by belonging to, or coming from a similar social environment (e.g. same social class, education and thus associations) (see social exchange, a form of collusion in China), which is referred to as *guanxi* (Li 2018).
3. *Ideological identification*: whilst magistrates/judges do not actively participate or campaign for a political party or individual, in some jurisdictions, they can in others. This can be broken down into (1) Judges have/hold political views but make no political statements/campaign for a specific political party and thus claim independence. (2) Judges are allowed to be a member of a political party, as in USA, campaign and express views which are often reflected in the punishment of offenders and matters of personal responsibility above and beyond class affiliation.
4. *Role substitution*: magistrates/judges confronted by collusion in the political system use the power of the judiciary to enforce laws and threat of punishment, and so challenge political power.
5. *Institutional impartiality*: impartiality, as demanded by the law.

These represent a broad understanding of judicial corruption in Italy (Della Porta 2001; Della Porta et al. 2004), Ghana (Braimah 2016), India (Raj 2017) and China (Li 2018). Regardless of the jurisdiction where some elect judges, with some by executive appointment, and some a combination of both elected and appointed; such as the USA; both systems can lead to corruption.

In the electoral system in the USA political and party leaders has some influence in the selection of judicial candidates; this is done via public endorsement, and use of party campaign funds (Kang and Shepherd 2011). In the USA judges(s) are often nominated at a party convention (Miller 2004). This is to 'open the process,' to the public and considered more democratic, but in practice it is the 'acceptable' candidate that is elected judge. S/he will be nominated, and the convention stacked with amenable colleagues, and party members in search of personal promotion. The vote can thus be a sham as party members simply vote for the already preferred candidate. It is possible to restrain public endorsement and also spending campaign funds (Kang and Shepherd 2011) but these fail to prevent compliant and/or corrupt judges becoming elected.

There is also the system of executive appointment. This is used in combination with elected judges in some jurisdictions such as USA. Here the appointment of a corrupt and/or incompetent and bias judge can perhaps be attributed to the politician (at a local level in a federalized structure) or the President of a country who selects the judge and/or suggests the judge via public endorsement (Mishler and Sheehan 1993, 1996; Alt and Lassen 2008). However, corruption has to be exposed and proven, which for a judge is extremely difficult. Executive appointments also have flaws; a judge might serve for years beyond the official appointment and thus political accountability is diluted and the president will no doubt be out of office if the judges' shortcoming and/or corruption are exposed. A judge might also be ethical to start with but become corrupt years later. Rather than nominate a candidate based on quality a local/national official that wants to create a legacy (a salient factor in the case of the federal judiciary) (Miller 2004), quality may be eclipsed by expediency. The process of legislative confirmation, while it may act as a partial check on quality, also produces partisan considerations into the appointment process.

Centralization of accountability is also diluted if a nomination is by collective body. If the confirming body is dominated by a different political party to those that nominate a judge, the confirmation process may be used as an opportunity to embarrass or punish a political adversary. Vested interests might also engage in some kind of political compromise: instead of nominating the best candidate one is put forward that is 'acceptable.' This process might prevent the appointment of judges at the highest levels, but is less successful in lowest courts.

It Italy informal mechanisms, institutional resources, professional culture, or lack of it, have contributed to corruption. Whilst an old example, the 'clean hands' investigation in Italy still has contemporary significance and is a useful illustration of how political interference in 'justice' can destabilize a state. For a detailed account (see Della Porta and Vannccui 2007) but briefly 'clean hands' investigated political corruption, links to organized crime and also the judiciary. To prevent investigation individual politicians attempted to diminish the power of the magistrates/judiciary by making members of the judiciary liable—civil not criminal—for cases under their control. Those implicated in the scandals sought amnesty schemes, and in 1993 Forza Italia under Berlusconi approved a parliamentary bill supported by the Minister of Justice to reduce judges' powers of arrest. This was withdrawn due to a judicial campaign and public opinion and protests and political interference but illustrates that the rule of law can be temporary rather than permanent.

Corruption is often unearthed where financial incentives and other 'offers' are available. In Italy magistrates/judges have been compensated for 'favours' such as financial rewards; in Ghana such favours are 'sex for justice' (Braimah 2016). These 'favours' can also be rewarded via indirect benefits such as promotion. This, however, makes magistrates/judges subject to political pressure if the appointment was based on collusion (see case in South Korea) (*The Economist* 2019). The reach of corruption and collusion is thus informal and hard to detect. A magistrate/

judge that uncovers political-judicial corruption is under threat from powerful individuals/organizations. If considered unable to understand 'political needs' a magistrate/judges can be isolated by senior corrupt members of the profession by simply moving s/he to another post/ location. In addition if an investigation by police, magistrates/judges appears to be heading in an unwanted direction—e.g. uncover corruption—cases can be reallocated to those more compliant and/or transferred to a jurisdiction that is inclined to suppress the matter.

Furthermore, the judiciary/magistrates and public prosecutors regardless of the system—adversarial or prosecutorial—work with organized crime. This can be because the state is so corrupt (Gutauskas et al. 2004) and lacks a rule of law, at least in practice, and judges keep rejecting prosecutors' requests to arrest criminals, and/or are blackmailed due to impudent acts e.g. attend a brothel (Plywaczewsky 2004). Such corruption occurred in Bulgaria, particularly between 1999 and 2006 where prosecutors blocked criminal cases reaching court and yet were later discovered to be managing criminal networks (Bezlov and Gounev 2014).

There is often a suggestion to pay law enforcement/judges/prison officers more than it is possible to 'earn' elsewhere to prevent corruption. Besley and McLaren (1993) and Mookherjee and Png (1995) have suggested that offering a wage above what can be earnt via corruption is a way to eliminate bureaucratic corruption. This, however, is slightly flawed; this is an economic view of judicial behaviour and it fails to really take account of the benefits that judges can accrue such as political power beyond financial 'rewards'. The social environment will also impact on judicial action and once the private sector has accepted corrupt judges and paying efficiency wages (payment to corrupt judges above the level of what can be 'earnt' by corruption), if at all, will be unable to completely remove corruption from the judicial process.

Corruption also reaches beyond actual criminal cases to arbitration courts where conflicts are settled between businesses and/or businesses and public bodies. In Italy the system of arbitration is often slow and inefficient and thus overloaded with cases. This has created a demand for extra-judicial arbitration. Judges' 'favours' are obtained legally as businesses and/or a public body nominate the judge(s) in the case, whilst, of course paying the arbitration fees to judges. If fees and favours fail to work straightforward bribery is still an option. This seems to have been embraced in Italy and elsewhere such as Bulgaria where personal networks influence judicial appointments (Bezlov et al. 2007).

Even if there is a system with a specific level of deterrence, and internal and external system of monitoring and salary structures judges can and will extort for 'judicial services' if there is a concentration of administrative and judicial roles, a complex procedural system, a lack of transparency in procurement of external services, defective information systems in courts and lack of a jurisprudence database, a lack of alternative dispute resolutions mechanism and/or bureaucratic and lengthy wait for a verdict on case(s). In such a framework, the capacity of a public official, a judge, is able to extract illicit rents depending on the concentration of market and organizational functions under judicial control. In this type of context—complete or partial—the corrupt incentives are provided by the public organizational, procedural, substantive, and market mechanisms within which corruption can flourish.

In a case of collusion where both those involved benefit the taxpayers/public are defrauded, exposing such collusion is extremely problematic. For example, paying a bribe to a public body to purchase a company product(s)/services (see Chapter 7) is a business investment; the bribe is covered and money made beyond the bribe since the product(s)/services are bought above market value. Furthermore, the impact of such an act of corruption is distributed amongst a population that is often unaware of the corruption. Illegal funds are swiftly transferred into the nether world of the financial system and evidence of collusion and corruption become impossible to establish, particularly in a court of law.

Therefore, corrupt individuals have no interest in reporting corruption, which is understandable, but if the system is so corrupt bribes will be offered, particularly if an investigation, accusation and/or charge of corruption is levelled. The diffusion of political corruption reduces moral costs (Miller 2017) as a corrupt system makes it far more acceptable for in this case, the judiciary to engage in corruption and view such acts as 'normal' and part of an unwritten code. Personal circles of reference (Li 2018), informal contacts and association (Bezlov et al. 2007) become a normative system on which judgments are reached. In such a system, prevention of corruption is impossible, and challenging such a system is difficult with powerful vested interests blocking legal and cultural amendments to future transformation of a system.

The presence of a strong professional culture that is underpinned by promoting the rule of law can inhibit corruption rather than completely prevent it, but is limited if a 'value' system in the judiciary is one that corruption is acceptable (Polinsky 1980; Chang and Liu 2007). Once set in motion social acceptance can snowball by encouraging more judges to participate in illegal corrupt acts. In such a situation no state anti-corruption measure will be successful. There are procedures in place in Italy, however, that prevent complete political control of the judiciary. A system of promotion is based on years of service rather instead of passing favourable judgments (Della Porta 2001; Della Porta and Vannucci 2007), but favourable judgments can help, in any system, with rapid promotion. There is also a formal rule of compulsory prosecution. However, whilst compulsory this is no indication that all cases are investigated. It can be seen as a bulwark to prevent political manipulation of the law, but if informal links override professional conduct, then this is a law on paper rather than one in action. The same can be said of political cases in France (Lalam 2014) where the Ministry of Justice has some control of judges and has thus reduced independent investigation.

It is assumed that if there is a social value system in place for members of the judiciary (Akerlof 1980) and if breached a sanction should be forthcoming. This could be via peer disapproval (Hollander 1990; Posner 1983, 1997) and personal guilt (Elster 1989) as much as a criminal sanction, but all of this is based on the assumption that there is a 'professional' value system. Individual politicians, particularly under investigation, simply attempt to delegitimize those investigating (Braimah 2016) by deflecting attention claiming a magistrate/judge is politically, ideologically bias, and then emphasizing superior legitimacy as an elected representative of 'the people' rather than an appointed, elected judge, if relevant to that jurisdiction.

Judicial independence will help in preventing corruption, but institutional resources can only help so much and will shape reaction towards the politically powerful. Judicial actions are effected by (formal) institutional independence as well as by (informal) political dependency, with behaviour shaped by the professional culture. Institutional resources, informal contacts and the professional culture all then play a role in the development of collusion. More important though have been informal political contacts: the composition of the magistracy/judges and political protection, the promotion of judges, ideological commitment to a political view, and clientelistic relationships (Della Porta and Vannucci 2007; Antonopoulos and Tagarov 2014; *The Economist* 2019). Different types of bribes—financial, sex, property, exclusive holiday, shares, bonds and stocks and promotion—buy the 'right' outcome of a case from a corrupt judge. Placed into a context where political corruption has interacted with the lack of a professional culture it is hardly surprising corruption abounds. Independence alone is insufficient to prevent manipulation of criminal cases, and legal amendments only slow down or temporarily thwart corruption rather than prevent it.

In the next section of this chapter, however, I raise the possibility that independence itself is part of the problem (Hanssen 2004) of judicial corruption. With little or no oversight other than by its own professional body judges engage in a variety of corrupt acts.

Judicial Corruption: At Liberty to Be Corrupt?

The USA is a nation that prides itself on liberty and the separation of political and judicial powers. I am aware that the Supreme Court judges are political appointments instead of completely independent and that the checks and balances in place such as questioning a potential appointment are limited. However, I am far more concerned about everyday judicial corruption that affects individuals in the criminal justice system. Political interference, patronage and bribery effect judicial judgments but is independence any assurance that 'justice' is served (Baum 2003; Berkowitz and Clay 2006)? Drawing on the USA it seems that 'justice' is at best erratic. Miller (2004: 432–433) has highlighted how judges can and do commit corrupt acts in the USA. These are:

(1) Corrupt influence on judicial action
(2) Fiduciary appointments
(3) Abuse of office
(4) Incompetence and neglect of duty
(5) Overstepping of authority
(6) Interpersonal abuse
(7) Bias, prejudice
(8) Personal misconduct
(9) Conflict of interest
(10) Inappropriate behaviour in judicial capacity
(11) Lack of candor and
(12) Electioneering/buying of office.

I do not consider all of these above corrupt; some fall under incompetence, but this can lead to corruption. These types of corruption obviously blur but offer a useful tool for analyzing the breathed and depth of judicial corruption.

Corrupt influence on judicial action is where judges have informed suspects of an impending search of their property, reducing bail for suspects requested by a personal contact, pocketing fees in exchange for illegal licenses, dismissing parking and speeding tickets for family and personal contacts, sitting in judgment on family members case(s), phoning other judges to recommend release of a criminal suspect, or to pass a 'favourable' sentence on a particular criminal, and tampering with and altering official records (Miller 2004: 434). All of these acts of corruption ruin criminal and civil justice legitimacy but the rewards for these acts are as diverse as the acts; sex with defendants, straightforward cash, reducing sentence on an offender as a favour to a political contact, accepting 'free tickets' for sporting events from lawyers on a case they are presiding judgment on. These acts are primarily individual acts of corruption but as above the context and culture can be conducive to corruption.

Financial rewards are available for the judge to dispense as well; appointing a woman/man the judge is having an affair with in court at state expense without, of course, disclosing the relationship, requesting dates from criminal defendants and/or victims of domestic violence, soliciting bribes, failure to disqualify cases that include some personal interest, appointing family members as a court mediator(s) and a triumvirate of judges, lawyers and political connected individuals involved in arranging and employing each other, placing people into a position of power (Bezlov et al. 2007)—power of promotion/demotion—and work in private law firms. Using personal contacts, however, is part of 'doing business', (Brooks 2016) but the issue here is: is this acceptable in criminal justice? A sinecure, depending on the person employed, is a threat to company credibility, but in criminal justice is a threat to criminal justice and legitimacy.

Such behaviour is manifest in abuse of office where judges have sentenced people to prison for contempt, or involved in a personal dispute such as paying rent on property owned by the judge, and setting bail as high or low as possible based on a 'favour' to a lawyer or political contact. These examples might be excused as a character flaw but incompetence can also reign in a court of law where some judges fail to understand process, procedures and even laws (Miller 2004: 439–440). In addition important paperwork is lost, court accounts are incomplete, and clerical personnel adjudicate in criminal cases, and judges engage in personal investigations of crime(s), summarily trying defendants, passing sentence and putting people in prison before conviction, and contact with witnesses before, and after a case. Treating people in such an unprofessional manner might not be considered corrupt but damages the legitimacy of criminal justice.

Magistrates and judges also commit crime: shoplifting, embezzlement, planting evidence on a competitor for office, if based in a jurisdiction that elects judges, engage in forgery (e.g. tax returns and mortgage procurement) and fail to declare a conflict of interest. Furthermore, inappropriate behaviour ranging from judges visiting pornographic material online in chambers, having sex with court employees and convicted offenders, and sex with defendants (Braimah 2016) and a failure to report convictions such as drunkenness and/or abuse and acts of violence.

In some jurisdictions judicial office is based on a local election such as in the USA. Such a system is open to abuse where judges or prospective judges engage in partisan conduct, dispense lucrative appointments, and patronage. Such acts are often linked to party politics and 'donations' to the right organization can secure the judicial nomination. Criminal justice in the USA is based on the proposition that the judiciary should be independent from political interference. This independence safeguards the public from state oppression and supposedly protects the criminal justice system by the administration of private interests. This, I suggest, however, as seen above is limited. In such a system judges are insulated from oversight and the quality of judges behaviour is sometimes corrupt with some judges spending years in office in receipt of 'financial rewards' and power, and become entrenched and difficult to remove from office. As Miller (2004: 457) has stated American judges' powers are "small in extent but vast within the ambit" of what a judge can do in passing sentence on the population.

The independence of trial judges interacts with the quality of judicial practice but if judges are not independent state interference is possible (Brinks 2008; Yadav and Mukherjee 2016) where influence will distort the outcome of cases. This might affect the development of laws, and detract from public confidence in the judicial system; however, unchecked or limited oversight on judicial power leads to abuse in the judicial system. State managed criminal justice or powerful independent judges, if unconstrained by check and balances in a system can lead to corruption. It could be the corruption of the system, or pockets of corruption, but its outcome regardless of the route it has travelled reaches the same destination.

Extortion or Bribery: A Judges Tipple?

In the above two sections of this chapter I have highlighted how political interference and an independent judiciary can be corrupt subject to internal and external sources of political power, culture and lack of professionalism. Whilst what will follow here is in reference to judicial corruption it is also relevant to state and private prosecutors, law enforcement, prison officers and lawyers. The judiciary has limited physical contact with offenders than state and private prosecutors, law enforcement, prison officers and lawyers, and if the judiciary is corrupt, which it sometimes is, expectations placed on others working in a criminal justice system to refrain from corruption is more than unrealistic.

In cases of corruption it can be difficult to distinguish between extortion and bribery. It is useful, however, to distinguish between procedure and substance (Ayers 1997). A crude distinction is to state that extortion is initiated by judges whilst bribery is initiated by a defendant(s). However, if it is known that a judge is receptive to bribery defendants could possibly consider a bribe and/or initiate contact.

It is possible to view this as moral desert (Miller 2017) or simply manipulation of power based on social and political position such as Ghana where the judiciary is often referred to as "second to God" (Braimah 2016: 13). For example, if a defendant is on trial for a crime and the available evidence should (instead of must) be proof beyond a reasonable doubt to secure a conviction. For such a defendant, a bribe, if the judge is susceptible, should reduce the probability of conviction (Lindgren 1988). If a judge extorts financial inducement s/he is threatening to increase the probability of conviction unless rewarded in some fashion. Extortion thus consists of paying to avoid unfair treatment.

Extortion and bribery entail payments from a defendant to a judge with the defendant paying to secure, or in the hope of, avoiding a prison sentence or any kind of sanction to avoid unfair treatment and conviction. If a 'pure' bribe is negotiated, the defendant, in the absence of 'understanding' with a judge or intermediary (family member of lawyer), anticipates a 'fair' trial. If 'pure' extortion is negotiated, the defendant, in the absence of 'understanding' with a judge or intermediary, anticipates an unfair, prejudicial trial (Ayers 1997). This then is the threat/offer dichotomy central to the philosophical discussion of coercion. This is the moral desert: a judge agreeing to a bribe is morally corrupt regardless of whether an understanding is based on extortion or a bribe. But in the defendants view is paying to secure better than 'fair' treatment more repugnant than paying to circumvent unfair treatment?

However, under what Ayers (1997) has called 'pure' extortion the judge upon payment only has to judge in a 'fair' instead of prejudicial or bias manner. This is difficult to assess; if a defendant is still convicted after payment the sentence might be warranted, with little the judge could do. Instead of paying a bribe or extortion there could be a combination of both. If a judge extorts a defendant that is then justifiably convicted a defendant could inform law enforcement of the judge, but by combining extortion with bribery a judge will potentially reduce the chances that a defendant will complain. Furthermore, a judge is unable to assure acquittal: it is imprudent to release an overwhelmingly guilty person and/or pass a very low sentence based on the evidence without provoking public criticism and suspicion of potential corruption, but this disappointingly occurs (Bezlov and Gounev 2014; Gomez-Cespedes 2014; Braimah 2016). A corrupt judge can therefore discharge, release and convict even if bribed and/or has extorted. A particularly harsh judge can extort payment simply because of a reputation. This will no doubt occur if an investigation into judicial corruption is known but if a judge starts to pass unduly harsh sentences that is uncharacteristic of them this can also arouse suspicion of potential corruption, particularly on specific people (Tyler 2014).

An analysis of judicial corruption could be: payment is made to avoid injustice, and extortion reduces the individual/organization's moral culpability for participating in extortion or a combination of bribery and extortion; paying to sidestep 'unfair', bias is excusable, but the payment becomes no less excusable if the judge wants to make sure that the defendant is acquitted, and even if a bribe is paid to a judge an investigation into judicial corruption, or a single judge can still convict regardless of the level of evidence to appear honest and tough on offenders, depending on the jurisdiction. Therefore, due to a range of potential outcomes the bribery and/or extortion by a judge, is a risk rather than an assured outcome. Furthermore, if a bribe to secure a favourable commercial outcome is seen as 'too high' the majority of organizations public demand for judicial services decline and the opportunity to extract illicit payments therefore decline.

If a judge has accepted a bribe should a retrial occur? A judge might convict based on an insufficient bribe, if the jurisdiction allows, or deflect detection if an investigation is underway. Individuals and organizations will and do pay via extortion or bribery for a favourable (Gomez-Cespedes 2014) outcome but state prosecutors also have a vested interest in the outcome of a case and could challenge a retrial based on judicial corruption; and should an individual/organization that has knowingly paid a bribe have the same constitutional/legal protection? Here we can see both the complex nature of corruption and its consequences. Judges can and are bias and prejudicial (Miller 2004) but to accept a bribe or solicit, extort for personal benefit in civil or criminal cases damages the legitimacy that the judicial branch of office and criminal justice systems claim to have.

Furthermore, if an individual/organization is acquitted by a judge but we later discover a bribe was paid should a retrial occur? After all, the acquittal could have been based on legal representation, the evidence or lack of it, poor witnesses and documentation presented by prosecutors. The individual/organization paid simply to 'make sure' it would be acquitted, or as sure as it could. In addition an individual might have completed their sentence even after paying a bribe or extorted and a retrial is impossible; financial reparation might be possible (Jenkins 2013) but depending on the jurisdiction difficult to secure.

To make this even more complex we simply have to consider the use of an intermediary. For example, a family member bribes a judge and the trial subsequently ends in an acquittal. Or a defendant pays his lawyer to bribe a judge, but the lawyer pockets the money instead, and the defendant is acquitted in a 'fair trial' without knowledge of what has happened. In these examples who is corrupt? These are legal and philosophical debates that are for another book rather than here (see Miller 2017). They do, however, highlight how difficult it is to unearth and convict individuals/organizations and judges and lawyers that are corrupt. If a judge is exposed as corrupt it calls in doubt all trials—those sh/e was bribed in and extorted from, and also those cleared of corruption. One corrupt judge will have presided and passed judgment and sentence many individuals/organizations in various cases in a career, and now because of known corruption all judgments passed regardless of the level of evidence and obvious guilt of some defendants, harms the legitimacy of criminal justice.

All of the above is based on a 'western' democratic system—natural or imposed—but there are cultural differences that need to be considered. In Ghana it is expected that traditional leaders are showered with gifts such as livestock and/or money as part of paying homage to maintain custom and tradition. In such a culture there is little distinction between a gift and a bribe and these gestures are extended to public office holders and often presented to influential individuals at festivals. Gifts are often presented to judges, but without prior deals attached. But in the recent scandal, Braimah (2016) has highlighted how defendants charged with narcotics offences, which is a non-bail offence in Ghana have been bailed. Furthermore, in such a corrupt system judges pay more attention to personal and familial relationships rather than objective justice and it is perhaps more dishonourable for a judge to discount the wishes of a family member than strictly adhere to the law (Pepys 2007).

Therefore, regardless of the state and cultural values the impact of judicial corruption is highly damaging to the legitimacy of criminal justice. The impact of corruption reaches beyond the individual to family to community to citizens. In some jurisdictions judges are bribed and/or extort; if justice is for sale with some judges can we put a numerical value on a crime, a life? Even if bribed a judge might still convict for the reasons cited above. Ending this section I suggest that we need to look beyond the bribery of judges and consider extortion as well. The difference between bribery and extortion is sometimes blurred as both are present in cases of corruption; instead we should view them, where relevant as intertwined aspect of judicial corruption.

Preventing Judicial Corruption

The potential solution to reducing judicial corruption is in the selection, retention, supervision and removal of judges. As such these fall under case specific, public systemic and private solutions.

For example, impeachment is the traditional case-specific way of dealing with corrupt judges. Impeachment has value (Miller 2004) in that it is a well-recognized, traditional method for disciplining judges in the USA. It is also a high-profile process that allows significant public participation and input but is viewed as a process that can become too political. Under impeachment a judge is either convicted and removed or acquitted and allowed to remain in office. These polar choices limit the range of sanctions available, short of removal, in cases in which a judge's conduct is subject to censure. A judge can also resign and potentially avoid impeachment. Impeachment is limited to serious cases of corruption, which is understandable, but it fails to deal with incompetent judges or those that are ideologically biased, nor does it address cases of private misconduct by judges unless extremely serious in nature. Impeachment is only really of use for judges in high positions; it does not work for the low-level posts.

A potential remedy to corruption is removal from the case and/or disqualification. Disqualification though is often based on precise criteria, which might be difficult to substantiate. A system can be in place that prohibits a judge from a case such as personal interest but is of little use if the judge(s) fail to declare a personal interest and there is little or no oversight of this process. If also fails to remove bias and/or prejudicial judges (Tyler 2014), and also challenge them for incompetence or inappropriate behaviour. Furthermore, it also fails to address those that abuse the position for personal benefit, and if sought there is always the potential, particularly if the judge is corrupt and or ideologically biased that s/he will be hostile towards those that requested disqualification.

Whilst in some systems of justice there is the right to appeal a sentence that can correct poor collective—police, judges and jury—decisions in a case, this is often a lengthy and bureaucratic process. Via appeal the judiciary can claim to be independent but it is still judges reviewing a judge. For example, judges have been suspended in Ghana for acts of supposed corruption with all allowances revoked but are in receipt of some judicial salary and public payment of rent (Braimah 2016). Even if a judge makes an error due to incompetence a corrupt sentence might still stand. The appeals process is costly and many guilty and innocent people, as both challenge judgments, simply accept a bias outcome as unable to incur expense of appeal if state funds to challenge a ruling are limited or non-existent. The right of appeal is over-inclusive (Miller 2004): it might expose some corrupt judges but will also capture adequate judges that sometimes make errors. Errors, particularly if the outcome is a lengthy one or even a death sentence have serious ramifications but an appeal only exposes the judge for passing judgment on one case rather than all cases.

Whilst a judge is (or should be) legally liable for committing crime(s) similar to other citizens in a jurisdiction this is rare. Outside their judicial roles, judges are liable as other citizens for crimes and breaches of contract but judicial immunity often shields them from liability for civil damages if acting as judge. Perhaps then we are left with an internal disciplinary procedure but here as elsewhere e.g. policing, those tasked with judicial oversight are either lax, bias and/or the system of oversight has been captured by the judges (Wang 2017) that they are supposedly policing. Lacking resources and/or political will we are mostly informed of the outcome of an investigation into a judge rather than the process. In addition all documentation is withheld and confidential. This is slightly understandable, as some challenges to the judiciary will be petty but an investigation 'behind closed doors' decreases the legitimacy of the rule of law. It is possible that public confidence in the rule of law (if there is one) will be undermined but any disciplinary process that excludes members of the public to some extent can also appear corrupt, particularly if the outcome is one that is clearly biased in favour of the judiciary.

Prosecutorial Corruption

State prosecutors have immense power depending on the jurisdiction. Of course, in dictatorships this is self-evident (Brinks 2008), but in democratic states prosecutors have discretion in the 'direction' investigations might head, selecting the crime(s) for a charge, and some influence on the sentence/punishment imposed. Public prosecutors are supposed to represent the public interest, but this is subject to interpretation; is the public interest punishment and/or rehabilitation or both, or is this dependent on the crime committed, and by whom?

In the USA elected state prosecutors are often expected to maintain a high conviction rate. Failure to do so might lead to the loss of elected office (Banks 2017). State prosecutors are therefore subject to a number of stresses—please the public, law enforcement, colleagues, and political connections, and victims. It is hardly surprising that some prosecutors are therefore corrupt. This understanding is not an excuse for corruption but recognition of the context in which state prosecutors act, and pressure to deliver leads to corruption of the criminal justice system. For Gershman (2001) state prosecutors should have a duty to the 'truth' and act as a 'minister of justice' as a representative of the state. This, though I consider to be an idealistic interpretation of how state prosecutors act. Unable to cover all acts of potential corruption by state prosecutors here I review those that subvert 'justice' on regular basis—power of discretion to charge or waive, disclosure (or not, as is sometimes the case) evidence and plea bargaining.

Discretion in charging suspects in the USA is protected by almost absolute immunity (Banks 2017). Freedman (1975) many years ago made a point that is still salient now; and that is charged with a crime results in a damaged personal reputation, regardless of a failure to convict. The emotional strain of a criminal trial as well as the financial burden, depending on the system, is set in motion when an indictment is sought. But an indictment could be brought on little more than a vague all-encompassing notion that the suspect is possibly guilty, hearsay is accepted as evidence and/or law enforcement have secured a 'confession' by corrupt conduct.

The problem here is that often there are few controls on state prosecutors, particularly in the USA where it is the "single most un-reviewed exercise of the power of the criminal law available to an individual in the American system of justice" (Gottfredson and Gottfredson 1988 in Banks 2017: 1338). There are, of course, checks and balances to address but a state prosecutor(s) can reject a case because the state is unable to secure a conviction, or seek prosecution based on little evidence because of the race of the suspect and victim (Tyler 2014). Selective prosecution then is based on 'improper' motives, bias and prejudicial attitudes and is an abuse of official power. This abuse though can be based on a conflict of interest, failure to enforce the law(s), vindictive accusations.

This leads onto the power of discretion to disclose or not disclose evidence (Gier 2006). Whilst it is considered appropriate, and in some jurisdictions a constitutional duty to disclose information to defense lawyer(s) state prosecutors can and do delay passing on relevant information, fail to disclose all information, wait for defense to request specific information (The Secret Barrister 2018), and suppress information to secure a conviction. These acts could be based on the view that the individual is innocent but prosecutors' seek a conviction and thus fail to disclose evidence to the defense (Jenkins 2013). These acts can result in denial of 'fair trial' on which democratic criminal justice should be based (or so we are told).

To make this increasingly complex some prosecutors might have a practice of 'open case file' where the prosecution file is disclosed, others will adopt a restrictive approach because of fear that such an approach will effect personal conviction rates (Yaroshefsky and Green 2012: 275) on which future success e.g. elected back into office is dependent. It is possible to disbar a prosecutor(s) for inappropriate conduct but it is rare (Ridolfi 2006), as with law enforcement and judges that sanctions are employed. Close relationships, particularly with law enforcement but also the judiciary could influence a prosecutors' willingness in covering up abuses, brutality, perjury and unlawful interrogation.

Failure to disclose evidence, particularly evidence that highlights an individuals' innocence is a clear case of prosecutorial misconduct, and I suggest outright corruption. To withhold and/or delay passing information might seem a 'legal tactic', part of the culture in criminal justice, but for suspects, offenders and victims this is hardly a 'fair' trial. In fact the Innocence Project highlights in USA (see Innocenceproject.org for a continuous updated commentary on unreliable jailhouse testimony, inadequate defense, false confessions, misapplication of 'science data and state misconduct) all of which is damaging, to criminal justice legitimacy and notions of justice.

Furthermore, prosecutors might influence a jury by knowingly making a statement in court that will be inadmissible. This is where innuendo, casting doubt on a witness statement and credibility harm criminal justice. In addition combined with appealing to bias, and prejudicial views (Tyler 2014) in a jury rather than seeking the 'truth' (see Chapter 4 for discussion on what is the truth), prosecutors can secure convictions on the most tenuous evidence.

This notion of justice is also thwarted by the power to engage in plea bargaining. The aim is often to achieve a compromise but also to secure some kind of conviction and sanction. In spite of legal and moral (Miller 2017) expectations of a prosecutor(s) to contest a case in court there are an array of tactics that are used before a trial. State prosecutors might engage in overcharging a defendant as a plea-bargaining tactic, to threaten and intimidate them to confess, and/or charging with more than one offence out of the same incident whilst intending to accept a plea to the least serious charge. Is this legitimate? If state prosecutor(s) can convict someone employing such a method in a case with little chance of conviction then is this little more than 'criminal justice poker': conning people and playing a hand beyond its power? In this situation who benefits? The victim might be disappointed as the 'offender' (or what they consider to be the guilty party) has lowest sentence possible, the public is dissatisfied with a low-level sentence, but a guilty person could secure the lowest possible sanction for an array of crimes and an innocent person convicted/sanction for a crime. Here, I suggest, only the prosecutor(s) have any kind of preferable outcome.

But why engage in such a practice? There is often a volume of criminal justice 'traffic', cases to review before a decision is made. Plea bargaining is presented as of benefit to offenders but in reality it saves prosecutors time and, in eliminating the expense and time of a trial, prevents the criminal justice system from becoming overloaded and reduces it costs. Such a method can also benefit prosecutors if the prosecution case is weak. Such a method can possibly work with unsophisticated young people, mentally ill, vulnerable in some capacity but powerful organizations will challenge accusations in court and public (Brooks 2016) and often reduce sanctions (Warrne 2016).

Furthermore, if cases are downgraded to secure a conviction is criminal justice providing a service to the victims? The practice of negotiating pleas, however, appears to have evolved within the criminal justice system in an unregulated, ad hoc manner in the USA. The essence of plea bargaining is that individuals are placed into a position where a choice has to be made between a risk of conviction, even if innocent, and thus confess to a crime for which they are innocent, or risk potential conviction in a court of law. Bargaining then has adverse consequences—it is in effect a coercive system where some innocent people plead guilty out of fear because of promises of leniency and it shifts sentencing policy from the judge and legislatures to a state prosecutor(s) and blurs the boundary of state power. This could possibly been seen as part of the shadow state (see Chapter 8) where a defendant's innocence and/or guilt is decided without investigation, evidence, or fact determined by an impartial body. In the absence of a public trial criminal justice messages—censure, condemnation, shame, held to account (Walker 1991) are all missing': as such criminal justice is simply a back room deal that has abandoned the public role of criminal justice.

This type of deal, even though public, is now available in parts of the United Kingdom. Referred to as a Deferred Prosecution Agreement (DPA) it is where a prosecutor with permission and under supervision of a judge can 'agree' with an organization, which could be prosecuted for an economic crime, has its sentence deferred. Certain conditions apply but key features are that the organization should make full reparation from criminal behaviour without the collateral damage of a conviction (e.g. sanctions or reputational damage that could ruin a company and investments of innocent people), and under the supervision of a judge is convinced that the DPA is in the interests of 'justice' and that the set conditions are 'fair, reasonable and proportionate.' However, reasonable and proportionate are vague; established in 2014. I can see the financial benefit to the criminal justice system but DPAs might simply be a way for businesses to act in a corrupt manner, and only pay a fine? Currently then, it makes sense to act in a rational and corrupt way; profit is secured by an act corruption, the financial penalty is substantial but ineffective as the cost of paying this penalty, if caught and convicted, is often less than the profit secured (Brooks 2016).

Conclusion

In this chapter, I have illustrated the range and types of corruption in the judiciary. As with all corruption such acts are not to be placed in isolation but the context in which they occur. This is not to dismiss the acts of corruption but to understand culture and that process and procedures only have limited power to reduce corruption. In addition, whilst we expect judicial corruption in non-democratic nations it was highlighted here the types of judicial corruption in western systems of criminal law, particularly the USA damage the legitimacy of criminal justice. Judges hold immense positions of power, regardless of the country or political system and can extort and secure bribes to pass judgment. However, no matter how small the corruption, judicial corruption is perhaps more damaging than that of corrupt law enforcement. If judicial power is corrupted then it is impossible claim there is a system of justice.

References

Akerlof, G. A. (1980). A Theory of Social Custom, of Which Unemployment May Be One Consequence. *Quarterly Journal of Economics, 94*, 749–775.

Alt, J., & Lassen, D. D. (2008). Political and Judicial Checks on Corruption: Evidence from American State Governments. *Economics and Politics, 20*(1), 33–61.

Antonopoulos, G., & Tagarov, N. (2014). Greece: The Politics of Crime. In P. Gounev & V. Ruggiero (Eds.), *Corruption and Organized in Europe: Illegal Partnerships*. Abingdon: Routledge.

Ayers, I. (1997). The Twin Faces of Judicial Corruption: Extortion and Bribery. *Yale Law School Scholarship Repository Paper 1500, 1*(1), 1213–1253.

Banks, C. (2017). *Criminal Justice Ethics: Theory and Practice*. London: Sage.

Baum, L. (2003). Judicial Elections and Judicial Independence: The Voter's Perspective. *Ohio State Law Journal, 64*, 13–41.

Berkowitz, D., & Clay, K. (2006). The Effect of Judicial Independence on Courts: Evidence from the American States. *Journal of Legal Studies, 35*, 399–400.

Besley, T., & McLaren, J. (1993). Taxes and Bribery: The Role of Wages Incentives. *Economic Journal, 103,* 119–141.
Bezlov, T., & Gounev, P. (2014). Bulgaria: Corruption and Organized Crime in Flux. In P. Gounev & V. Ruggiero (Eds.), *Corruption and Organized in Europe: Illegal Partnerships.* Abingdon: Routledge.
Bezlov, T., Gounev, P., Petrunov, G., Tzenkov, E., & Tzvetkona, M. (2007). *Organized Crime in Bulgaria: Markets and Trends.* Sofia: Centre for the Study of Democracy.
Braimah, A. I. (2016). Are Judges Corrupt? An Empirical Analysis of the Ghana Judiciary. *Journal of Humanities and Social Science, 21*(8), 12–21.
Brinks, D. M. (2008). *The Judicial Response to Police Killings in Latin America: Inequality and the Rule of Law.* Cambridge: Cambridge University Press.
Brooks, G. (2016). *Criminology of Corruption: Theoretical Approaches.* Basingstoke: Palgrave Macmillan.
Chang, J. J., & Liu, C. (2007). The Negligence Rule in the Presence of Judicial Corruption and Social Norms. *Atlantic Economic Journal, 35,* 203–215.
Darden, K. (2008). The Integrity of Corrupt States: Graft as an Informal State Institution. *Politics and Society, 36*(1), 35–59.
Della Porta, D. (2001). A Judges' Revolution? Political Corruption and the Judiciary in Italy. *European Journal of Political Research, 9*(1), 1–21.
Della Porta, D., & Pizzorno, A. (1996). The Business Politicians: Reflections from a Study on Political Corruption. *Journal of Law and Society, 23,* 73–94.
Della Porta, D., & Vannucci, A. (1997). The Resources of Corruption: Some Reflections from the Italian Case. *Crime, Law and Social Change, 27*(23), 1–254.
Della Porta, D., & Vannucci, A. (2007). Corruption and Anti-corruption: The Political Defeat of 'Clean Hands' in Italy. *West European Politics, 30*(4), 830–853.
Della Porta, R., Lopez-de-Silanes, F., Pop-Eleches, C., & Shleifer, A. (2004). Judicial Checks and Balances. *Journal of Political Economy, 112,* 445–470.
Elster, J. (1989). Social Norms and Economic Theory. *Journal of Economic Perspectives, 3,* 99–117.
Freedman, M. (1975). Judges Frankel's Search for the Truth. *University of Pennsylvania Law Review, 123,* 1060–1082.
Gershman, B. (2001). The Prosecutor's Day of Truth. *Georgetown Journal of Legal Ethics, 14,* 309–354.

Gier, K. (2006). Prosecuting Injustice: Consequences of Misconduct. *American Journal of Criminal Law, 33*(2), 191–222.
Gomez-Cespedes, A. (2014). Spain: A Criminal Hub. In P. Gounev & V. Ruggiero (Eds.), *Corruption and Organized Crime*. London: Routledge.
Gutauskas, A., Juska, A., Jonstone, P., & Pzzuto, R. (2004). Changing Typology of Organized Crime in Post-socialist Lithuania (the Late 1980s-Early 2000s). *Global Crime, 6*(2), 201–221.
Hanssen, F. A. (2004). Is There a Politically Optimal Level of Judicial Independence? *American Economic Review, 94*, 712–729.
Hollander, H. (1990). A Social Exchange Approach to Voluntary Cooperation. *American Economic Review, 80*, 1157–1167.
Jenkins, S. (2013). Miscarriages of Justice and the Discourse of Innocence: Perspectives from Appellants, Campaigners, Journalists, and Legal Practitioners. *Journal of Law and Society, 40*(3), 329–355.
Kang, M. S., & Shepherd, J. M. (2011). The Partisan Price of Justice: An Empirical Analysis of Campaign Contributions and Judicial Decisions. *New York University Law Review, 86*, 69–130.
Lalam, N. (2014). France: From Local Elites to National Leaders. In P. Gounev & V. Ruggiero (Eds.), *Corruption and Organized Crime*. London: Routledge.
Li, L. (2018). The Moral Economy of *guanxi* and the Market of Corruption: Networks, Brokers and Corruption in China's Courts. *International Political Science Review, 39*(5), 634–646.
Lindgren, J. (1988). The Elusive Distinction Between Bribery and Extortion: From the Common Law to Hobbes. *UCLA Law Review, 35*, 815.
Maravall, J. M., & Przeworski, A. (2001). *Democracy and the Rule of Law*. Cambridge: Cambridge University Press.
Miller, G. P. (2004). Bad Judges. *Texas Law Review, 83*(2), 431–487.
Miller, S. (2017). *Institutional Corruption: A Study in Applied Philosophy*. Cambridge: Cambridge University Press.
Mishler, W., & Sheehan, R. (1993). The Supreme Court as a Counter-Majoritarian Institution? The Impact of Public Opinion on Supreme Court Decisions. *American Political Science Review, 87*(1), 87–101.
Mishler, W., & Sheehan, R. (1996). Public Opinion, the Attitudinal Model, and Supreme Court Decision-Making: A Micro-Analytic Perspective. *Journal of Politics, 58*(1), 169–200.
Mookherjee, D., & Png, I. P. L. (1995). Corruption Law Enforcement: How Should They Be Compensated? *Economic Journal, 105*, 249–283.

Nagle, L. (2010). Corruption of Politicians, Law Enforcement, and the Judiciary in Mexico and Complicity Across the Border. *Small Wars and Insurgencies, 21*(1), 95–122.
Pepys, M. N. (2007). Corruption Within the Judiciary: Causes and Remedies. In *Global Corruption Report 2007: Transparency International Excerpt*. Cambridge: Cambridge University Press.
Plywaczewsky, E. (2004 [2006]). Organized Crime in Poland: Its Development from Real Socialism to Present Times. In L. Paoli & C. Fijnaut (Eds.), *Organized Crime in Europe*. Dordretcht: Springer.
Polinsky, A. M. (1980). Strict Liability vs Negligence in a Market Setting. *American Economic Review, 70*, 363–367.
Posner, R. A. (1983). *The Economic Theory of Justice*. Cambridge: Harvard University Press.
Posner, R. A. (1997). Social Norms and the Law: An Economics Approach. *AEA Papers and Proceedings, 87*, 365–369.
Raj, A. S. (2017). Cultural Roots of Corruption: Efficacy of Judiciary in Combatting Corruption in India. *Indian Journal of Public Administration, 57*(3), 797–805.
Ridolfi, K. (2006). *Prosecutorial Misconduct: A Systematic Review. California Commission on the Fair Administration of Justice: Preliminary Report*. Sacramento, CA: California Commission.
The Economist. (2019, January 26–February 1). Judging the Judges. *The Economist*.
The Secret Barrister. (2018). *The Secret Barrister: Stories of the Law and How It's Broken*. London: Macmillan.
Tyler, J. C. (2014). Blind Injustice: The Supreme Court, Implicit Racial Bias and the Racial Disparity in the Criminal Justice System. *American Criminal Law Review, 51*, 689–713.
VonDoepp, P. (2005). The Problem of Judicial Control in Africa's Neo-patrimonial Democracies: Malawi and Zambia. *Political Science Quarterly, 120*, 275–301.
Walker, N. (1991). *Why Punish*. Oxford: Oxford University Press.
Wang, Y. (2017). Relative Capture: Quasi-Experimental Evidence from Chinese Judiciary. *Comparative Political Studies, 51*(8), 1012–1041.
Warrne, E. (2016). *Rigged Justice 2016: How Weak Enforcement Let's Offenders of Easy*. Washington, DC: Office of United States Senate and Office of Elizabeth Warren.

Yadav, V., & Mukherjee, B. (2016). *The Politics of Corruption in Dictatorships*. Cambridge: Cambridge University Press.

Yaroshefsky, E., & Green, B. A. (2012). Prosecutors' Ethics in Context: Influences on Prosecutorial Disclosure. In L. C. Levin & L. Mather (Eds.), *Lawyers in Practice: Ethical Decision Making* (pp. 269–292). Chicago: University of Chicago.

7
An Archipelago of Profit: Custodial Institutions and Corruption

Introduction

Corruption in custodial institutions is a major issue in criminal justice systems. By the time an offender(s) reach a custodial institution to serve a sentence or wait on remand or detained until deported, the criminal justice system could have lost all or some of its legitimacy as an objective system, depending on the jurisdiction. Whilst legitimacy is important to maintain some kind of control in a custodial institution, it is, as was highlighted in Chapter 2 a complex issue. In a custodial institution legitimacy is on multiple levels: the legitimacy of officers to control and order inmates, management to order and control/supervise officers, and inmates to order and control inmates (Liebling 2000, 2005, 2007, 2008). The relationships between and within these is complex and can be based on respect, fear, threats of violence, corruption, collusion and compromise (Sykes 1958; Kauffman 1988; Gottschalk 2015; Lessing 2016). The problem though is that corruption is committed on and by both inmates and officers with three themes a habitual problem: smuggling of contraband, 'inappropriate' prison employee and inmate relationships and violence.

G. Brooks, *Criminal Justice and Corruption*,
https://doi.org/10.1007/978-3-030-16038-8_7

The smuggling of illegal items in a custodial institution by visitors, transferred inmates, officers and/or civilian employees is a conduit of corruption (Brooks 2016). Whilst smuggling is difficult for some such as transferred inmates, it is not impossible, but someone in a position of power—access to the outside world—officers and civilians exploit this position of power (Centre for the Advancement of Public Integrity 2016) and smuggle food, narcotics and mobile/cell phones into institutions. Such smuggling is achieved via bribery—inmates' family members paying officers in return for smuggling contraband, with sexual relationships, willing or bartered, conducted between civilian personnel in prison and inmates. Overshadowing these is always the threat of violence. Violence and the threat of it, is used by both officers and inmates to control and subjugate individuals and/or specific inmates such as sex offenders. The application of violence, however, is common in custodial institutions around the world regardless of what system—democratic or dictatorial—people are incarcerated in.

Before I continue and to avoid confusion I will refer to custodial institutions in this chapter rather than prison, Youth Detention Centre, and Immigration Detention Centre, unless stated otherwise. The reason for this is that regardless of the status of the inmates all are in institutions subjected to rules and regulations under the control of officers with disciplinary power. Furthermore, I will use the term prison officers (the same as Banks 2017: 178) rather than correctional officers or prison guards. All terms describe the institution but also the role of the institution but often, I suggest, incorrectly. For example, correctional officers signify that officers 'correct', by deterrence and/or rehabilitate individuals in a custodial institution, but this is ambiguous as such institutions record of recidivism is poor. Guards conjures up notions of protection rather than correction, but in custodial institutions all officers in one sense 'guard' people and/or entrances/exits, but working in an institution is more than simply 'guarding' a population of inmates. A custodial population has diverse and complex needs and no institution can claim to have homogenous inmate needs or roles to control its captive population with the roles of officers multi-faceted.

However, regardless of these needs there are common characteristics of all custodial institutional environments. These are volatility secretive, and often brutal. A custodial institution is volatile because of the nature of placing numbers of vulnerable and also violent individuals behind bars and subsequent abuse by inmates on inmates and by officers on inmates. As with a closed institution corruption is often hidden and the use of violence by inmates and officers is a habitual problem that no custodial institution wishes to be made public. In addition smuggling contraband is also secretive or known but smuggling is a threat to inmates and officers inside and outside an institution as mobile phones allow inmates to still coordinate crime(s) on the outside (Centre for the Advancement of Public Integrity 2016). Smuggling allows individuals to breach the walls and therefore corruption in custodial institutions affects us all regardless on what side of the walls we are located. This reach beyond the physical structures of prison though is only possible with complicit involvement of officers or civilian employees and/or lack of control of an inmate population that is a threat to criminal justice (Lessing 2016). These 'relationships' muddy the waters of how we define corruption in the prison sector, and it is to this problem I now turn.

Corruption in Custodial Institutions: A Problem of Definition

As was noted in Chapter 2 trying to define corruption is problematic. Corruption in criminal justice might be the use of arbitrary power because it presupposes the use of power to achieve a purpose beyond what it was intended for. Examples might include employing or promoting an unqualified person because s/he is a relative of an officer or warden of a prison or is sexually attracted to an individual and/or sees them as compliant. Such 'soft' corruption is perhaps nepotism and is prevalent in public and private sector businesses, but as was noted in chapter two regarding legitimacy the public sector is expected to be beyond such preferential treatment. The impact of employing the 'incorrect' person for a post in criminal justice though can aggravate a situation: a poorly trained or inappropriate individual dealing with an inmate with mental health issues can become a major issue because of this 'soft' corruption. In addition officers can dispense preferential treatment to inmates for a variety of reasons such as sharing the same religion; and yet at the same time officers can engage in the denial of civil rights and privileges to inmates because of religion/race/offence committed.

In a broad sense corruption can be broken down into: *Legal corruption* and the use of extralegal methods. Such oppression is common in non-democratic states but is also part of living in democratic states: examples might include manufactured prison rule violation, increase the threshold of indictments, and permitting physical abuses to be inflicted on inmates (or officers). *Ethical corruption* is the failure of officers to exhibit compassion and care for inmates under supervision. Examples here might include ignoring an inmate's request for medical attention, and withholding information that could help with an inmates' release. *Economic corruption* is the abuse of authority for personal benefit; examples include a prison warden producing a procurement contract that fits a specific private sector vendor, the exploitation of inmates by inmates threatening them with violence unless the family pays a bribe, smuggling and selling contraband to inmates, and the unauthorized use of prison equipment (a vehicle, a truck, or a tractor) by a prison warden/officers.

A similar typology of corrupt acts to be found in custodial institutions is acts of misfeasance, malfeasance, and nonfeasance (Braswell et al. 1984). Acts of misfeasance are where prison officials or 'outsiders' who are associated with the prison commit illegitimate acts for personal profit. Examples are similar to those of economic corruption above where an executive director, a prison warden, or a member of the prison board awards a building contract/food supply/or maintenance contract based on bribery. This type of corruption is mostly on the 'outside' of the prison, and benefits key individuals, but will, depending on the type of contract such as the provision of food also impact on the inmates.

Acts of malfeasance are criminal acts or acts of misconduct that officials knowingly commit in violation of state laws and/or agency rules. These almost always constitute the inappropriate use of authority and such violations are mostly, but not exclusively committed by officials in low/or middle management levels. Here prison officers might commit theft, embezzlement, smuggling contraband in and out of prison, extortion, official oppression, and the exploitation of inmates or family for payment, products or services. As such acts of malfeasance are legally, ethically and economically corrupt.

Acts of nonfeasance are acts of omission or avoidance knowingly committed by officials. These are far more subtle acts and are common across the institution. Braswell et al. (1984: 234) cited two types of such acts: (a) ignoring inmate violations of institutional rules such as the smuggling in of narcotics into a prison by inmates or visitors; and (b) failure to report misconduct/abuse/violence by other officers out of either personal loyalty, repayment for a previous favour or fear of reprisals. Acts of nonfeasance are products of four factors: absence of moral courage on the part of the official(s) to prevent misconduct and fail to act in anticipation of some future personal profit (profit in this sense can mean financial benefit but also future promotion), co-option by a company, or a person, in anticipation of a share in an illegal profit to be made; maintaining an illegitimate personal relationship with an inmate; and indifference to corrupt act(s) in a manner consistent with an organizational culture (Ashforth and Arnad 2003). Whilst some acts of nonfeasance are breaches of ethical codes, some, such as smuggling are breaching laws and illegal, which in turn some officers financially benefit from and so is part of economic corruption, too.

The problem then with trying to define corruption in custodial institutions is one act cuts across attempts to define a single act. Smuggling contraband is illegal (a breach of laws) for which an officer(s) is paid with by money or sex and so is also a form of economic corruption. This smuggling will occur under the threat of potential violence to either the inmate, officers involved in smuggling or even family members outside the institution. Rather than attempt to define individual acts of corruption as illegal, unethical or economic it is better to see corruption as part of an ongoing, negotiated power struggle in a confined physical space where sometimes officers and inmates control the institution (Lessing 2016). To attempt to prevent corruption in custodial institutions seems naïve in such a volatile, combustible closed environment: the best hope seems to be to manage an intractable problem reducing corruption where possible.

The Propensity of Prison Corruption: An Intractable Problem?

Custodial institutions are often a unique physical structure in a city, town or countryside and impossible to miss. They are located in a city, town or community but not of it (Souryal 2009). Subsequently there is a sense of difference, and unless incarcerated in one, employed or visiting the majority of the public have no comprehension of life in prison. Instead public knowledge is based on misleading and often incorrect newspapers ideological views and readership. As such there is no doubt a level of public acceptance of corruption 'behind' institutional walls.

Much of the literature on corruption views the public sector as the conduit of corruption which is misleading (Brooks 2016). Public sector employees, particularly in the criminal justice system, are expected to faithfully adhere to and execute all laws without bias or prejudice. If laws are breached corruption is damaging to the public sector, as confidence in justice is broken, and public corruption, especially when routinely committed, reflects badly on the ability of a criminal justice agency to administer justice competently. As a result, legitimacy to punish is diminished and/or lost.

Prison officials work behind the walls and in an environment that is somewhat closed to public examination, unless assessed by a regulatory state body. Behind closed walls it is possible as it is in police cells, to commit acts of corruption and suppress much of the evidence associated with corrupt acts. Working in a prison, however, regardless of the type of offenders, is stressful (Liebling 2005, 2008). Given the task of managing an often "reluctant, resistant, and sometimes hostile inmate population" (Braswell et al. 1984: 235) physical conflict is possible. This situation, in some jurisdictions such as Brazil (Lessing 2016) where control of some institutions is lost to inmates is a longstanding problem. But this has perhaps increased with overcrowding in some jurisdictions such as USA (Banks 2017) and elsewhere around the world. Regardless of the type of custodial institution, however, placing huge numbers of inmates in closed confined cells leads to the prisonization (Clemmer 1940) of offenders. Consequently, a 'criminal outlook' and shared culture of manipulation and violence and exploitation are common, depending on the jurisdiction, but also the prison (e.g., maximum security prison see Shalev 2009) both by prison officers and inmates. In such a volatile situation it is understandable that cynicism and small acts of corruption potentially lead to rampant corruption by officers.

Kauffman (1988) noted prison officers attitudes toward inmates and other colleagues and produced a typology of five 'types' of prison officers. Kauffman named these types but here it is the role(s) and attitudes I consider important. Some officers were considerate of colleagues, but critical of the manner in which they dealt with inmates. These officers adopted a helping strategy as a means of coping with the prison environment, and expressed their sympathy for inmates. Some officers held positive attitudes toward inmates but negative attitudes toward their fellow officers and were interested in working with people, and showed compassion for inmates. Yet others were hostile/aggressive toward inmates and identified closely with fellow officers. Here, such officers saw prison as a world of conflict, a 'them and us' situation between inmates and officers. As perhaps with any stressful employment, but noticeable in some law enforcement/prison officer(s) role there was burnout, and such officers held negative attitudes toward officers and inmates and were unable to cope, if at all. Finally, there were those that simply coped with the stress of the role by closing down, ignoring transgressions.

Managing inmates in a custodial institution, however, is to confront major issues such as overcrowding (Banks 2017), the spread of AIDS, ageing inmates, and 'gang' membership (Lessing 2016) and affiliation and use of narcotics. These complicate order maintenance and potential for violence. In addition with pay, particularly in the private prison sector, which is low (Eisen 2017), officers might be tempted to supplement income. The incentive to be corrupt for some will happen, and smuggling in contraband is a simple way to make 'extra' and regular income. A note of caution is needed here, however; regardless of how much some officers and management earn a little extra income is always tempting, particularly with such a captive audience hidden behind walls.

This is where the role of ethical management of a prison is an important issue. A recurring theme in the literature on corruption is that a company engages in rampant and systemic corruption because management is openly corrupt. The prison system is no different. A prison policy statement is only useful if more than a paper statement. It is straightforward to have a mission statement, written rules of conduct and a system of reporting corruption, depending on the jurisdiction, but if these are not acted on if corruption is suspected and/or known then such rules lose all validity and legitimacy. Measures can be implemented to reduce incidents of corruption in custodial institutions such as increasing officers' income but this alone is insufficient. In addition to prevent employing the 'incorrect' type of person to work in a prison that might abuse inmates, psychological tests of prospective candidates are useful, but not infallible.

It is important to remember though that working in a prison is stressful for officers. In what is often a volatile environment where officers' deal with individuals that have committed horrendous crime(s), and repeat offenders, particularly the young, return year-after-year a culture of cynicism is understandable? To tackle such a problem there needs to be a clear and consistent application regarding ethical principles and the disciplining of workers if offenders see incarceration as partially legitimate, and the development and presence of a professional association or union to move beyond its own interests and effectively monitor its members and upper management adherence to legal and ethical practice. Public officials, particularly working in criminal justice are expected to exhibit a developed standard of integrity at all times. For the public sector, which is expected to deliver services under a set of rules and standards such as a code of ethics emphasizes the primacy of principle rather than expediency, 'truth' instead of deception, and social utility instead of personal and/or organizational reward. Concomitantly, if a conflict arises between matters of fact and matters of value, all criminal justice professionals are expected to follow the facts (Souryal 2007). This, however, is an ideal, an ethos that is impossible to always deliver. Corrupt individuals and organizations see the standards of civil behaviour as irrelevant; irrelevant in a specific case, or irrelevant to people from social and/or ethnic backgrounds.

Furthermore, the highly political nature of custodial institutions makes it difficult to obtain reliable information on corruption. Acts of corruption such as theft of products, smuggling in contraband, or sex with inmates are understandably hidden by the custodial institution. Incidents of this nature are mostly resolved administratively where the culpable party are sometimes dismissed rather than sanctioned (Souryal 2007). These issues—attempting to work to an ideal, smuggling contraband, sex with inmates, overcrowding and violence—are an intractable problem in the prison sector but the majority of these are hidden behind the walls of an institution. However, placing some offenders behind walls still fails to diminish personal and organizational power to influence beyond institutional walls. It is this ability and reach of organized criminal elements that can corrupt the management of the institution but also the whole judicial process to which I now turn.

Corruption *in* and *Beyond* Prison Walls

Organized crime is a known and visible aspect of corruption of the criminal justice system with violent criminal and 'political' organizations challenging and corrupting law enforcement and judicial power before a sentence is determined. But criminal organizations (Lessing 2016) are also capable reaching beyond institutional walls to influence the outcome of events and judicial process, once incarcerated.

In this section I review the power of prison officers but mostly criminal organizations to order and control the life of those on the inside of a custodial institution, and therefore corrupt the prison system, but also wield significant power outside the custodial institution, where, at a minimum, street crime is subjected to a form of tax or tribute, violence is reduced or increased based on control of those incarcerated, and criminal markets controlled.

In his conceptualization of power in prison Hepburn (1985: 146) suggested five types of power; these were legitimate, coercive, reward, expert, and referent power. These types of power were used to describe prison officers but can be applied to inmates to some extent as well. Legitimate power is where officers are invested with power to command. As such it is the position of prison officers in an institutional structure that confers such power. However, as was seen in Chapter 2 legitimacy and consent is complex, and if the institution is controlled by inmates (Lessing 2016) it is possible legitimate power is usurped. Coercive power is based on the capacity to punish inmates, yet again, inmates can and do punish inmates for transgressions of 'criminal codes' as well as prison officers. The power to reward, and this in itself is an example of power—ability to confer or withhold—punishment, concessions to inmates; but also here, organized 'gangs' in prison can also behave in this way, and confer a type of trade (narcotics) on individuals, and brutally punish transgression(s). There is also some notion of expert power, this is perhaps relevant to a type of prison e.g. a therapeutic environment, but expertise can be subjected to bureaucratic procedures and as such some expertise is lost. For a skilled criminal though e.g. cybercrime expertise is respected and sought after. Then there is referent power; this is where officers exercise power because of respect from inmates. This is based on personality of officers, knowledge and treatment of inmates. Earning legitimacy in such an environment is a lengthy process, but regardless of the character of the prison officer(s) if the institution is lost to the inmates no officers will have legitimacy (Lessing 2016).

Power then has to be negotiated (Sykes 1958: 42) and officers are in a "continuous struggle to maintain order". Physical power, while seeming an obvious way to enforce rules, is simply ineffective, and prison officers need a system of rewards and punishments to negotiate order with the inmates. Such a system needs to be consistent in it application otherwise corruption is possible. Dispensing rewards, and this can be dependent on what the reward was dispensed for, is potentially dangerous. A reward to an inmate might be used as a form of blackmail at a later date to ensure rewards, and/or a reward might cause a dispute and violence between inmates unless equably distributed, at least in the eyes of the inmates, and 'valuable rewards' (narcotics) in particular potentially cause more conflict and can endanger other officers by bringing in contraband to the prison; lastly, if the reward is seen as insignificant it will fail to secure compliance. All of this could perhaps be applied to a 'criminal code' in a prison and thus a system of control and compliance by inmates or officers in a custodial institution is similar.

Criminal 'gangs', particularly in Latin America, are now operating within and across multiple institutions. They affect the structure of local—inside and outside the prison—criminal markets controlled often by a centralized body. Sophisticated criminal 'gangs' and networks control life within a custodial institution is a key resource for organized criminal, and political reach and power on the outside corrupting all of the criminal justice system. The Eme (Mexican Mafia prison gang) controlled some units in institutions in the prison sector in the USA the 1980s, but have since reached beyond the walls and established control of Los Angles Latino street districts (Mateo 2011; Cruz 2012) and beyond. The reach of criminal organizations was and is helped by contemporary criminal justice policy, where anti-gang 'crackdowns' lead to a rise in incarceration rates and lengthy sentences. A rapid influx of inmates helped prison 'gangs' establish control of the institution. Institution codes are supplanted by criminal codes and in such a situation power has passed from the institution to the criminal 'gang(s)' that can arrange and preplan or reduce the level of inmate violence, in multiple institutions or on the street.

Evidence that 'institutionalized gangs' have established control in a prison are very complex but criminal control is possible by adapting to a changing environment and circumstances (Hagedorn 2005: 153–169). Simply reducing incarceration rates and/or improving institutional conditions will not diminish criminal control and power, particularly within a custodial institution. Even if it were possible this depends much on the institution—public or private—and its ability to control and enforce institutional codes of conduct. These codes, however, are often overlooked and circumvented by prison officers, and/or control usurped by the inmates. Successful 'gangs' consolidate power by use of violence and the elimination and subjugation of known potential rivals (Lessing 2016). The early stage of a struggle for power and control is violent, but once achieved violence will decrease (Sykes 1958; Jacobs 1978). A hegemonic (Gramsci 1971) rule can thus control key aspects of institutional life—control of contraband, power to reward and punish inmates.

State and/or institutional policy can inadvertently aid the consolidation of power; by segregating inmates by gangs(s) it can increase control and power of a part of the prison, but segregating gang(s) members and placing them around the institution can also lead to reach beyond a part of the institution to all of the institution, and hegemonic control. In addition, as illustrated by Skolnick et al. (1990), Human Rights Watch (2004), and Lessing (2016) incoming offenders are often placed in units based on some notion of gang affiliation, which might be based on neighbourhood and/or racial background. This, however, is problematic: it puts unaffiliated offenders under a gang(s) control and tutelage and jurisdiction. There is also the problem of propagation. Gang members and non-gang members—are moved around a custodial system in an attempt to break the power and hold on units and whole institutions. This can also lead to the reach of and propagation of criminal networks. This can be achieved via transfer, release and re-arrest and imprisonment. Transfer of inmates within the state system in the USA is common but this has spread to private institutions with substantial overcrowding of the current system (Eisen 2017), which has exacerbated the problem rather than solve it. This propagation, however, within and between states is only part of the problem; offenders are also transferred between nations as Valdez (2011) highlighted with the deportation of 'gangs' from California institutions in the 1990s to Mexico and Central America where the reach and control of institutions has increased.

Prison gangs then, can and do corrupt custodial institutions but also usurp the power to control the incarcerated population. It is, however, the ability to reach beyond institutional walls that corrupt the criminal justice system itself. Organized criminal 'gangs' with sophisticated networks of communication can influence 'life on the outside' whilst 'living on the inside' of an institution. Rules and codes of conduct are laid down, a set boundary and types of crimes are set and sanctioned, and of course, violence is used as a mechanism of fear and control by prison officers but also inmates that threaten other inmates and family members on the outside. The reach is such that gang members and even unaffiliated offenders are often controlled by other high-ranking gang members. Many gang members will encounter the criminal justice system at some point in a criminal career, and spend some time in an institution where inmate 'criminal justice' and retribution is inescapable (Rafael 2007). The projection of power is thus based on the control of inmates, but also non-incarcerated potential and/or future inmates.

'Tough on crime' political mantra and policy, however, contributes to this propagation and reach of power. Highlighted by Lessing (2013) anti-gang laws and an increase in incarceration and length of sentence and poor institutional conditions can cause an unstable environment that offenders' control. In this way inmates usurp officers and control fellow inmates. This is exacerbated by law enforcement sweeping tactics that catch intended offenders but also low level offenders in the net (Cohen 1985). In El Salvador Mano Dura was a harsh anti-gang initiative that criminalized gang membership and awarded substantial powers to law enforcement. This increased the incarceration rate but law enforcement often failed to distinguish members from non-gang members (Van Hofwegen 2009) and such an approach appears to have significantly contributed to the organizations power and reach (Cruz 2012). By widening and enclosing the net low level incarcerated offenders are offered protection by prison gangs. Pro-incarceration, whilst politically popular, fails to see that such an approach can help consolidate control of institutions, which in turn increase the reach beyond the institution corrupting both inside custodial institutions and the network of public and private custodial institutions and also beyond the prison walls (Lessing 2016), depending on the jurisdiction.

The reach of incarcerated power in El Salvador is so extensive prison inmates coordinated a public sector transport strike from prison. As this was happening incarcerated offenders demanded better conditions and veto of the anti-gang law(s) (Wolf 2012) and launched a wave of disruption and riots in other institutions. Whilst law enforcement were deployed to custodial institutions street level collaborators confronted law enforcement officers and damaged urban infrastructure. Eventually the state made key concessions and the violence stopped (Lessing 2016). It is this reach beyond the institutional walls that is a major problem for some jurisdictions. Criminal markets offer substantial financial rewards for the most successful, which are often the most violent, particularly as rivals attempt to secure power. Once achieved in a prison a reach beyond institutional walls is possible with parts of the city and/or regions controlled by those 'on the inside.'

Control of a unit or whole institution has occurred and corrupted the prison system before, but it is the reach beyond these walls and parallel powers providing order, justice, retribution but also medicine, clothes, textbooks and protection of mostly the poorest in a favela. From inside an institution then, an organized gang supplants the state as the system of justice but also system of education and medical provision (Arias 2006; Mateo 2011). This allows incarcerated individuals and gangs to control and coordinate orchestrated internal (in the institution) and external (outside of the institution) violence. This orchestrated violence is used as a tool to negotiate prison conditions, potential amnesty of individuals and organizations, reduce length of sentences etc. To be able to coordinate riots on the streets of a city, shutdown businesses, burn public transportation and assault police stations is an 'effective political cudgel' (Lessing 2016: 1). Such power bequeaths 'gangs' enormous leverage in negotiations with corrupt states where street violence is controlled more by criminal gangs than the police e.g. Brazil, El Salvador, Honduras and Nicaragua, to name a few.

Systemic factors though prevent such a problem from progressing beyond a partial negotiated armistice. Organized crime can reduce the level of violence its employs but stopping extortion, prostitution, thefts is impossible as these are a source of revenue. In addition, 'new' presidents secure power such as in El Salvador in 2015 that refused to negotiate with offenders and instead placed them into solitary confinement. Even though it is difficult, if not impossible, to communicate from solitary confinement it is noticeable that violence increased once high profile members were placed in solitary (Katz and Amaya 2015; Lessing 2016) lending credence to the conjecture that units in custodial institutions and the whole institution, and even multiple institutions are corrupted and that the reach is such that in some states there is a parallel system of justice run by organized criminal 'gangs.'

Such a situation is difficult to deal with but with the reach of such gangs beyond institutional walls leaves some states with the option of how to learn how to work with or manage the problem. Repression has perhaps helped caused some of this problem, along with corrupt political systems, military coups, corrupt law enforcement and judiciary and poverty. The outcome though is still the corruption of the criminal justice system.

Privatization: The Corruption of State Legitimacy?

In Chapter 2, I considered state power, legitimacy and privatization; in this section of the chapter all three are considered in reference to private custodial institutions. Before I continue though clarification is needed on what is meant by privatization. Privatization is the process that shifts 'responsibility' of public sector roles via contracts to the private sector. This privatization can be specific services such as medical, mental health, education, providing food for inmates and prison officers, services and maintenance of a prison or detention centre or complete ownership of a prison/detention centre and management of them: in the later example the private company owns and runs the institutions. Either way the private sector should secure the contract by a competitive bidding process. This is immediately vulnerable to corruption with the process often less than visible, with information passed to vested interests via bribery. The rise in privatization of whole or sections of a criminal justice system has occurred because of the ideological rise in the private sector and free market, overcrowding of the public prison sector based on penal populism, and the price of incarceration. Most of the literature here will refer to the USA but where relevant I will make reference to other jurisdictions.

The Corrections Corporation of America (CCA) (now known as CoreCivic) has operational and management and control of eighty-nine 'correctional' institutions in 2017; GEO Group (once Wackenhut) one hundred and four correctional, detention and reentry (reentry is release from an institution and transition to civilian life) institutions, with Management and Training Corporation (MTC) twenty-six institutions in USA. CoreCivic and Geo Group also reach beyond the USA and have contracts in the United Kingdom, Australia and South Africa.

On a local, state level this impact of privatization is even more pronounced. CoreCivic runs Crowley prison in Colorado, one of four it has in the state: but this prison alone contributes $1.6 million in property tax per annum in revenue, which is more than half the taxes paid in the county (Eisen 2017). The impact of the private sector, particularly in the USA on one state is substantial: it employs people and pays taxation which is hard for some states to refuse. However, with such reach and impact the private sector can influence policy at both at state level and ultimately nationwide. The reach of the private prison and detention sector in the USA and search for profits then is in no doubt. This has been referred to as the meeting of pinstripes and prison stripes (Barron 1985 in Eisen 2017) and whilst the extent of the private 'correctional' sector can have a major influence on criminal justice prison policy, particularly in some states, this impact is often difficult to quantify, and is contested. Although the law draws a clear distinction between 'public' and 'private,' both perform many of the same tasks. This is balkanization (Heywood 2015) of the prison sector since what was once the sole province of the state criminal justice system is now, and under some circumstances, performed by the private sector in democratic states alone or with the public sector.

Whilst some consider that "CEO profits and shareholders' returns have no place in the criminal justice system (Jones 2014 in Eisen 2017: 13) profiting from prisoners is hardly new. However, a tough on crime narrative has without doubt helped caused overcrowding in prison systems around the world (Banks 2017: 184–186), and this political, criminal justice policy is linked to the development and expansion in the private prison sector. This is not the only reason, though as "The construction of the carceral state was the result of complex set of historical, institutional, and political developments. No single factor explains it rise, and no single factor will…it demise" (Gottschalk 2015: 14), if in fact, it will decline?

This contemporary catalyst for the privatization of the prison sector, particularly in the USA started in the 1980s (Burkhardt 2014). Even though there is reference to the benefits of privatization such as flexible and innovative in providing prison capacity it appears the main concern was the cost of the prison population. Furthermore, some states public institutions were under court orders for a failure for cruel and unusual punishment in prison (Eisen 2017). This was, however, mostly caused by high incarceration rates. Some inmates, depending on the crime, were released early, but many could not be released in the community. It is here that the seed of the privatization was planted. Rising crime rates based on public policy, were thus a financial windfall for the private sector.

Whilst the price of incarceration, however, is substantial, both economically and socially the current estimated cost of running criminal justice in the whole of the USA is $260 billion per annum (as of 2017) (Eisen 2017). However, is it morally justified and thus legitimate to use the private sector to imprison and/or detain suspected offenders, actual convicted offenders and people that have breached immigration rules? There are a number of issues to consider. The private prison and detention sector is profitable because of the low cost of its employees. It has no union representation, a lack of public accountability, and is built on the need for high rates of incarceration to secure a profit. This will mean that the private sector has an interest in punitive criminal justice. Paid on per capita basis to house inmates, reform to criminal justice is a threat to private sector profits. Many private contracts are structured on predetermined occupancy rates e.g. the state pays for full capacity of prison even if under-utilized. In such circumstances is it tempting to perhaps put people in prison? Some contracts have one hundred percent inmate occupancy and thus states will either put people in prison, or pay for under-utilized capacity and space. Why such contracts were considered appropriate for the states is unclear but such a system is clearly flawed regarding criminal justice. These types of contracts only benefit the private sector.

There is also now little competition as the majority of the private prison and immigration detention sector in the USA is controlled by CoreCivic, Geo Group and MIT. As such, they now wield substantial influence on how many institutions are built, where inmates are housed, and what town a new prison is built in. The private sector is also flexible and moved beyond prison walls to managing community rehabilitation.

Furthermore, the private sector also has the power to increase an inmates' sentence if breaching an institution rule. This is encouraging the private sector to claim offenders' breached rules and infractions to extend a sentence for profit e.g. a long prison sentence is more profitable than a brief one. Is the private sector then, primarily based on numbers of inmates for profit rather than rehabilitation and/or reintegration? Understandably the private sector disputes this version of its role in the prison sector, and claims that it is a safety-valve to contain inmates and reduce overcrowding in public institutions, is flexible and can react to changes in the prison and immigration detention centre population without additional costs. This is, I suggest, misrepresenting the available current evidence, though. The issue of cost is one often promoted by the private sector; however, this can depend on what is counted. To start with the private sector is in competition with the public sector but not the private sector as so few organizations now have the ability to offer services on the scale expected. Such concentration of 'power' leads to a lack of competition; the private sector thus fails to offer competition on which it claims costs are reduced and services enhanced (see Chapter 2 for private sector legitimation strategy) (White 2015; Fitzgibbon and Lea 2017). In some states such as Mississippi one company is running the entire private prison sector and therefore with concentration of market share there is no pressure/competition to reduce costs.

In addition a few powerful organizations lobby for legislation that favour its business model. In 2015 (Eisen 2017) three major private organizations spent a combined $2 million on lobbying alone. This it is understandable, for them, but disappointing that such organizations might lobby for an increase in sentences—a punitive system—that is financially beneficial to them. Whilst possible to calculate potential financial benefits to the private sector expansion leads to uncalculatable social costs to inmates and family members. This, however, is an excellent representation of the new penology (Feeley and Simon 2006). Here we see that competition is a myth and the private sector costs are reduced by employing as few 'officers' as possible and paying employees a low wage to maintain security in a prison (*The Economist* 2018). This can lead to the temptation to succumb to bribery in some form, but also lose control of the prison to inmates. In Idaho in 2013, and Mississippi in 2014 a private prison company misreported its numbers of employees working in the prison. The FBI launched an investigation and discovered prison officers in Mississippi were negotiating with prison 'gang leaders' to maintain order. This is a clear case, I suggest, of corruption of the prison sector and criminal justice system (Centre for the Advancement of Public Integrity 2016).

Comparing both public and private sectors is difficult and both sectors do not always count the same costs. For example, it is important to include capital costs of the prison and monitoring costs to oversee the contract as well. Security costs should be included but the private sector, particularly in England and Wales only deals with low-level offenders. As such security costs are below those in a high-security public prison. In addition with ageing prison populations around the world medical treatment will increase the total cost of running a prison. The biggest hurdle to a clear comparative analysis though is that the private sector can refuse to release the details of its operations, including the cost of the services they claim to offer. Regardless of the method employed to present costs or savings in custodial institutions it is clear that competition, a central claim that will reduce costs is now at best misleading. Only a few major organizations now dominate the private prison and detention sector around the world, and as such there is no competition. Therefore be it managing all of a custodial institution or the part of it can lead to security and safety issues and extortive practice(s).

Extortive practices are apparent in providing services to the prison sector and inmates. For example, the prison telecommunications business in the USA is a case in point in extortion. Inmates can only make calls with a company that has an exclusive contract with the prison. Three organizations in the USA control this part of the industry—Securus, Telmate and Global Tel Link (Eisen 2017). Often, but not always the public sector is compromised because of the contract it has with a private sector organization; a common system is where the private sector will have inflated costs for it service above market rates for inmates such as telephone/video calls. To state the obvious inmates are captive in prison and captive also of the private sector service, which is the only one available. The county or the state pays a commission for the services but the private sector pays a percentage in commission to the state. Due to the inflated cost of the service both the private sector and state prison sectors secure some profit. As we can see these schemes are based on profit sharing with the public sector whilst charging inmates above-market-rate costs of service. Such an incentive is hard to resist in an underfunded public sector. This I consider to be an abuse of power where inmates have no choice but to accept inflated costs.

Furthermore, some private sector prison organizations business model—a Real estate Investment Trusts (REITs) mean they pay little in taxes; instead profit is passed on (approximately ninety percent of taxable income) to shareholders. In such a model there is little cash to cover regular and necessary security and procedural operations, and as such a need to rely on revolving credit from banks to pay employees and shareholders. This can be an advantage, though. In 2015 GEO Group paid $7.4 million in international, federal and states taxes of its $1.84 billion revenue (Eisen 2017). This is where the appeal is, as REITs allow flexible compliance with its business. To highlight the reach of business beyond state criminal justice systems and its potential effect on the private prison sector are loans underwritten by the banks that also own shares in GEO Group and CCA. Banks can thus profit from interest and fees and loans and by owning or investing clients' money in the private prison sector. For a detailed and informative account of the private sector though see Private Corrections Working Group (see www.privateci.org) for a review of private prison corruption.

The private sector, however, is not the only special interest in seeking high incarceration rates. California Correctional Peace Officers Association (CCPOA) contributed more than $100,000 to help pass the California 'three strikes' sentence that leads to lengthy mandatory prison sentences, and have made $22 million in political campaign contributions, more than GEO Group and CCA combined (Eisen 2017) in the past 30 years. Thompson (2011) has suggested that unions supporting mass incarceration is misleading and instead put forward the suggestion that American prison officers organized because of low wages, and endured poor working conditions and injury. This however, I suggest, fails to explain why a union is so supportive of long prison sentences, unless of course it too has a vested interests in high rates of incarceration. A captive audience needs supervision and regardless of the sector—public or private—a reduction in inmates could be seen as a threat to company profit (private sector) and/or threat to secure employment (public sector).

As we all can see the reach of the private sector in the prison and detention sector is substantial. It also commits acts of corruption. This however, is because it is the private sector rather than the prison sector. The public prison sector is also capable of committing corruption. The difference between the two, however, is perhaps the search for profit. A public or a private prison/detention centre will have officers that accept bribes, smuggle contraband in to and out of a custodial institution, engage in threats, intimidation and violence, and have inappropriate relationships with offenders. It has become increasingly difficult to separate the public and private sector; they are not distinct sectors but interlinked where contracts are awarded to the private sector legitimately or via corruption. Whilst we can all suffer from business corruption and still be unaware of it, it is perhaps the inmates and family members that encounter corruption in and out of the prison in the form of abuse, withdrawal of services, inflated costs of keeping in contact. But unless we are incarcerated or have a family member in a prison/detention centre there is little call to challenge corruption on a marginalized, captive audience.

Conclusion

In this chapter, I considered the problem of trying to define corruption in a custodial institution. This was broken down into legal, ethical and economic corruption and also misfeasance, malfeasance and nonfeasance, that highlighted many avenues and types of corruption. As such corruption in the prison sector was seen as an intractable problem. Due to the nature of a prison environment smuggling, 'inappropriate relationships' and violence are commonplace. The application of violence by inmates, however, has reached beyond the prison walls in some jurisdictions to the extent that the criminal justice system is compromised. The chapter ended with a review of the potential avenues of corruption in the private prison sector. This highlighted that in neo-liberal jurisdictions, the reach of the private sector is such that it has consolidated and now only a few private sector organizations control institutions around the world. The consequences of this change have yet to materialize to a significant extent but if expansion is to continue issues of legitimacy and the power to punish, I suggest should be revisited.

References

Arias, E. D. (2006). The Dynamics of Criminal Governance: Networks and Social Order in Rio De Janeiro. *Journal of Latin American Studies, 38*(2), 293–325.

Ashforth, B. E., & Anand, V. (2003). The Normalization of Corruption in Organizations. *Research in Organizational Behavior, 25*, 1–52.

Banks, C. (2017). *Criminal Justice Ethics: Theory and Practice*. London: Sage.

Braswell, M., McCarthy, B., & McCarthy, B. J. (1984). *Justice, Crime, and Ethics*. Cincinnati, OH: Anderson.

Brooks, G. (2016). *Criminology of Corruption: Theoretical Approaches*. Basingstoke: Palgrave Macmillan.

Burkhardt, B. (2014). Private Prisons in Public Discourse: Measuring Moral Legitimacy. *Sociological Focus, 47*(4), 279–298.

Centre for the Advancement of Public Integrity. (2016). *Prison Corruption: The Problem and Some Potential Solutions.*. New York: Centre for the Advancement of Public Integrity, Columbia Law School.

Clemmer, D. (1940). *The Prison Community*. New York: Rinehard.

Cohen, S. (1985). *Visions of Social Control—Crime, Punishment and Classification*. New York: Basil Blackwell.

Cruz, J. M. (2012). The Transformation of Street Gangs in Central America. *ReVista* (Winter), pp. 16–18.

Eisen, L. B. (2017). *Inside Private Prisons: An American Dilemma in the Age of Mass Incarceration*. New York: Columbia University Press.

Feeley, M., & Simon, J. (2006). The New Penology: Notes on the Emerging Strategy of Corrections and Its Implications. *Criminology, 30*(4), 449–474.

Fitzgibbon, W., & Lea, J. (2017). Privatization and Coercion: The Question of Legitimacy. *Theoretical Criminology, 22*(4), 545–562.

Gottschalk, M. (2015). *Caught: The Prison State and the Lockdown of American Politics*. Princeton, NJ: Princeton University Press.

Gramsci, A. (1971). *Selections from the Prison Notebooks* (Q. Horae & G. N. Smith, Trans.). New York: International Publishers.
Hagedorn, J. M. (2005). The Global Impact of Gangs. *Journal of Contemporary Criminal Justice, 21*(2), 153–169.
Hepburn, J. (1985). The Exercise of Power in Coercive Organizations: A Study of Prison Guards. *Criminology, 23*(1), 145–164.
Heywood, P. M. (2015). *Routledge Handbook of Political Corruption.* Abingdon: Routledge.
Human Rights Watch. (2004). *Real Dungeons: Juvenile Detention in the State of Rio De Janiero.* New York: Human Rights Watch.
Jacobs, J. B. (1978). *Stateville: The Penitentiary in Mass Society.* Chicago: University of Chicago Press.
Katz, C. M., & Amaya, L. E. (2015). *The Gang Truce as a Form of Violence Intervention.* San Salvador: FUNDE.
Kauffman, K. (1988). *Prison Officers and Their World.* Cambridge, MA: Harvard University Press.
Lessing, B. (2013). *A Hole at the Center of the State: Prison Gangs and the Limits to Punitive Power* (CDDRL Working Paper No. 143). Stanford: Stanford University Press.
Lessing, B. (2016). *Inside Out: The Challenge of Prison-Based Criminal Organizations* (pp. 1–23) (Brookings Local Orders Papers Series). Washington, DC: Brookings Institution.
Liebling, A. (2000). Prison Officers, Policing and the Use of Discretion. *Theoretical Criminology, 4*(3), 333–357.
Liebling, A. (2005). The Late Modern Prison and the Question of Values. *Current Issues in Criminal Justice, 16*(2), 202–219.
Liebling, A. (2007). Why Prison Staff Culture Matters. In J. M. Byrne, D. Hummer, & F. S. Taxman (Eds.), *The Culture of Prison Violence.* New York: Pearson.
Liebling, A. (2008). Incentives and Earned Privileges Revisited: Fairness, Discretion, and the Quality of Prison Life. *Journal of Scandinavian Studies in Criminology and Crime Prevention, 9,* 25–41.
Mateo, J. (2011). Street Gangs of Honduras. In T. Bruneau, L. Dammert & E. Skinner (Eds.), *Maras: Gang Violence and Security in Central America* (pp. 105–22). Austin: University of Texas Press.
Rafael, T. (2007). *The Mexican Mafia.* New York: Encounter Books.
Schlosser, E. (1998). The Prison Industrial Complex. *The Atlantic*, pp. 1–24.

Shalev, S. (2009). *Supermax: Contorlling Risk Through Solitary Confinement.* Cullumpton: Willan.
Skolnick, J. H., Correl, T., Navarro, E., & Rabb, R. (1990). The Social Structure of Street Drug Dealing. *American Journal of Police, 9*(1), 1–41.
Souryal, S. S. (2007). *Ethics in Criminal Justice: In Search of the Truth.* Cincinnati, OH: Anderson.
Souryal, S. S. (2009). Deterring Corruption by Prison Personnel: A Principle-Based Perspective. *The Prison Journal, 89*(1), 21–45.
Sykes, G. M. (1958). *The Society of Captives: A Study of a Maximum Security Prison.* Princeton, NJ: Princeton University Press.
The Economist. (2018, August 25). The Stench of Failure. *The Economist*, p. 19.
Thompson, H. A. (2011). Downsizing the Carceral State: The Policy Implications of Prison Guard Unions. *Criminology & Public Policy, 10*(3), 771–779.
Valdez, A. (2011). The Origins of Southern California Latino Gangs. In T. Bruneau, L. Dammert, & E. Skinner (Eds.), *Maras: Gang Violence and Security in Central America.* Austin: University of Texas Press.
Van Hofwegen, S. L. (2009). Unjust and Ineffective: A Critical Look at California's Step Act. *Southern California Interdisciplinary Law Journal, 18,* 679–702.
White, A. (2015). The Politics of Police 'Privatization': A Multiple Streams Approach. *Criminology and Criminal Justice, 15*(3), 283–299.
Wolf, S. (2012). Mara Salvatrucha: The Most Dangerous Street Gang in the Americas? *Latin American Politics and Society, 54*(1), 65–99.

8

The Probation Service: Corruption in the Community

Introduction

In this chapter, I start by highlighting the types of corruption that can and do occur in probation services in the community, and the process and procedures to address and prevent corruption. There is then a reflection on the legitimacy of state probation services contracted out to the private sector and rise of the shadow state particularly in neoliberal states, and reach to control and punish offenders in the community. By shadow state here I mean operating beyond the criminal law and justice institutions via institutional annexation and legal hybridity where increased civil and administrative pathways lead to incarceration and civil 'alternatives' to criminal statutes; and the incorporation of criminal law into administrative legal processes in ways that enhance state carceral power (Feeley and Simon 1992; Anderson 2009; Harris et al. 2010; Beckett and Harris 2011; Beckett and Murakawa 2012), which has caused 'mass probation' (Phelps 2017: 51), particularly in USA and is perhaps less a "potential solution to the problem of over-incarceration" than "part of the continuum of excessive penal control" (Doherty 2016: 291). This leads onto perhaps the most intrusive form

G. Brooks, *Criminal Justice and Corruption*,
https://doi.org/10.1007/978-3-030-16038-8_8

of surveillance in the community; electronic monitoring (EM) (Graham and McIvor [2017] for Scotland, Bartels and Martinovic [2017] for Australia and Moss [2018] for Ireland). It is here that I primarily highlight the reach of corrupt practice in the private sector, but note that management of state contracts and oversight are also problematic.

The Potential for Corruption in the Community

I am unable to offer a detailed analysis of how probation is viewed in every jurisdiction, but for a broad brush stroke, or 'airplane view' (see Durnescu 2013; McNeill 2013; Nellis 2014a; Aebi et al. 2015). However, whilst useful to have a snapshot of probation services the main thrust of this chapter is on the potential for corruption in the community and/or prison where probation officers, in some jurisdictions work, and the decline in rehabilitation as a core concept of probation in neoliberal jurisdictions such as the USA. This is a crude distinction but whilst probation still has elements of rehabilitation it is often, in neoliberal jurisdictions seen as an arm of criminal justice that could, and should incapacitate, but in the community and used to control expanding numbers of offenders and also 'dangerous' offenders in the community (Garland 2001; Feeley and Simon 2006; Phelps 2017).

There is 'diversity at the edge' of probation services where local traditions emphasize different aspects of community punishment and rehabilitation such as offender mediation and victim rights in the Czech Republic, Slovenia, Slovakia and Croatia, with some states preference for 'front door' community sanctions such as alternatives to custody with some a preference for 'back door' options—community sanctions and measures that reduce time spent behind bars such as conditional release (Durnsecu 2013). These options are where social, cultural and political issues coalesce with a sole public sector probation service or commissioned private sector or market competition for resources that effect the 'back' or 'front' door approaches to probation, but also the avenues for corruption.

As with all types of corruption a definition of the problem is useful. Drawing on the National Offender Management Service (NOMS) (now called Her Majesty's Prison and Probation Service since 2017) that included both the prison and probation systems in England and Wales corruption was defined as 'the misuse of their role in order to plan or commit a criminal act, or a deliberate failure to act to prevent criminal behaviour'. Examples of corruption include (but are not limited to) 'unauthorized or improper drafting and amending of all reports, records and licence conditions, unauthorized disclosure of information, accepting or seeking bribes, inappropriate relationships, blackmail, taking or seeking money or other favours for any reason, or theft of money or property' (NOMS 2016: 3). Benefits can include financial, emotional, sexual or other personal and/or any work-related reason(s). The definition even prohibits acts which it refers to as noble cause corruption such as instances where an employee considers they have a 'moral obligation or entitlement to break the rules' (NOMS 2016: 3). In addition, it is expected that all employees—this includes probation officers but also contracted employees, private sector partners, volunteers etc.—to report corruption they witness, suspect or hear about. This can include unsubstantiated, unproven or unspecified information and can be reported via a telephone hotline, email or confidential address.

All information regarding acts of corruption and crime, it is claimed, will be treated in confidence. However, whilst anonymity is offered at the start of the reporting stage, the information (which could be on a fellow colleague) could be used for internal and external bodies and anonymity will cease as evidence in a disciplinary panel or court of law will become necessary. With this in mind, will probation officers expose a fellow colleague? This is doubtful as literature on exposing corruption regardless of the sector highlights how badly individuals are treated for exposing corruption (Glazer 2002; Miceli et al. 2008; Brooks et al. 2013) but for criminal justice (see Heck 1992; Rothwell and Baldwin 2007).

In the NOMS corruption prevention document, there is a list of examples of corrupt acts. These are not exhaustive but help illustrate the range of potential corrupt acts that probation officers could engage in whilst supervising offenders in prison and the community. These are bribery, blackmail such as a threat to disclose sensitive information, e.g. expose an offenders conviction for a sex offence; whilst referred to as blackmail here this is similar to extortion in

Chapter 6 and judicial corruption. Perverting the course of justice such as producing and/or manufactured documentation and false statements, yet again, this is similar to law enforcement and testilying (see Chapter 4), conveying into or out of a prison without authorisation a firearm or component of one or ammunition, or knife, or narcotics, alcohol, mobile phones, technology such as data sticks, tobacco and prohibited items such as letters and magazines. Furthermore inappropriate relationships with offender(s) and non-offender(s) such a close relative of offender are also prohibited (NOMS 2016: 11–12).

This list and potential for corruption in the community is complicated by having a public sector probation service dealing with high risk offenders, a commissioned private sector with low/middle risk offenders, and/or voluntary bodies in England and Wales. No criminal justice agency, however, is completely free of corruption; it is more a case of the extent of corruption. This differs though depending on the context and 'type' of probation service and its ethos and treatment of offenders. By having different services provided by different public/private and voluntary bodies under formal contracts, which need to be monitored makes a difficult service—trying to manage a variety of offenders in the community with different needs—complex. Any system that is excessively complex and needs detailed supervision is ripe for corruption; combined with poor oversight corruption is, I suggest, inevitable. The legitimacy to punish and/or supervise offenders in the community is damaged, but offenders elicit little sympathy in some jurisdictions, and here the rise of the shadow state and its potential for corruption are manifest.

Probation and the Rise of Shadow State

Due to the potential reach of corruption and its flexible nature, what kind of 'surveillance' can be achieved to keep the public, private and voluntary sector and contracted employees from engaging in acts of corruption? With the expansion in the use of probation in supervising offenders in the community in states that have a low and/or high use of custody and in some jurisdictions a high caseload of offenders to deal with, is the criminal justice system capable of managing this problem? Furthermore, with the rise of the shadow state (Anderson 2009; Harris et al. 2010; Becket and Harris 2011; Beckett and Murakawa 2012) and privatization of criminal justice in neoliberal jurisdictions (Teague 2011; Dominey 2012) has the private sector simply become an extension of under contracted state power?

The withdrawal of public services has produced, as was no doubt intended, openings for the private sector to fill in neoliberal jurisdictions. It has been suggested that we are (or already have) witnessed the emergence of a 'shadow state' (White 2013) and a powerful private sector presence in criminal justice matters. In neoliberal states, it is contended that the prison and probation systems should be in competition with a more diverse range of organizations that offer criminal justice services (Nellis 2014a). These organizations (Human Rights Watch 2014) are primarily out to make a profit before a service is provided (White 2015; Fitzgibbon and Lea 2017). This is the nature of the private sector; to state the obvious, if it fails to make a profit it will cease to exist as a company and so will its service.

The problem as noted in Chapter 7 on the prison is that there is a myth of competition and innovation in the private criminal justice sector. In England and Wales G4S, Serco and Sodexo, until recently dominated the management of private custodial institutions and EM. Rather than increasing competition as intended it has brought about the emergence of a private sector EM control instead of state monopoly which it was supposed to replace. Furthermore, substituting state responsibility for offenders in the community for the private sector encouraging investment in order to secure private profits represents a fracture of the social contract upon which the probation service was built (Nellis 2014a) (e.g. rehabilitation).

There is, of course, some concern regarding the legitimacy of letting the private sector have the right to punish. This right to punish is still meant to be controlled by the state but the fundamental normative question is whether it is right for the state to delegate the administration of punishment to a profit-driven private sector organization. The nature of the private sector is that it is responsible to its shareholders rather than the public (Genders 2002). Whilst the state can hold the private sector to account via contracts and thus potentially control performance it is questionable if it is capable of providing this assurance. Whilst there is a sense that 'heated debates about the ethics of privatisation have faded' (Crewe and Liebling 2012: 25) there is little on the corruption of contracts and treatment of offenders by the private sector in probation services in sociology and criminology literature (Nellis 2014a).

A key aim of the probation service in neoliberal states is to punish offenders in the community and keep them under surveillance; rehabilitation has not completely disappeared but been downgraded (Nellis 2014b). However, the private sector rather than the voluntary sector needs and seeks external legitimacy via state contracts, and recourse to claim efficiency and innovation and internal legitimacy via its treatment of offenders. This later legitimacy though is also an expectation on public probation services. McNeill and Robinson (2013: 118) emphasized that community sanctions should achieve rehabilitation and desistance as well as punishment and retribution. This legitimacy is linked to individuals' active cooperation with a community sentence and it is doubtful that a private agency is seen as equally legitimate as a public probation service. This internal legitimacy is important; if lacking legitimacy by offenders it supervises it has the potential to impact on compliance and breach, which in turn effect payment by results (PBR), e.g. prevent recidivism on which the private sector is judged. Therefore—and here is the temptation to commit acts of corruption—private sector attitudes to compliance and breach could be influenced by the need to hit certain measures of success in order to avoid a financial penalty rather than rehabilitate offenders.

Evidence to support this view is the change in probation services in England and Wales where under *Transforming justice—A key revolution in the way we manage offenders* (Ministry of Justice 2013) some £600 million worth of contracts (approximately 60% of the entire probation budget) was put out to tender and awarded to what are referred to as a Community Rehabilitation Company (CRC). There were 21 CRCs that had the task of supervising an estimated 200,000 low and medium risk offenders (as of 2014) which were to reduce recidivism under a system of PBR. CRCs were also responsible for providing support for an estimated 45,000 offenders released from custody with sentences of less than 12 months (as of 2014) (Criminal Justice Joint Inspection 2016). The probation service was left to deal with supervising high risk offenders and the provision of court reports: the core functions of probation. However, such a move has proved problematic with a private sector failure to deliver the service(s) in the community culminating in the suspension of the scheme in 2018. The promised results were unrealistic (Moore and Hamilton 2016; Maguire and Raynor 2017; Taylor et al. 2017), more aspirational than deliverable (Maguire and Raynor 2017) and have highlighted a flawed process that has a narrow grasp of supervision in the community (Moore and Hamilton 2016).

This is not to dismiss the private sector as a potential partner (Fletcher and Batty 2013) but appears to be a lack of understanding, either because of ideology or the private sectors inability to fulfil its contract. Furthermore, there is a lack of appreciation and understanding of risk where high risk offenders are managed by the probation service with medium and low risk offenders by private and voluntary organizations but little awareness of the issues of movement of offenders between these classifications. Perhaps this lack of understanding combined with the reach of the private sector where the complexity of supervision is reduced to an instrumental 'pay by results' (Dominey 2012) approach has contributed to the rise of potential and actual corruption.

The involvement of the private sector in criminal justice, and specifically PBR is based on the contention that services subjected to a competitive, free market environment will offer more cost-effective, innovative, and efficient responses to the persistent problem of high rates of reoffending. The proclaimed aim is that the criminal justice system contracts services and programmes that 'work' in reducing reoffending, and also rehabilitation and desistance. In time, this could perhaps be achieved, but it seems to be intended to transfer some financial risk and possibly the risk of responsibility of individuals' offenders from the state to the private sector, regardless of what is achieved.

Payment by results, however, has also put the voluntary sector at a disadvantage. Only private sector organizations of some size will have the capacity to bear the associated financial risk of 'running' a major initiative in the community such as EM. In addition, a major private sector organization can bid for the contract and then if successful contract out to voluntary organizations that have the expertise in service delivery. The concept of PBR also appears to shift the focus of work with offenders from processes to outcomes (Dominey 2012). Many voluntary organizations have reasoned that credit should be noted for work with hard to reach and high risk offenders and those payment systems should value 'distance travelled' as well as reconviction (e.g. how far the offender has made progress and responded under treatment), but under a system based on commercial principles this is rarely valued.

Furthermore, the private sector could strategically invest only in offenders that have the potential to yield an outcome (Damm 2012) whilst 'parking' problem offenders with complex needs with the probation service. A binary measure that can be assessed and credited or debited appeals to the neoliberal approach and combined with private sectors deskilling (Fitzgibbon and Lea 2014) of probation paying its own employees a low wage, similar to private prison officers (see Chapter 7) there will be the temptation to engage in corruption to supplement low wages. It is, of course, this de-professionalization of probation, the standardization of procedures and the transformation of core tasks in the direction of guarding and risk control—in a word 'Taylorisation' (Braverman 1974)—that renders it amenable the current wave of *neo-privatization.*

The expression of neoliberal reach in criminal justice and payment is reflected in the USA where those on probation pay fees, which can be collected by the private sector. Offenders on probation thus pay for 'services'. However, the American Parole and Probation Association (APPA) distinguishes between 'programme fees' which are uniformly set and charged to all on probation and 'service fees' which are only charged to those in receipt of specific (and expensive) services, such as Global Positioning Satellites (GPS) tagging. These fees are collected by an array of 'collection' bodies from offenders, which have the potential for corruption. Failure to pay can result in breach of an order (Anderson 2009; Harris et al. 2010; Beckett and Harris 2011) and return to prison or carceral clawback (Carlen 2002) and the state alone or via the private sector captures (Dal Bo 2006) individuals into the inner sanctum of criminal justice. The consequences are a dispersal of punitiveness (Cohen 1985). This is not necessarily the intended aim of criminal justice but it is a consequence.

There has been debate (Teague 2011) regarding the appropriateness of fees but community corrections affirm that the revenue raised leads to reduced caseloads, and that payment of fees instal a sense of responsibility in offenders (APPA 2011). For the APPA's collections are simply a means to help achieve its mission, but not the mission itself. It should be noted, however, that supervision fees sometimes produce the majority of a community correction agency's total operational budget (Teague 2011) and therefore the APPA stance is perhaps based on self-interest rather than its mission.

Probation/community correction services thus have a vested interest in payment of fees, but some offenders, regardless of the cost, have chaotic lifestyles and live in poverty and will find it difficult, if not impossible to raise funds for their own supervision. The pressure to pay fees will in some circumstances propel an offender to commit crime, or even more crime, but with a probation/correction agency reliant on supervisees' fees, it is possible that there is little incentive for early termination of supervision if warranted. Failure to appear at a supervision meeting and/or payment leads to probation officers issuing a probation violation for failure to appear (Bannon et al. 2010: 24) which in turn sees the offender returned to prison. Here, probation officers can threaten to breach an offender for a failure to adhere probation conditions or failure to pay fees, and if corrupt demand a 'favour', a service in place of payment of fees.

Some states in the USA have also passed legislation that allowed courts to prolong probation terms for failure to pay debt even if the offender has fulfilled all other conditions of their order, and even if there is evidence that the supervisee lacks the financial wherewithal to clear the supervision debts. The outcome of this is inevitable—individuals stay enmeshed in the criminal justice system and incarcerated—not for new crimes, but for technical violations of probation conditions, including payment conditions (Bannon et al. 2010: 25). Is this a legitimate use of a criminal justice sanction?

The notion of legitimacy is, however, perhaps context specific. For example, many American probation officers carry weapons. In some states, it is mandatory to carry a weapon while others allow individual officers the choice to be armed. Hanser (2010: 142) has even claimed that armed probation officers still offer 'an integrative approach towards community supervision'. By combining private sector intervention with state armed probation officers and payment of fees is perhaps reflective of a carceral, surveillance private sector approach that is American probation. However, it is difficult to come to a definite conclusion about the US probation system as it is a federalized nation where states have substantial 'local' control.

Neo-liberal policy has moved to a new phase, quite unique to the Anglo-American version formed by the alliance between probation and the voluntary sector. The strategy involves effectively killing *both* and replacing probation voluntary relationships with a new alliance of state control and *security industrial complex*. This new combination of state and private sector will make both traditional probation and voluntary sector skills a distant memory (Fitzgibbon and Lea 2014) and consolidate a risk management and security strategy in probation services. What is happening and in some of parts of criminal justice systems in Anglo-American jurisdictions is that neo-liberalism involves both a privatization of and a strengthening of the state and is best described as *neo-privatization and marketization*. Competition for the running of criminal and community justice services is an inevitable part of this process of marketization (Reynolds 2000; Clear et al. 2009). In this commercial secured post-conviction market (Teague 2011) it is hardly surprising that the private sector has such reach and involvement in criminal justice.

Private sector involvement in England and Wales in probation is also now well established: in October 2012 Serco, partnered with the London Probation Trust, secured a four-year contract from the Ministry of Justice worth £37m, for supervision of unpaid 'community payback'. 'Operational innovation', it was claimed by Serco 'should reduce cost, not increase it' (Fitzgibbon and Lea 2014: 29). However, the more skilled, labour intensive, traditional forms of rehabilitation and reintegration, which cost are often avoided by the private sector. The contracts sought and secured by the private sector in criminal justice have been primarily based on low-level low costs such as the management of young offenders' prison and children's homes, electronic tagging and curfew enforcement. This can and will no doubt lead to the potential for the private 'capture' (Dal Bo 2006) of the voluntary sector and absorption of it into the private sector and criminal justice system.

Furthermore, and it is here that corruption can be an incentive; if reporting offenders' breaches incur delays or a financial penalty or even future loss of contract, the private sector can act in a corrupt way, e.g. fail to record and report a breach, and submission of incorrect bills for tagging (Fitzgibbon and Lea 2014: 33). Large organizations can (as was seen in Chapter 7 on prison systems) employ such calculations and even lose a contract now and then as it has the capacity to absorb the loss. Outcomes need to be measured and thus the private sector understandably will pay attention to these above rehabilitation. The *why* has an individual offended is of less importance than *how* should it be prevented. The two, however, should not be viewed as separate. Reintegration is a long-term aim, particularly for offenders with multiple issues, but the effect of PBR is to hit the set objective. Success is simple risk management and public protection and it does not matter why offenders reoffend or avoid conviction. Under a dominant economic discourse of risk where measures of reconviction and cost reduction are valued the principle of moral engagement that underpinned the voluntary sector (Mythen et al. 2013: 364) is marginalized or replaced by the pursuit of profit.

Suggestions that G4S or other private sector organizations can increase their market share in probation by efficiency savings are simply not credible (Fitzgibbon and Lea 2014). 'Privatization' and 'the market' are an extension of state control. This is not the retreat of the state or its withdrawal but a 'diffusion of control' where the state becomes one 'node' alongside a variety of private sector nodes. Attention on privatization only captures the withdrawal of the state from, in this case, the provision of the public probation services while ignoring the active role of the state in setting up and, most important, legitimating new structures, their tasks and methods of operation (Fitzgibbon and Lea 2014, 2017). These 'private' organizations are therefore best considered as part of a *new state apparatus*, part of the process of *neoliberal state* in which probation joins policing, as part of an expanding apparatus of surveillance and control: a 'criminalisation of social policy'.

In this context, rehabilitation is a way of managing risk and not an end in itself. Rehabilitation is only used to the extent that it is able to offer sufficient public protection, reduce risk, and be cost-effective (Cracknell 2018). Rehabilitation becomes a tool, to justify increased sanctions, particularly on persistent offenders and leads to a punitive system that expands the criminal justice net and social control. This is the shadow state, but rather than rely on the public sector to deliver its desire for control the neoliberal approach seeks to reduce costs as much as possible by encouraging the private and voluntary sectors to supervise offenders in the community. The reach of the private sector and shadow state is most noticeable in the use of electronic surveillance to monitor offenders in the community, and so is its corruption.

Electronic Monitoring, the Private Sector and Corruption

First developed in 1983 by Judge Jack Love in New Mexico (Jones and Newburn 2002) EM is now a widely used application in criminal justice systems around the world. EM is the use of remote surveillance technologies to pinpoint the locations and/or movements of offenders and/or defendants (Nellis 2014a). It is used in Canada, Taiwan, Singapore, Australia, New Zealand, England and Wales, Denmark, Finland, Sweden, the Netherlands, Germany, Belgium, Portugal, Italy, Argentina, Israel, Estonia, France, Northern Ireland and Scotland (Paterson 2008; Nellis 2014a; Graham and McIvor 2017; Bartels and Martinovic 2017). Its use, however, as a standalone sanction or part of a package of conditions is dependent on the social and cultural context of the use of EM. This social and political context is important as it can establish EM as a rehabilitative 'tool' or punitive sanction or a combination of both, and if it is controlled by the probation service or police and prison services as in Belgium and Catalonia (Nellis 2014a) and/or the private sector or under contract to the private sector (Nellis et al. 2013) as in England and Wales. However, rather than dwell on the historical development of EM (see Paterson 2008; Nellis et al. 2013; Nellis 2014b). Instead, I reflect on the potential for corruption in this section of the chapter by analyzing the cost effectiveness of EM, its legitimacy as a method of crime control both by the state and private sector and management of private sector contracts.

I primarily assess the neo-liberal nations such as England and Wales and USA as its use of EM because there has been a process since the 1980s where the state subcontracts some of its sovereign responsibilities to commercial organizations. England and Wales also has the largest EM scheme in Europe and as such is important here. This approach emphasizes the role of the state as an administrator (Fisher 2006) of a service, rather applying the service. In England and Wales and the USA, provision of criminal justice is subject to competition with the public sector understood simply as one node of security as are commercial, voluntary and statutory sectors (Johnston and Shearing 2003) but the international expansion of the private sector in criminal justice, beyond these neo-liberal states is underpinned by international trade and influence of the World Trade Organization (WTO) and World Bank that has often claimed corruption is a problem only for the public sector. This, however, is nonsense as the private sector regardless of the sector is capable of corruption with no public sector involvement (Brooks 2016). Criminal justice, however, was not exempt the promotion of international trade and helped underpin the expansion and development of the presence of multinationals with crime control interests in the EM market such as G4S. The impact of nation states, particularly the USA, and private sector lobbying has challenged public sector control of criminal justice and private sectors drive for expanding markets in surveillance and private security, and pluralization of criminal justice services.

The birth and development of EM can therefore be understood as the political construction of space for commercial organizations to enter the jurisdiction of probation services, and reflect different approaches to its use (Nellis 2014a) around the world. There has and still is significant resistance to the use of what can be referred to as e-control and supervision but this seems dependent on the culture and state and non-state networks in situ (e.g. Greece and Germany have shown antipathy towards all technical surveillance perhaps due to years of military dictatorships).

EM in England and Wales, and elsewhere therefore cannot be simply understood as either state inspired or the product of market forces. Although the state can via ideology and legislation engender the market space for commercial organizations to enter the crime control system, it also struggles to retain control over policy and formal contracts. This is why the state has been referred to as a private security pimp (Zedner 2006) by creating commercial-public hybrid organizations whose positions in the market of crime control are legitimized via national contracts whilst loosely regulated at the local level.

This leads on to the much-promoted view that EM is cost effective under contract. The earliest types of EM were based on a radio-frequency; these were considered 'expensive' and 'inefficient.' The development of GPS, however, is far more accurate in placing offenders in position/location(s), and appears to cost less (Bartels and Martinovic 2017) than the 'old' technology. In addition, EM is always compared to prison, which it costs less than, but this, I suggest, is an insufficient reason for its use. EM is also often supported by claims that it also reduces recidivism but such claims are still inconclusive, as it can depend on how offenders are treated, what conditions are placed on the offender(s), political and criminal justice climate of the country and state supervision of contracted private sector. In 2006, Premier-Serco (now Serco) was challenged on its failure to account for breaches of EM on time. The response of Premier-Serco (as it was known at the time) is telling: it openly admitted that it was 'not subject to performance deductions under the old contract for failures to report breaches on time' (House of Commons Committee of Public Accounts 2006). There were insufficient incentives to comply with the contract due to the absence of financial penalties (Paterson 2008). This can embolden any company that seeks profits to conceal malpractice (Moss 2018) with private sector employees showing little attachment to EM work (Hucklesby 2011). These breaches of contract or 'sound' but poor management of contracts, depending on your view, failed to slow the use of the private sector as criminal justice in England and Wales appears to be primarily concerned more with reducing public expenditure, regardless of the consequences than quality of supervision (Macrae et al. 2011) where PBR is the dominant discourse.

The control of the EM market in England and Wales was, and mostly still is dominated by G4S and Serco. Little has changed with the suspension of the CRC mentioned earlier. Criticism of EM was that it is expensive (a conservative view) and that it lacks legitimacy (a liberal view). Whilst this is a crude distinction and views on the use of EM are complex fears of a dystopian future appears to have receded with a cultural shift in attitudes and use of EM (Nellis 2014a). This, however, fails to account for breaches and overcharging the state for services. These have been downplayed and instead it is the type of contracts and management of them that is considered the problem.

There was some political concern regarding overcharging where The House of Commons Public Accounts Committee (this body is responsible for overseeing state expenditure) expressed displeasure at Serco and G4S who, between them, had been paid a total of £700m in 2005–2013 for EM. Price Waterhouse Cooper (PwC) was employed to review these organizations (more private sector involvement) and the MOJ procurement unit that had been managing the contracts. G4S and Serco state contracts were thus placed under review; Serco withdrew from the then forthcoming EM tender, with G4S, at a later date only after it was referred by the Justice Minister to the Serious Fraud Office in 2013 for, as viewed by MOJ, its refusal to cooperate with the initial PwC audit (Nellis 2014b). Neither G4S or Serco were charged but Chris Grayling (then Justice Minister) replaced MOJ employees considered responsible for mismanagement (Hansard 2013: Col. 581) of contracts, but the private sector continued to expand. The PwC audits of G4S and Serco EM contracts, and Ministry of Justice contracts, however, remain confidential.

What information that was released revealed that G4S and Serco saw an opportunity due to poor oversight and imprecision in the EM regulations to maximize profit (Nellis 2014b). The issue of 'overcharging' was broken into 'charging on the basis of the number of orders rather than subjects;' charging a monitoring fee when EM had ceased;

charging monitoring fees even if installation or failed to work (NAO 2013: 11). Both G4S and Serco admitted engaging in such practices, believing it to be compliant with the contract.

There is some justification here because G4S and Serco could not close an order without state notification that an order had finished, which in many cases it failed to receive, particularly in respect of EM-bail (Nellis 2014b). Some of the continuous charging, however, went on for 'months or even years' (NAO 2013: 11). A few individual examples here will help illustrate the costs of EM: G4S charged the Ministry of Justice 612 days of monitoring, costing £3000, even though the offender was on a custodial sentence. G4S, however, continued to bill for such an offender, as they were unable to secure 'cessation paperwork' from the court; Serco continued to bill the Ministry of Justice for five years, at a cost of £15,500 after a failed EM installation (NAO 2013: 12). It seems that the main issue though was the allegation that the state was billed for 3000 phantom offenders; the MOJ was billed for tagging 18,000 offenders per day under the £700m contract when only 15,000 were monitored (Nellis 2014b). Whilst G4S and Serco were criticized the MOJ was not immune as it was noted that there was a lack of oversight.

As noted above, the official view emphasized remedies to 'manage' the private sector rather than reassertion of state control. However, for G4S and Serco such exposure had negative commercial and reputational consequences. Failure in other outsourced contracts such as disorder at HMP Oakwood, mismanagement of HMP Thameside, murder of a conference delegate in Scotland by badly vetted security, and accusations of sexual impropriety at an immigration removal centre slowed but failed to stop the use of the private sector in EM and other criminal justice roles. G4S publicly apologized for the mismanagement of the EM contract and offered the Ministry of Justice a £24.1m 'credit note', but this was rejected as inadequate. Serco's repaid £65.5 plus Value Added Tax for overcharging on EM. In March 2014, G4S repaid £109m, a sum that covered the cost of investigations into its business, as well as overcharging for EM (Nellis 2014b). These breaches of contract, however, still allowed both G4S and Serco to bid for future criminal justice contracts. This is hardly surprising as with the volume of offenders on EM and costs of upgrading and developing technology and/or purchasing it excludes the public sector but also the voluntary sector involvement.

Traditional knowledge bases and institutionalized forms of expertise—the probation service and previous commercial organizations—are ruthlessly dispensed with as EM is upgraded and probation downgraded (Nellis 2014a: 503–504). EM is not just a penal phenomenon; it reflects a moment, a readiness to use technology into particular spheres of social life. This readiness—a receptive embrace of technical devices and systems—is not developed out of penal discourses, but out of attitudes towards normalized, everyday communication, utility and ubiquitous use (Nellis 2014b). Once a particular technology has its champions, particularly a state-backed commercial sector the 'old ways' of supervising offenders in the community is regressing in some jurisdictions. Attempting to reduce the costs of the prison system, but not necessarily the numbers incarcerated, EM is a helpful extension of state control (Geohegan 2012) and surveillance in partnership with the private sector in neo-liberal jurisdictions but with corruption or poor business practice(s) in the private criminal justice sector the legitimacy to punish in the community should raise some moral doubts as to its use.

Conclusion

This chapter has illustrated that 'probation' alone or in combination with other conditions is used in very different ways in different states. This is based on social, historical, political and cultural antecedents. What is perhaps apparent is that neo-liberal states seek private sector involvement in criminal justice beyond providing 'hardware'. This extension of the state as both an agency involved in direct supervision of offenders and administrator of contracts and oversight of the private sector is an extension of state control or shadow state. Furthermore, I illustrated private sector corruption or 'bad business practice' with the overcharging of EM. If considered a failure this has failed to prevent its expansion in neo-liberal states. As Cohen (1985) noted, failure does not halt the spread of the net of social control; instead, it continues a search for new and more innovative forms of intervention. These 'new' forms are often based on technology, which are purchased—hardware and/or services—from the private sector. The problem now and in the future is to prevent corruption of state-run probation via offenders and/or private sector utilizing bribery—small or substantial sums—from individuals and organizations and sexual favours from perhaps offenders to reduce conditions of licence or breach of contract. There is, however, the need for more research on all these issues but with the reach of the shadow state will the public and private sector criminal justice employees use invested power for personal benefit? It is human to err, and currently, the management of criminal justice in preventing corruption in the community is poor even in a democratic nation.

References

Aebi, M. F., Delgrande, N., & Marguet, Y. (2015). Have Community Sanctions and Measures Widened the Net of the European Criminal Justice Systems? *Punishment and Society, 17*(5), 575–597.

American Probation and Parole Association (APPA). (2011). *Supervision Fees.* Lexington, KY: American Probation and Parole Association.

Anderson, H. A. (2009). Penalizing Poverty: Making Criminal Defendants Pay for the Court-Appointed Counsel Through Recoupment and Contribution. *University of Michigan Journal of Law Reform, 42*(2), 323–380.

Bannon, A., Nagrecha, M., & Diller, R. (2010). *Criminal Justice Debt: A Barrier to Reentry.* New York: Brennan Center for Justice at New York University School of Law.

Bartels, L., & Martinovic, M. (2017). Electronic Monitoring: The Experience in Australia. *European Journal of Probation, 9*(1), 80–102.

Beckett, K., & Harris, A. (2011). On Cash and Conviction: Monetary Sanctions as Misguided Policy. *Criminology & Public Policy, 10*(3), 505–537.

Beckett, K., & Murakawa, N. (2012). Mapping the Shadow Carceral State: Toward an Institutionally Capacious Approach to Punishment. *Theoretical Criminology, 16*(2), 221–244.

Braverman, H. (1974). *Labor and Monopoly Capital*. London: Monthly Review Press.

Brooks, G. (2016). *Criminology of Corruption: Theoretical Approaches*. Basingstoke: Palgrave Macmillan.

Brooks, G., Walsh, D., Lewis, C., & Hakkyong, K. (2013). *Preventing Corruption: Investigation, Enforcement and Governance*. Basingstoke: Palgrave Macmillan.

Carlen, P. (2002). Controlling Measures: The Repackaging of Common-Sense Opposition to Women's Imprisonment in England and Canada. *Criminology and Criminal Justice, 2*(2), 155–172.

Clear, T. R., Cole, G. F., & Reisig, M. D. (2009). *American Corrections*. Belmont, CA: Thomson Wadsworth.

Cohen, S. (1985). *Visions of Social Control*. Cambridge: Polity Press.

Cracknell, M. (2018). Post-release Reforms for Short Prison Sentences: Re-legitimising and Widening the Net of Punishment. *Probation Journal, 65*(3), 302–315.

Crewe, B., & Liebling, A. (2012). Insider Views of Private Sector Competition. In V. Helyar Cardwell (Ed.), *Delivering Justice: The Role of the Public, Private and Voluntary Sectors in Prisons and Probation*. London: Criminal Justice Alliance.

Criminal Justice Joint Inspection. (2016). *An Inspection of Through the Gate Resettlement Services for Short Sentence Prisoners*. London: HM Inspectorates of Probation and HM Inspectorates of Prisons.

Dal Bo, E. (2006). Regulatory Capture: A Review. *Oxford Review of Economic Policy, 22*(2), 203–225.

Damm, C. (2012). *The Third Sector Delivering Employment Services: An Evidence Review* (Working Paper 70). Birmingham: Third Sector Research Centre.

Doherty, F. (2016). Obey All Laws and Be Good: Probation and the Meaning of Recidivism. *Georgetown Law Journal, 104*(2), 291–354.

Dominey, J. (2012). A Mixed Market for Probation Services: Can Lessons from the Recent Past Help Shape the Near Future? *Probation Journal, 59*(4), 339–354.

Durnescu, I. (2013). The Future of Probation in Europe: Common in the Middle and Diverse at the Edge. *Probation Journal, 60*(3), 316–324.

Feeley, M., & Simon, J. (1992). The New Penology: Notes on the Emerging Strategy of Corrections and Its Implications. *Criminology, 30*(4), 449–474.

Feeley, M., & Simon, J. (2006). The New Penology: Notes on the Emerging Strategy of Corrections and Its Implications. *Criminology, 30*(4), 449–474.

Fisher, T. (2006). Race, Neoliberalism, and Welfare Reform. *Social Justice, 33*(3), 54–65.
Fitzgibbon, W., & Lea, J. (2014). Defending Probation: Beyond Privatization and Security. *European Journal of Probation, 6*(1), 24–41.
Fitzgibbon, W., & Lea, J. (2017). Privatization and Coercion: The Question of Legitimacy. *Theoretical Criminology, 22*(4), 545–562.
Fletcher, D. R., & Batty, E. (2013). *Offender Peer Interventions: What Do We Know?* Sheffield: Sheffield Hallam Centre for Regional Economic and Social Research.
Garland, D. (2001). *The Culture of Control: Crime and Order in Contemporary Society*. Oxford: Oxford University Press.
Genders, E. (2002). Legitimacy, Accountability and Private Prisons. *Punishment and Society, 4*(3), 285–303.
Geohegan, R. (2012). *Future of Corrections: Exploring the Use of Electronic Monitoring*. London: Policy Exchange.
Glazer, M. (2002). Ten Whistleblowers: What They Did and How They Fared. In D. Ermann & R. Lundman (Eds.), *Corporate and Government Deviance*. New York: Oxford University Press.
Graham, H., & McIvor, G. (2017). Advancing Electronic Monitoring in Scotland: Understanding the Influences of Localism and Professional Ideologies. *European Journal of Probation, 9*(1), 62–79.
Hanser, R. D. (2010). *Community Corrections*. London: Sage.
Harris, A., Evans, H., & Beckett, K. (2010). Drawing Blood from Stones: Legal Debt and Social Inequality in the Contemporary United States. *American Journal of Sociology, 115*(6), 1753–1799.
Heck, W. P. (1992). Police Who Snitch: Deviant Actors in a Secret Society. *Deviant Behavior: An Interdisciplinary Journal, 13,* 253–270.
Home Affairs Committee. (2012). *Olympics Security*. London: The Stationery Office.
House of Commons Committee of Public Accounts. (2006). *The Electronic Monitoring of Adult Offenders* (Sixty-Second Report of Session 2005–2006). London: HMSO.
House of Commons Hansard Debates. (2013, July 11). *Electronic Monitoring*, Cols. 573–583.
Hucklesby, A. (2011). The Working Life of Electronic Monitoring Officers. *Criminology and Criminal Justice, 1*(1), 59–76.
Human Rights Watch. (2014). *Profiting from Probation*. New York: Human Rights Watch.
Johnston, L., & Shearing, C. (2003). *Governing Security*. London: Routledge.

Jones, T., & Newburn, T. (2002). The Transformation of Policing? Understanding Current Trends in Policing Systems. *British Journal of Criminology, 42,* 129–146.

Macrae, J., Page, J., & McClory, J. (2011). *Transformation in the Ministry of Justice: Second Interim Report*. London: Institute for Government.

Maguire, M., & Raynor, P. (2017). Offender Management in and After Prison: The End of the 'End to End'? *Criminology & Criminal Justice, 17*(2), 138–157.

McNeill, F. (2013). Community Sanctions and European Penology. In T. Daems, D. van Zyl Smit, & S. Snacken (Eds.), *European Penology*. Oxford and Portland, OR: Hart Publishing.

McNeill, F., & Robinson, G. (2013). Liquid Legitimacy and Community Sanctions. In A. Crawford & A. Hucklesby (Eds.), *Legitimacy and Compliance in Criminal Justice*. Abingdon: Routledge.

Miceli, M. P., Near, J. P., & Dworkin, T. M. (2008). *Whistleblowing in Organizations*. New York: Routledge.

Ministry of Justice. (2013). *Transforming Justice: A Key Revolution in the Way We Manage Offenders* (Consultation Paper CP1/2013). London: Ministry of Justice.

Moore, R., & Hamilton, P. (2016). Silo Mentalities' and Their Impact on Service Delivery in Prison-Community Transitions: A Case Study of Resettlement Provision at a Male Open Prison. *The Howard Journal of Crime and Justice, 55*(1–2), 111–130.

Moss, B. (2018). Electronic Monitoring and Monitoring Probation: The Case of Ireland. *European Journal of Probation, 10*(2), 120–135.

Mythen, G., Walklate, S., & Kemshall, H. (2013). Decentralizing Risk: The Role of the Voluntary and Community Sector in the Management of Offenders. *Criminology and Criminal Justice, 13*(4), 363–379.

National Audit Office. (2013). *The Ministry of Justice's Electronic Monitoring Contracts*. London: The Stationary Office.

National Offender Management Service. (2016). *Corruption Prevention—How to Identify, Report and Manage Staff Corruption in the National Probation Service*. London: NOMS.

Nellis, M. (2014a). Understanding the Electronic Monitoring of Offenders in Europe: Expansion, Regulation and Prospects. *Crime, Law and Social Change, 62*, 489–510.

Nellis, M. (2014b). Upgrading Electronic Monitoring, Downgrading Probation: Reconfiguring 'Offender Management' in England and Wales. *European Journal Probation, 6*(2), 169–191.

Nellis, M., Beyens, K., & Kaminski, D. (2013). *Electronically Monitored Punishment: International and Critical Perspectives*. London: Routledge.

Paterson, C. (2008). Commercial Crime Control and the Electronic Monitoring of Offenders in England and Wales. *Social Justice, 34*(3/4), 98–110.

Phelps, M. S. (2017). Mass Probation: Toward a More Robust Theory of State Variation in Punishment. *Punishment and Society, 19*(1), 53–73.

Reynolds, M. O. (2000). *Privatizing Probation and Parole* (NCPA Policy Report). Dallas, TX: National Center for Policy Analysis.

Rothwell, G. R., & Baldwin, J. N. (2007). Whistle-Blowing and the Code of Silence in Police Agencies: Policy and Structural Predictors. *Crime and Delinquency, 53*(4), 605–632.

Taylor, S., Burke, L., Millings, M., & Ragonese, E. (2017). Transforming Rehabilitation During a Penal Crisis: A Case Study of Through the Gate Services in a Resettlement Prison in England and Wales. *European Journal of Probation, 9*(2), 115–131.

Teague, M. (2011). Probation in America: Armed, Private and Unaffordable? *The Journal of Community and Criminal Justice, 58*(4), 317–332.

White, A. (2013, January 7). The Shadow State: Probation Chiefs Voice Doubts About Outsourcing. *New Statesman*.

White, A. (2015). The Politics of Police 'Privatization': A Multiple Streams Approach. *Criminology and Criminal Justice, 15*(3), 283–299.

Zedner, L. (2006). Liquid Security: Managing the Market for Crime Control. *Criminology and Criminal Justice, 6*(3), 267–288.

9

Vigilantes: The Corruption of the Justice System

Introduction

This chapter will highlight how some nations have lost control of all or parts of the state criminal justice system and conceded the role of punishment to organized crime, militias, and paramilitary organizations (Davis 2006; Meagher 2007; Monaghan 2008; Pratton 2008; Grillo 2011; Grayson 2011; Topping and Byrne 2012; Mullins and Wither 2016). This chapter explores the context in which vigilantes occur and corruption of criminal justice where social order is maintained outside the recognized legal order of justice and where extra-judicial punishment is used to enforce criminal and 'social' rules. The notion of what 'justice' is and how it should be enforced leads to a discussion on what the criminal justice system can, and is able to do, and the definition of 'justice'.

I do not consider individuals that entrap sex offenders here, which is a vigilante action or organized public gatherings to protest a local issue or disorganized impromptu gatherings of local citizens to protest on a specific issue such as building a sex offender unit in a local prison. The latter example is a public protest within the official system of law and I

G. Brooks, *Criminal Justice and Corruption*,
https://doi.org/10.1007/978-3-030-16038-8_9

am concerned with 'organisations' that challenge and subvert state control of criminal justice. There is also anti-vigilantism to consider where the fear of sex offenders in the community is hijacked by newspapers, but mostly by the criminal justice system. Whilst some newspapers and social media sites call for the most punitive sanctions possible (and some that are not possible), events are exploited regarding the control of sex offenders in the community about ownership and jurisdiction of the problem. The criminal justice system can thus deflect public disclosure of sex offenders by claiming that vigilantism will cause sex offenders to disappear and thus become difficult to track and monitor, leading to a potential increase in violent assaults. But if 'managed' by the criminal justice system presenting sincere concern(s) about 'dangerous' offenders law enforcement can come to control the situation. In this chapter, however, I primarily consider organized vigilantes that challenge the legitimacy of the state to exercise power and offer an alternative system of justice as this is a corruption of a criminal justice system.

Vigilantes challenge state social control and legitimacy and prevent and punish crime in a local community/region, but can move from protecting a community/region to preying on it (Baker 2002; Gore and Pratten 2003; Meagher 2007; Pratten 2008). Vigilantism can thus be subject to the same process as a legitimate system of justice; it starts out to protect, loses credibility and legitimacy because of brutal punishment, threats, intimidation and corruption and imposes itself on those it set out to defend.

What Is Vigilantism?

Vigilantes are an unusual problem for law enforcement; in some circumstances law enforcement understands, and tacitly accepts illegal acts committed by vigilantes and shares some satisfaction in the ad hoc punishment on suspected and/or known offenders. However, militias, and paramilitary vigilantes, as seen by some in a community, often break the law in punishing these suspected or known offenders, and sometimes perception of what is seen as 'criminal' behaviour is different to that of a state legal system. This puts law enforcement, but also a prosecution service in an awkward position. Do these organs of state arrest and indict vigilantes, and possibly risk a confrontation with a local community under vigilante protection or accept vigilantes and embolden punishment of offenders seen as beyond law enforcement reach? Even a well-equipped law enforcement body, particularly in a democratic nation, has difficulty in preventing offending with crime often unpunished.

This, however, is no justification for vigilante action, and yet in non-democratic and democratic nations, vigilante acts are committed leading to a different system of justice controlled by highly organized militias and paramilitary organizations that command and control a geographical region and offer an alternative system of justice, which is often popular with local citizens (see Tankebe and Asif [2016] for police legitimacy and vigilantism in Pakistan). Vigilantism is associated with individuals or politically organized alternative systems of justice outside, beyond and/or part of a legitimate system of judicial law enforcement. Whilst vigilantism is context specific e.g. historical, social, cultural and political it has some common characteristics. These are:

1. Planning and premeditation of acts.
2. Private citizens and/or individuals and/or a collection of individuals engage in voluntary acts.
3. Resemble a form of 'autonomous citizenship' and, as such, can constitute a social movement.
4. Use, or threaten to use, physical violence.
5. These threats, acts of intimidation breach legitimate laws.
6. These establish an alternative system of 'justice' that offer a form of social control to a local and/or regional population providing security both from criminal elements and official state law enforcement, which are often seen an ineffectual and corrupt.
   (Johnston 1996; Monaghan 2008; Topping and Byre 2012; Reed 2015; Mullins and Wither 2016; Moncada 2017).

As such, there is a context to vigilantism. These are that the local community, a set geographical locale has been brutalized by a conflict such as civil war. This has occurred for a number of years and citizens have become institutionalised to violent crime. In addition, within such a context crime can be differentiated into 'political' and 'normal' crime. 'Political crime' can also be differentiated; it can be 'working' with law enforcement to inform on a community and/or members of an illegal organization, or 'working' for the illegal organization defined by state laws and rules. Then there are normal crimes such as theft that is dealt with by the formal justice system or informal vigilante justice system, depending on local citizen's view of official law and judicial enforcement. This could be a matter of faith, or lack of it, in local law enforcement to apprehend the offender(s) and the judicial system to punish them, and ultimately, which system—formal or informal—a member of the public will approach. Two systems of justice can thus run in parallel, an official and/or informal system of law enforcement. If dissatisfied with an official law enforcement response, if approached, members of a local community could approach vigilantes to mete out punishment. However, when the legitimacy of the state and its effectiveness are integral to the conflict—both security and legal systems—community access is often foreclosed (Monaghan 2008). A direct consequence of this is that a community seeks informal justice or an alternative system of justice, which is influence by the violent environment in which they reside. This can change though as restorative schemes replace violence (Gormally 2001; McEvoy and Mika 2001; Mika and Zher 2003; Mitchell 2008), but these too can have a limited impact on the legitimacy of criminal justice because of years of mistrust and on ongoing law enforcement corruption (Davis 2006). These approaches are not exclusive but sometimes combined, depending on the circumstances, e.g. the stage of a peace process, if there is one, that official and informal systems of justice are part of Tonge et al. (2011) and the need for critical engagement (McEvoy and Mika 2002, Kucera and Mares 2017; Hearty 2018) for it to succeed.

Before progressing though it has to be noted that no matter how controversial, vigilante action can enjoy a considerable degree of public approval (Reed 2015; Tankebe and Asif 2016). This, of course, depends on the act(s), and local community to whom they appeal. Impulsive vigilantism, either by individuals or by a set of people that cluster around a specific issue, is normally isolated, short-lived and transitory.

However, unstructured vigilante action often puts innocent people at risk of extreme violence—such as the Paulsgrove estate in Portsmouth (Williams and Thompson 2004), United Kingdom in 2000 where a small number of residents briefly mistook an innocent person for a sex offender.

If vigilantism is highly organized, particularly around a political vacuum, the situation for law enforcement becomes problematic and dangerous. Organized militias and paramilitary vigilantism has the potential to be very hazardous since the perception or reality of extreme bias, corrupt law enforcement and judiciary leads to a rejection of the state system. It is here rather than a small scale temporary disturbance, a local protest of a single issue which law enforcement can either control, reassert control, or fail to that causes entrenched vigilantism. The state can reassert its position and legitimacy if vigilantism is brief and people coalesce around a local issue, but the more entrenched the rejection of official law enforcement the vigilantes usurp and assume the responsibility of law enforcement and offer an alternative system of justice.

With a long-established view that law enforcement and some members of the judiciary are corrupt in Mexico (Grillo 2011) and Nigeria (Meagher 2007) where state power is used to extort and abuse members of the public for personal or institutional benefit distrust and rejection of local law enforcement by local inhabitants is hardly surprising. With little or no option, local inhabitants have to defend themselves from corrupt law enforcement, organized crime and wayward individuals. In such circumstances where there is a breakdown of law and order and official law enforcement is brutal and violent ineffectual vigilante action could be the only possible option to a local community/region to defend itself from organized crime and law enforcement. In some circumstances, this is not a move to co-opt or usurp power but protect a community from those that are powerful and corrupt as in Mexico (Ríos 2013; Ochoa and Tomas 2016).

Once such power is secured, some vigilantes will be loath to relinquish it. This is really only relevant to highly organized, political vigilantes, where some have progressed into terrorism and confront and contest state security law enforcement such as happened in Northern

Ireland, and highlighted by Mexico and Nigeria. This 'relationship' with vigilantes is thus complicated but once law enforcement has 'lost control' of a locale or region, particularly if corrupt it is hard to secure legitimate control once more. Many organized vigilantes profess to offer a service that official law enforcement has failed to. This breeds resentment and mistrust but even if vigilantes are hostile towards law enforcement, in some circumstances vigilantism is sometimes popular with law enforcement; paramilitary members of organizations in Northern Ireland can 'punish' normal criminal offenders without recourse to legal and judicial standards bringing 'justice' to both injured member(s) of the public and enforcing law and order, in an alternative rather than official system. Official law enforcement can thus have a complex relationship with vigilantes: they are a threat to state security and state legitimacy, but can control local populations to keep crime under control and mete out punishment that official law enforcement is incapable or unable to unless it breaks legal rules and conduct. Such a situation has been noted in Northern Ireland to which we now turn.

Northern Ireland

There is a wealth of information on Northern Ireland on paramilitary vigilante factions—Loyalist and Republican—(Gormally 2001; Knox 2001, 2002; McEvoy and Mika 2001; Monaghan 2002, 2004, 2008; Mika and Zher 2003; Mitchell 2008; Topping 2008b; Topping and Byrne 2012; Reed 2015; Mullins and Wither 2016) is a small sample of available literature, and whilst drawing on this excellent work I will offer only a brief contemporary account of the historical development of paramilitary organizations here. This is not to dismiss the importance of this literature; instead it is best to read the original articles. What I offer here is a narrow analysis of why a system of justice is seen as corrupt and how paramilitary organizations became the system of local law enforcement that citizens—not all of them—turn to if a normal crime has occurred.

In a referendum in 1998, the Irish Republic endorsed a peaceful solution to the conflict in Northern Ireland (Hearty 2018). This heralded a political solution to the intractable problem and endless cycle of political violence. A political compromise helped British and Irish states resolve 'differences' with a wide-ranging and mutual acceptance of the principle of consent, e.g. Northern Ireland is part of the United Kingdom (but remains so only as long as a majority of the population wishes). The Irish constitution was thus amended to reflect this understanding, and power was devolved, in December 1999 to an elected Northern Ireland Assembly with a wide range of executive and legislative powers. In an attempt to construct a peaceful as possible society in Northern Ireland political prisoners were released, reviews of policing and criminal justice promised, a new independent Human Rights and Equality Commission established, and a commitment to complete and total disarmament of all paramilitary organizations. This later point demanded that paramilitary organizations had to work with the Independent International Commission on Decommissioning (IICD). Failure to resolve this issue caused a temporary suspension of the Northern Ireland Assembly and Executive in February 2000 and August 2001 which resulted in a political impasse and the reimposition of Direct Rule from Westminster, but by September 2005, the PIRA had satisfied the IICD's Chair, General de Chastelain that it had 'put all of its arms beyond use' (IICD 2005: 2). There were claims that PIRA simply allowed vigilantism as a pretext to control the narcotics markets, providing 'licences' to a selected few allowed to 'trade'. The paramilitary organizations, however, were careful to obscure involvement in 'common criminal acts' (Mullins and Wither 2016) and the narcotics market as this could harm its own claim to protecting the local community and thus its legitimacy.

The population of West Belfast had little confidence in official law enforcement (Hearty 2018); the Royal Ulster Constabulary (now Police Service of Northern Ireland) was viewed as a sectarian system of law enforcement, or more pointedly an illegitimate and occupying presence with no interest in supporting the local population. With little or no legitimacy there was a demand for a 'better' system of justice, and in these circumstances the I.R.A., which was the only organization with the resources to offer one in its own enclaves became a de facto informal system of justice. This system of justice though is extremely violent

(Monaghan 2004, 2008; Topping and Byre 2012). Such a situation, and one that is found elsewhere (see below), is that with violence a part of life for the majority of the population and distrust of law enforcement paramilitary violence to maintain the 'peace' in a community was mostly acceptable. In the case of Northern Ireland, it was telling that the Secretary of State in 1999 claimed 'the peace we have now is imperfect, but better than none' and that we now have 'an acceptable level of violence' (Mowlam 1999 in Mullins and Wither 2016).

In such a context 'normal' crime such as car theft, and narcotic offences should have been the province of official law enforcement and the formal justice system but when the legitimacy of the state and its effectiveness and impartiality of its organs (the police, security services and legal system) are integral to the nature of the conflict, this is foreclosed. A consequence of this is that informal justice mechanisms and responses to 'normal' crime are usurped. The informal system is, however, heavily influenced by the violent environment within which it became established.

Since the start of 'The Troubles', alternative systems of justice developed mostly in working-class districts of Northern Ireland. This often involved, and still can, a range of punitive measures for low-level offences and antisocial behaviour and what are referred to as nuisance, e.g. youths gathering at street corners, verbal abuse of citizens and the dumping of rubbish to serious crime(s). These violations, however, are defined by paramilitary organizations. A system of punishment became so established that a tariff system developed in both republican and loyalist districts. This system reflected the formal (state) criminal justice system but in a more extreme form with a scale of sanctions that start with threats or warnings, enforced curfew, public humiliation, exile and punishment beatings, such as kneecapping or, in exceptional circumstances, execution. The punishment ordered is influenced by mitigating factors such as age, past criminal record, and family background. In practice, however, the level of punishment can be arbitrarily brutal or lenient, often dependent on whether the offender had paramilitary affiliation (Monaghan 2008; Topping and Byre 2012).

Furthermore, exile was also a sanction employed as part of this informal system; this exile or expulsion of criminals or antisocial elements echoes British criminal justice policy in the seventeenth and eighteenth century and use of transportation to Australia and USA many of whom were Irish. Banishment could vary from months to years or permanently on orders and threats of violence from paramilitary organizations. The initial rationale for this informal justice system within Northern Ireland differs between the republicans and loyalists. For the republican community, it is the lack of legitimacy law enforcement had and still has with some in west Belfast. This is because of its previous policing of Northern Ireland as an unwelcome and occupying presence; but for loyalists, informal justice helps assists the police (Monaghan 2002) in dealing with crime.

Due perhaps to the length of the conflict and lack of legitimacy law enforcement had in some parts of Northern Ireland a policing vacuum emerged. In this context, paramilitary organizations were called on by local inhabitants to deal with 'normal crime' and acts of violence in and on local estates. The system, however, is a highly retributive system of community-based justice (Knox and Monaghan 2002). In such a context punishment in an informal system is often popular as justice is swift and visible (Silke 1999, 2001). In some way the control of a community becomes, for the paramilitary organization a public relations exercise; swift and harsh, brutal punishment is popular (Monaghan 2004). It is perhaps useful to view such a system as popular by some members of a community rather than all, and that such a system will only maintain its legitimacy if it represents the majority of its local community/region. The issue of legitimacy and public consent was reviewed in Chapter 2 and formal state institutions and vigilantes seek this acceptance to 'police' a community/region. If vigilantes are too brutal, however, consent is replaced by fear and the public have simply moved from a formal system to an informal system of enforcement. Whilst official law enforcement is imperfect a local community under a brutal system of informal justice is sometimes usurped and manipulated by ambitious political individuals or military leaders such as in Nigeria (Meagher 2007).

Law enforcement and the police in particular still occupy a symbolic position at the centre of the conflict in Northern Ireland. There is still a significant lack of legitimacy in parts of West Belfast (Topping 2008a; Topping and Byrne 2012). Substantial political progress has been made with policing in republican strongholds (Hearty 2018) but the change from a counter-insurgency system of law enforcement to community policing is still problematic. However, a problem for the PSNI is that if sections of the public distrust them, and fail to report crime, there is little that the PSNI can do. This leads to a level of dissatisfaction on part of some of the public, which a paramilitary organization can fill. It is in the interests then of paramilitary organizations to complain and encourage local criticism of law enforcement, and then appropriate the role of informal police. The state police in Northern Ireland then is perhaps in an impossible position; it needs the local community to come forward and report crime and act as witnesses, but due to its previous role in the conflict is seen as highly suspicious and illegitimate by some, and has to compete with an informal system of justice which is popular in parts of Belfast. Whilst the changes in policing in Northern Ireland were welcome by the republican community police/law enforcement service, no matter how much political support it has it still has to contend with a post-conflict landscape where bitter social, political and religious divides continue. The same can be said of Nigeria.

Nigeria

Law enforcement and the judiciary in Nigeria were and are still seen as primarily corrupt by its citizens (Heerten and Moses 2014). Whilst political corruption is a clear cause of corrupt law and judicial enforcement I examine vigilantism at state level here and in particular the Bakassi Boys. As with all corrupt systems of law enforcement that fail to protect its citizens, or prey on them, its credibility is irreparably damaged or completely lost. The causes of militias in Nigeria are said to be: colonialism, the Nigerian Civil War (1967–1970), religious, ethnic (Muslims dominate in the North and Christians in the South of Nigeria) and tribal routes and competition for control of oil. Touching on these 'reasons' helps 'set the scene' in Nigeria but these should be read as an accumulation and competing causes of vigilantism.

Before colonialism existed in Nigeria a framework of trust and protection within and across local, regional ethnic enclaves existed in

Nigeria. Credit networks based on clan and ethnic lines had an established system of trade. As such a decentralized system of precolonial Nigerian religious, ethnic and tribal links were bound by 'a dense network of tiny capillary veins' (Isichei 1976: 67). An institutional matrix of religious, ethnic and tribal linkages thus provided an economic infrastructure. However, the problem of ethnic nationalism in Nigeria came with the advent of colonialism (Aluko 1998; Ake 2000) which created structural imbalances within the nation in terms of socio-economic projects, social development and establishment of administrative centres. This imbalance deepened conflict between ethnic groupings in Nigeria (Aluko 1998) that corrupt politicians regularly emphasize to secure power and control of limited resources. Ekeh (1987) explained that the reason African nations have a problem of nationwide, country loyalty, commitment and patriotism of its citizens is that it's social structure, political and law enforcement and judicial institutions were imposed rather than developed from within. Here again, we see a system of law enforcement as externally imposed and lacking legitimacy, as in Northern Ireland. In this context, though the system was both external and unfamiliar to its inhabitants; in Northern Ireland the system was familiar but unwelcomed.

With Nigerian Independence in 1960 and subsequent Civil War local power of the Igbo nation/state of 'Biafra' played a central role in the development of the region (Forrest 1994: 195–196; Brautigam 1997: 1006). In doing so the Igbo consolidated local power in its state. However, with ongoing conflicts and accumulation of power at local/regional level national state cohesion is constantly under threat. Local trade becomes potentially divisive, as it secures the dominance of lucrative income. This 'income' attracts organized crime, local leaders and ethnic militias. Cultural and economic divisions can and do cause resentment and conflict with individuals out for wealth, power and prestige (Anthony 2002). This, however, is not particular to Nigeria but a worldwide phenomenon. In Nigeria and elsewhere there is often political manipulation of ethnic loyalty, particularly in the struggle for oil resources (Shaxson 2007). These play a central role in outbreaks of violence but so do local issues, with organized crime in parts of Nigeria, a lack of law enforcement and/or corrupt law enforcement and judiciary.

It is in such a context local vigilantes arose. The Bakassi Boys in Aba, in southeast Nigeria are only one example. Originally established to protect traders from threats, intimidation and violence from organized crime and dissatisfied with local law enforcement's inability or more particularly unwillingness to deal with crime, local market traders simply requested protection from threats, intimidation, theft and violence. However, whilst this started a movement to protect local traders it became an ethnic militia; this in itself is not unusual in Nigeria where ethnic and religious groupings seek 'self-defence', because they have no trust in the ability of democratic institutions to settle their conflicts (Gore and Pratten 2003; Lawal 2005). Ethnic nationalism is common in all plural cultures but subject to manipulation, especially by corrupt political leaders that pursue personal interest above communal, region or state development. The interplay of ethnic nationalism has also made the sharing of the national revenue a much more volatile and sensitive issue.

In the case of the Bakassi Boys local law enforcement came to accept what was seen as a local rival 'policing' organization. The Bakassi Boys usurped sovereign state powers but only replaced violent criminals and local brutal and/or ineffectual law enforcement with a violent militia (Ukiwo 2002). Such violence is a threat to the economic interests of the local community/region that the Bakassi Boys were supposed to defend but instead violence already embedded in the social fabric of the region continued. Public executions were celebrated, and whilst law enforcement representatives were critical of lynch law where the Bakassi Boys acted in an arbitrary fashion, law enforcement were also seen as brutal. However, for Harnischfeger (2003) criticism of the Bakassi Boys was seen as simply an attempt by state law enforcement to discredit more successful rivals and claims to legitimate power. Furthermore, corrupt law enforcement had also lost a major source of illegal income as it was unable to demand payment in return for law enforcement and 'justice'. It could be suggested here that 'justice' was for sale and that the public preferred Bakassi Boys system of enforcement to that of state institutions. Local public consent to legitimately 'police' thus moved from state institutions to informal vigilantes.

The reason the Bakassi Boys secured such public support is threefold: (1) Law enforcement and the judiciary were unable or unwilling to protect citizens, and thus lost all respect. In such circumstances, western concepts of justice were discredited. With decades of state decline, under either military or civilian leaders, notions of human rights and justice seem unsuited to a Nigerian environment where the occult and in some regions of Nigeria, Islam hold sway. (2) Militias could not have established themselves without political patronage. However such patronage is then used to intimidate political opposition, but violence is also used by businessmen as democratic institutions failed to offer an effective system of disputes. (3) As people lack faith in the ability of the state to contain violence, ethnic and religious militias are formed and ethnic violence (Smith 2004; Meagher 2007) occurs.

As with Mexico (see below) law enforcement lacked legitimacy and lost control. Under previous military dictatorships, in Nigeria, it became normal to shoot convicted offenders in public, and engage in extra-judicial killings. This, however, to some extent still seems to happen. With a corrupt judicial system and sections of law enforcement which still seems exempt punishment unless 'laying hands on someone with influential' contacts (Harnischfeger 2003: 28) the majority of the public understandably might viewed the criminal justice system as corrupt.

Whilst law enforcement and the judiciary can be, and should be criticized a system of corrupt political patronage and poorly equipped police—in calibre of people, resources and public legitimacy—are causes of this corruption and rise in vigilantism. Some of this is considered historical, e.g. previous military dictatorships viewed 'forces' not under direct military command as rivals. Under military dictatorship members of the army refused to submit to the public legal system (Meagher 2007) and kept the numbers of police officers small, with the result that the police were hopelessly over-burdened, and unable to 'police' to citizens' needs. In such circumstances law enforcement insisted on payment for a public service, such as to investigate a crime, and/or extort via threat of illegal detention.

Instead, the Bakassi militia inspired confidence. The Bakassi methods, however, are similar to law enforcement. There was and is another element to consider here; that is the occult (Baker 2002; Harnischfeger 2003). By drawing on the occult the Bakassi Boys represented a precolonial tradition and laid claim to magical powers to help establish 'truth'. Judges were presented more as mislead by magical influences rather than engaging willingly in egregious corruption. Magical powers were carefully cultivated, including ritualized cruelty and instruments of justice, such as oracles, presented as pitiless powers pronounced judgement on the guilty as confirmed by the spirit world (Smith 2004).

Nigeria thus has a 'mixed' law enforcement and judicial system. One is the imposition of colonial rule that lacks the legitimacy in Nigeria whilst vigilantes draw on cultural legitimacy and the occult. Instead of providing justice, an ex-colonial model has been subject to corruption and thus lacks legitimacy. In cultures that have no written codes, such as the Igbo, there is a pragmatic relationship to justice rather than a 'western' rule of law without recourse to ideological principles or a morality based on universal claims. Seeking justice an individual can choose the judicial power; be it an oracle, priest of a powerful idol or council of elders. These approaches have persisted and as such different legal codes coexist, wherein some parts of Nigeria (the north of the country) religious or magical elements play a role in establishing the truth and public punishment (Meagher 2007, Moncada 2017).

Furthermore, in Nigeria, the separation of judicial and executive powers often appears to obstruct the course of justice where law enforcement sometimes fail to pass suspects onto the courts as judges acquit offenders if in receipt of payment (Meagher 2007). This is a justification why law enforcement imposes summary justice but can be seen as little more than an attempt to extort suspects instead of judges. In contrast to these state institutions, Bakassi Boys vigilante justice is seen as fast and efficient; here judgement is passed by the militiamen in secret but punishment is a public display of vengeance and power. The state of Nigeria is thus only partially in control of its own justice system but is competing with an alternative vigilante system that has usurped much of its legitimacy in parts of Nigeria.

I have described only one part of Nigeria here and its competing systems of justice. Nigeria is more an oligopoly of power that is shared between law enforcement, the military and vigilantes within and across Nigeria. The vacuum of state legitimacy (Obarisiagbon and Aderinto 2018) and its corrupt system has thus helped spawn an alternative system which methods—violence and brutality—are similar to that of the state justice system and law enforcement. Both state institutions and vigilantes have been manipulated for political gain though, and employed as a form of terror to control local and regional populations. State institutions attempt to draw on notions of public consent and legitimate political power to 'rule'; but vigilantes draw on local public consent but invoke the occult and magical rituals that speak to the local population in a way that helps legitimize an alternative vigilante system of competing justice.

Mexico

Referred to as the 'Narco state' (Grillo 2011; Atuesta and Ponce 2017) Mexico has a major problem with cartels ability to corrupt the political and judicial process. This problem is such that Campbell (2014: 1) has referred to a 'narco-propaganda' as a 'new' form of political discourse where a form of criminal behaviour is represented as a quasi-ideological expression of criminal organizations, along with police, the military and political partners that control vast parts of Mexico and have illegitimate criminal justice roles of state.

However, since it is impossible to review the whole of Mexico, and cartel corruption and criminal justice in Mexico I will examine one region in Mexico: Michoacán and Tierra Caliente—known for its vigilante resistance and defence from both brutal organized cartels and corrupt law enforcement. The state of Michoacán borders the Pacific Coast between the states of Guerrero to the south (where Acapulco is located) and Jalisco to the north. It is one of the 31 states plus the Federal District that includes Mexico City into which the country is divided.

The reason I have considered this region is that vigilantism in this part of Mexico is somewhat different to Northern Ireland and Nigeria. Rather than a cause of corrupt law enforcement or an occupying 'criminal' external system of justice, it is a reaction to both: caught between organized crime and corrupt law enforcement the citizens have neither protection from a criminal justice system nor a vigilante system. Therefore, local citizens formed into self-defence vigilantes because of breakdown in the rule of law and state law enforcement incapable of protecting its citizens. This situation has occurred because a military-style approach to combat organized crime since 2006 has failed; a military campaign was successful in killing and/or arresting leaders of organized crime but created a vacuum which new criminal networks appropriated. These 'new' reorganized (Ríos 2013) criminal networks coalesced into new groupings beyond the reach of the traditional criminal leadership established in previous decades (Atuesta and Ponce 2017). Fractured organized crime and corrupt law enforcement, judiciary (Ferreyra-Orozco 2010) and political representatives exacerbated a volatile situation. The lack of democratic state power and legitimate law enforcement control caused the vacuum which allowed organized crime in combination with local officials to control the region. Organized crime, however, had no legitimate control as seen earlier in this chapter and simply ruled by threats of violence. Vigilantism in this region of Mexico thus developed in response to both state and organized cartel control.

Vigilantism in this region of Mexico should be seen in this context. Vigilantism and cartels are part of a flawed and corrupt 'democratic' process. The Narco problem (Grayson 2009; Grillo 2011) is more than a demand for narcotics; it has developed and expanded due to a lack of legitimate political, law enforcement and judicial control. Due to weak official and/or corrupt institutions informal 'institutions' have developed by citizens to protect citizens from crime networks and corrupt law enforcement, as was evident in Nigeria.

Local/regional roles such as mayor, state congressman and senators are often dispensed as sinecures. Unable to rein in the power of corrupt local officials such as mayors, citizens were under the control of corrupt municipal and/or states, and local law enforcement. Abuse of state power with no effective system of checks and balances on power (Davis 2006; Grillo 2011; Grayson 2011; Campbell 2014) a system developed and become entrenched where the ability to control vast expenditures of public resources was used to bribe and purchase loyalty. A form of state capture (Dal Bo 2006) has thus occurred but contested by both cartels and corrupt public officials. Such powers are abused by those in office for personal enrichment and dispense favours to 'loyal' subjects and cartels, and fix the promotion of future public corrupt officials. As a result, politics is plagued by political clientelism where, in exchange for ratifying proposed legislation, individuals are awarded public contracts. The citizens have become little more than spectators of rampant corruption and victims of a state criminal justice system.

With judicial power mostly controlled by state 'leaders' that influence the appointment of magistrates, and judges at the state level, the subordination of judicial power to the executive causes mistrust about the legitimacy of criminal justice (Ferreyra-Orozco 2010). Judicial power, unless complicit in corruption is neutered and is unable to perform its role as the constitutional counterweight to executive power. Developed over many years a political culture based on clientelistic and paternalistic relations has become embedded in Mexico where services are rewarded only in exchange for votes. With low levels of education and a system based on unequal but mutual patronage clientelistic schemes of political control and resources (Abdulai and Hickey 2016; Berinsky and Lenz 2010) abound outside the legal framework.

With a combination of corrupt officials and threats of violence from organized crime, Tierra Caliente has seen corruption and the use of public administration as a mechanism for paying political favours. This has produced a governing apparatus that is corrupt and highly inefficient. State law enforcement lacks a robust legitimate presence, with no rule of law and unable or unwilling to challenge the power of criminal networks. Even if the police wanted to counteract organized crime few police officers are available. The police are also poorly paid and trained, and thus seduced by offers from organized crime that corrupts the criminal justice system (Boyce et al. 2015).

In such a political vacuum, criminal networks seize power and extracted 'rents' from the local population (Banister et al. 2015). All subjected to extortion in return for protection from other criminal networks that worked in collusion with state representatives. Organized crime thus emerged as political representatives funded electoral campaigns, mediated conflicts between private citizens, and fixed prices for products. Authority was exercised through local 'chiefs' (jefes de plaza) appointed by organized crime that extorted citizens, stole, engaged in kidnappings and murders (Boyce et al. 2015).

It is hardly surprising then that vigilante self-defence developed in Michoacán in 2013. Due to the absence of a democratic system or state with sufficient legitimacy to impose order based on the rule of law local representatives were subject to the most powerful 'officials' interests. It appears that 'ordinary' citizens had no option but to form into vigilante units to protect people and property from violence and extortion from either competing organized crime groups or law enforcement. This reflects, once again in this chapter, the lack of trust in, and legitimacy of, democratic mechanisms to conflict settlement, as well as the role of the state as mediator of peaceful social coexistence. However, if state law enforcement is corrupt, the political system corrupt and organized crime is unchallenged or 'works with' corrupt law enforcement/judicial system the role of law enforcement will fall to citizens.

With the state of Michoacán subject to competing and warring factions (Atuesta and Ponce 2017) informal channels between law enforcement and vigilantes were utilized. However, law enforcement used local vigilante knowledge to apprehend members of criminal networks rather than help local citizens, whilst members of the criminal networks infiltrated the vigilantes, in an attempt to seize and increase control of the state (Ochoa and Tomas 2016). Vigilantes were then corrupted by criminal networks, and captured by law enforcement. It seems then, for the future that vigilantism is part of life in Michoacán. With a lack of democracy and unstable network of state institutions there is a political and social vacuum that both criminal networks and vigilantes' now control. The lack of state, official legitimacy and absence of a rule of law, an effective judicial system, and a system of checks and balances are causes of vigilante action. With organized crime, vigilantes and law enforcement all trying to control the region (Atuesta and Ponce 2017), but with the only modest democratic progression to tackle widespread corruption an omnipresent and blatant abuse of power by Mexico's political class will continue. The current picture is one where vigilantes are the local protection for its inhabitants from organized crime and law enforcement. Without substantial political and economic changes, the future of Mexico will be characterized by violence and lack of state public security. Improving the quality of democracy and establishing and enforcing a rule of law is needed, otherwise 'normal' citizens will have to continue to form a system of local vigilantes for protection usurping ineffectual state powers.

Conclusion

In this chapter, I considered the condition in which vigilantes might occur. This started with common factors that can cause and lead to the development of vigilantes such as a lack of legitimate law enforcement and judicial system, corrupt political system, and power vacuum into which organized crime and/or vigilantes move and control. I provided three examples of ongoing cases of vigilantism in Northern Ireland, Nigeria and Mexico. Whilst these are context specific, e.g. based on historical, social, cultural and political circumstances state power is rejected, challenged and undermined. In all of them, the power to punish has shifted from the state to militias, paramilitary organizations and vigilantes, and/or is the case in Mexico the development of vigilantes as a system of protection from organized crime and corrupt law enforcement. Seen as an occupying and unwelcome force, or threat to ethnic survival or simply pushed into armed resistance because of corrupt law and judicial enforcement vigilantes, if seen as such, as this can be contested, corrupt the criminal justice system.

References

Abdulai, A. G., & Hickey, S. (2016). The Politics of Development Under Competitive Clientelism: Insights From Ghana's Education Sector. *African Affairs, 115*, 44–72.

Ake, C. (2000). *The Feasibility of Democracy in Africa*. Dakar: Codesria.

Aluko, M. A. O. (1998). Threats to Nationhood: The Nigerian Experience. *Journal of Nigerian Anthropological and Sociological Association, 1*(1), 78–84.

Anthony, D. (2002). *Poison and Medicine: Ethnicity, Power and Violence in a Nigerian City, 1966–1986*. Oxford: James Currey.

Atuesta, L. H., & Ponce, A. F. (2017). Meet the Narco: Increasing Competition Among Criminal Organizations and the Explosion of Violence in Mexico. *Global Crime, 18*(4), 375–402.
Baker, B. (2002). When the Bakassi Boys Came: Eastern Nigeria Confronts Vigilantism. *Journal of Contemporary African Studies, 20*(2), 223–244.
Banister, J. M., Boyce, G. A., & Slack, J. (2015). Illicit Economies and State(less) Geographies: The Politics of Illegality. *Territory, Politics, Governance, 3*, 365–368.
Berinsky, A., & Lenz, G. (2010). Education and Political Participation: Exploring the Casual Link. *Political Behaviour, 33*(3), 357–373.
Boyce, G. A., Banister, J. M., & Slack, J. (2015). You and What Army? Violence, the State, and Mexico's War on Drugs. *Territory, Politics, Governance, 3*(4), 446–468.
Brautigam, D. (1997). Substituting for the State: Institutions and Industrial Development in Eastern Nigeria. *World Development, 25*(7), 1063–1080.
Campbell, A. (2014). Narco-Propaganda in the Mexican "Drug War" an Anthropological Perspective. *Journal of Latin American Perspectives, 41*(2), 60–77.
Dal Bo, E. (2006). Regulatory Capture: A Review. *Oxford Review of Economic Policy, 22*(2), 203–225.
Davis, D. E. (2006). Undermining the Rule of Law: Democratization and the Dark Side of Police Reform in Mexico. *Latin American Politics and Society, 48*(1), 55–86.
Ekeh, P. (1987). 'Colonialism and Two Publics in Africa' a Theoretical Statement. *Comparative Studies in Society and History, 17*, 91–112.
Ferreyra-Orozco, G. (2010). Understanding Corruption in a State Supreme Court in Central Mexico: An Ethnographic Approach. *Human Organization, 69*, 242–251.
Forrest, T. (1994). *The Advance of African Capital: The Growth of Nigerian Private Enterprise.* Edinburgh: Edinburgh University Press for the International African Institute.
Gore, C., & Pratten, D. (2003). The Politics of Plunder: The Rhetorics of Order and Disorder in Southern Nigeria. *African Affairs, 102*(407), 211–240.
Gormally, B. (2001). *Conversion from War to Peace: Reintegration of Ex-prisoners in Northern Ireland.* Bonn: International Centre for Conversion.
Grayson, G. W. (2009). *Mexico: Narco-Violence and a Failed State?* New Brunswick, NJ: Transaction Publishers.

Grayson, G. W. (2011). *Mexico: Narco-Violence and a Failed State?* New Brunswick, NJ: Transactions Books.
Grillo, I. (2011). *El Narco: Inside Mexico's Criminal Insurgency*. New York: Bloomsbury.
Harnischfeger, J. (2003). The Bakassi Boys: Fighting Crime in Nigeria. *The Journal of Modern African Studies, 41*(1), 23–49.
Hearty, K. (2018). How the 'Suspect Community' Become Critical Engagers: The Reframing of the Irish Republication Narrative on Policing Northern Ireland. *Irish Political Studies, 33*(1), 21–42.
Heerten, L., & Moses, D. (2014). The Nigeria–Biafra War: Postcolonial Conflict and the Question of Genocide. *Journal of Genocide Research, 16*(2–3), 169–203.
Independent International Commission on Decommissioning (IICD). (2005). *Final Report of the Independent International Commission on Decommissioning*. Belfast: IICD.
Isichei, E. (1976). *A History of the Igbo People*. New York: Palgrave Macmillan.
Johnston, L. (1996). What Is Vigilantism? *British Journal of Criminology, 36*(2), 220–236.
Knox, C. (2001). Establishing Research Legitimacy in the Contested Political Ground of Contemporary Northern Ireland. *Qualitative Research, 1*, 205–222.
Knox, C. (2002). 'See No Evil, Hear No Evil' Insidious Paramilitary Violence in Northern Ireland. *British Journal of Criminology, 42*(1), 64–185.
Knox, C., & Monaghan, R. (2002). Violence in a Changing Political Context: Northern Ireland and South Africa. In E. Stanko (Ed.), *The Meanings of Violence*. London: Routledge.
Kucera, M., & Mares, M. (2017). Vigilantism During Democratic Transition. *Policing and Society: An International Journal of Research and Policy, 25*(2), 170–187.
Lawal, I. B. (2005). Judicial Corruption in Nigeria: An Appraisal. *Journal of Public and International Law, 1*(1), 42–58.
McEvoy, K., & Mika, H. (2001). Punishment, Policing and Praxis: Restorative Justice and Non-violent Alternatives to Paramilitary Punishments in Northern Ireland. *Policing and Society, 11*(3–4), 359–382.
McEvoy, K., & Mika, H. (2002). Restorative Justice and the Critique of Informalism in Northern Ireland. *British Journal of Criminology, 42*(3), 534–562.
Meagher, K. (2007). Hijacking Civil Society: The Inside Story of the Bakassi Boys Vigilante Group of South-Eastern Nigeria. *The Journal of Modern African Studies, 45*(1), 89–115.

Mika, H., & Zehr, H. (2003). A Restorative Framework for Community Justice Practice. In K. Mcevoy & T. Newburn (Eds.), *Conflict Resolution and Restorative Justice*. London: Palgrave.
Mitchell, C. (2008). The Limits of Legitimacy: Former Loyalist Combatants and Peace Building in Northern Ireland. *Irish Political Studies, 23*(1), 1–19.
Monaghan, R. (2002). The Return of "Captain Moonlight": Informal Justice in Northern Ireland. *Studies in Conflict and Terrorism, 25*(1), 41–56.
Monaghan, R. (2004). An Imperfect Peace: Paramilitary 'Punishments' in Northern Ireland. *Terrorism and Political Violence, 16*(3), 439–446.
Monaghan, R. (2008). Community-Based Justice in Northern Ireland and South Africa. *International Criminal Justice Review, 18*, 83–105.
Moncada, E. (2017). Varieties of Vigilantism: Conceptual Discord, Meaning and Strategies. *Global Crime, 18*(4), 403–423.
Mullins, S., & Wither, J. K. (2016). Terrorism and Organized Crime. *Connections: The Quarterly Journal, 15*(3), 65–82.
Obarisiagbon, E. I., & Aderinto, A. A. (2018). Kidnaping and the Challenges Facing the Administration of Criminal Justice in Selected States of Nigeria. *African Journal of Criminology and Criminal Justice, 11*(1), 41–54.
Ochoa, J. A., & Tomas, C. L. (2016). Democracy and Vigilantism: The Case of Michoacán, Mexico. *International Journal for Crime, Justice and Social Democracy, 5*(4), 17–28.
Pratton, D. (2008). The Politics of Protection: Perspectives on Vigilantism in Nigeria. *Journal of the International African Institute, 78*(1), 1–15.
Reed, R. (2015). *Paramilitary Loyalism: Identity and Change*. Manchester: Manchester University Press.
Ríos, V. (2013). Why Did Mexico Become So Violent? A Self-reinforcing Equilibrium Caused by Competition and Enforcement. *Trends in Organized Crime, 16*(2), 138–155.
Shaxson, N. (2007). Oil, Corruption and the Resource Curse. *International Affairs, 83*(6), 1123–1140.
Silke, A. (1999). Ragged Justice: Loyalist Vigilantism in Northern Ireland. *Terrorism and Political Violence, 11*(3), 1–31.
Silke, A. (2001). The Devil You Know: Continuing Problems with Research on Terrorism. *Terrorism and Political Violence, 13*(4), 1–14.
Smith, D. J. (2004). The Bakassi Boys: Vigilantism, Violence and Political Imagination in Nigeria. *Current Anthropology, 19*, 3.
Tankebe, J., & Asif, M. (2016). Police Legitimacy and Support for Vigilante Violence in Pakistan. *International Journal of Comparative and Applied Criminal Justice, 40*(4), 343–362.

Tonge, J., Shirlow, P., & McAuley, J. (2011). So Why Did the Guns Fall Silent? How Interplay Not Stalemate, Explains the Northern Ireland Peace Process. *Irish Political Studies, 26*(1), 1–18.
Topping, J. R. (2008a). Community Policing in Northern Ireland: A Resistance Narrative. *Policing and Society, 18*(4), 377–398.
Topping, J. R. (2008b). Diversifying from Within: Community Policing and the Governance of Security in Northern Ireland. *British Journal of Criminology, 48*(6), 778–797.
Topping, J., & Byrne, J. (2012). Paramilitary Punishments in Belfast: Policing Beneath the Peace. *Journal of the Behavioural Sciences of Terrorism and Political Aggression, 4*(1), 41–59.
Ukiwo, U. (2002). The Changing Roles of Bakassi Boys in Eastern Nigeria: Democracy and Development. *Journal of West Africa Studies, 3*(3), 39–51.
Williams, A., & Thompson, B. (2004). Vigilance or Vigilantes: The Paulsgrove Riots and Policing Paedophiles in the Community: Part 1—The Long Slow Fuse. *The Police Journal, 77*, 99–119.

10

Lawyers and Criminal Justice

Introduction

Literature on lawyers mostly reflects notions of standards of behaviour—expected and absent—and seen as an issue of 'legal ethics' (Banks 2017). These views are particularly prominent in American literature where lawyers are trying, but fail to act 'properly' or as Simon (1988: 204–205) put it, are 'ethically ambitious'. Popular conceptions and discourse of lawyers working with organized crime and laundering illegal funds (Gottschalk 2016a) are also part of the literature. In criminology, and even with a growing awareness of professionals involved in crime or enabling it, or as I prefer to call it 'professional conduits of corruption' there is still a lack of literature on corrupt lawyers/solicitors particularly with the position they hold in criminal justice systems apart from a selection of articles by Middleton (2005, 2008), Middleton and Levi (2004, 2015), Lankhorst and Nelen (2004), Levi et al. (2005), Nelen and Lankhorst (2008), and Otusanya (2011).

This chapter then is primarily concerned with how lawyers, which is the term I use for legal representatives here unless stated otherwise that expedite criminal acts helping others, mostly, but not exclusively,

G. Brooks, *Criminal Justice and Corruption*,
https://doi.org/10.1007/978-3-030-16038-8_10

clients, but engage in crime for personal benefit and/or 'game' the legal system for a client or personal benefit. Lawyers or as referred to in England and Wales, solicitors, personal benefit can be payment for unethical and/or illegal advice to engaging in criminal acts such as fraud. Much of the business environment and knowledge and practice(s) employed in legitimate work are used in illegitimate work; e.g. helping clients legally reduce taxation and laundering illegal criminal funds to a tax haven. Analyses of lawyers' ability to commit crime and act as a conduit to legitimize illegal conduct are therefore important. This is perhaps even more so since Taylor (1988: 507) has characterized the courts of England and Wales, of which lawyers/solicitors are officers of the court, as a 'condition on which the administration of justice as a whole rests' which is also relevant to other jurisdictions.

This chapter starts with a review of legal, professional ethics such as partisanship, neutrality, relationship with client(s), confidentiality and perjury. I then briefly review types of crime committed by lawyers for personal benefit and then as a conduit of corruption (Brooks 2016) and risks to the legitimacy and credibility of criminal justice. The next section assesses this threat, if viewed as one, where defence lawyers employ every tactic—legal, breaching rules and illegal conduct—in defence of a client in a court of law. This is then placed into a theoretical framework of white collar crime trying to explain why professionals engage in criminal acts alone or in concert with organized crime.

Professional and Ethical: In Search of a Legal Ideal?

Professional ethics is an expression that has multiple possible meanings, but is often used to refer to rules governing professionals and professions. Establishing ethical standards is one approach in which a profession seeks to convince the public to entrust personal affairs and confidence to members of the profession (Banks 2017). Trust is a fundamental part of professionalism (Hough et al. 2010) because clients depend on the knowledge of the professional, regardless of the sector. In the legal profession this is a core value because confidence between a lawyer and client is crucial if lawyers are to secure knowledge (or as full as) of a client's involvement in a crime, if at all. Breaching a client's trust undermines confidence in the legal profession, but ultimately the criminal justice system. Literature often presents the role of the lawyer as one committed to the pursuit of justice and a contribution towards establishing an efficient legal system (Banks 2017), supporting the law as an institution, and as promoting procedural justice (Tyler 1990, 2003, 2011; Tyler and Huo 2002; Bottoms and Tankebe 2012). However, is this professional self-promotion, a form of managing a discourse that advances the power of profession as a public benefit but from which legal representatives handsomely profit? Only some lawyers earn stratospheric wages rather than the whole of the profession but regardless of position, the adversarial system in particular offers lawyers a measure of control within legal process and procedures, which can be abused.

The adversarial system reflects an individualistic ethic, and in some cases lawyers will act in a way that breaches established legal rules. Note that a rule is breached rather than broken here and the consequences can differ depending on the act committed. Lawyers can and do therefore engage in legal but perhaps morally reprehensible acts such as bullying to obfuscation of justice. This is presented as the principle of partisanship: pursuing clients' interests providing robust representation protecting the rights of individuals, and putting clients' interests above all other considerations.

This position, however, could cause a problem. How can a lawyer remain neutral if a client is morally corrupt? (as far as the lawyer is concerned). The lawyer is expected to put aside questions of client morality and represent them regardless. This is the principle of neutrality. The principles of neutrality and partisanship above are seen as supporting the notion of equality before the law. Wasserstrom (1986: 122) made it clear that criminal defence lawyers should be concerned only with the interests of the client, particularly if a criminal case, as the potential for incarceration is enough of a justification for a robust defence. However, such a justification makes lawyers instruments of clients (Hall and Holmes 2008) and the court trial; instead lawyers should deliver accurate as possible evidence? Whilst I respect both views I suggest they represent 'ideal type' scenarios instead of 'in the field' or courtroom legal practice. Lawyers, the same as law enforcement and judges, might have a culture of working practice but the culture of tax lawyers could be seen as a very different beast to a human rights lawyer(s).

Subordinated to clients' interests, regardless of the case, is to subvert the truth though, and in the USA lawyers are expected to take 'reasonable remedial measures' (Banks 2017: 131) if aware that a client has produced incorrect evidence. Here then, the view is that lawyers should avoid clients demands and employ procedural rules to secure justice (Hall and Holmes 2008). In addition there is the view that a client can and should be able to 'make a choice' and have the freedom to do so, and such a system is a moral benefit. Rather than allow lawyers to make a moral judgement on the case then the client can direct a lawyer. In practice, however, it is perhaps useful to follow the advice of the professional. A lawyer's moral compass, if they have one, should not be placed above that of a client, but such a position as above is a rationalization that lawyers should participate in an immoral objective, with a caveat that a lawyer can refuse to represent a client. This is reflected in the legal ethics of a lawyer–client relationship where neither should control the relationship. Instead the client should control what to do, and the lawyer is a technical advisor and counsellor. A lawyer, however, can 'push' a client in a direction that is far more suitable for them than the client. Relationships are not some linear progression where a decision (by client) is fulfilled by the lawyer. There is, as with all relationships differences of what are 'facts' and how to present them. In the USA, however, whilst the model is based on loyalty to the client's wishes lawyers can withdraw representation if 'a client insists upon pursuing an objective that the lawyer considers repugnant or imprudent' (Banks 2017: 130).

Even if withdrawing from representing a client lawyers are expected in USA to fulfil the promise of confidentiality. Breaching the duty of confidentiality breaches acting in the client's best interests, and it is important to note that this confidentiality is owned by the client and not to the lawyer, and thus only the client can waive it in the USA. If accused of crime, confidentiality is seen as important; without it a client could refuse to disclose relevant information, but regardless of this ethic lawyers no doubt represent clients based on limited information.

Clients, particularly criminal clients withhold information as a personal damage limitation exercise. Furthermore, the duty of confidentiality is not the same as lawyer–client privilege: confidentiality is an expectation that lawyers keep the client's confidences but lawyer–client privilege is where a lawyer can reveal information at trial, providing client confidences that are revealed are not used as evidence (Banks 2017).

However, the ethic of lawyer–client confidentiality is completely negated if the client consults the lawyer in furtherance of a crime. Lawyers are, but in narrowly defined circumstances allowed to disclose confidential client information to prevent future harm, particularly if it results in imminent death and/or substantial bodily harm, but is not permitted if it is an 'old' crime.

This section of the chapter was a brief review of ethical principles that lawyers are expected to adhere to. This, however, is an expectation, a set standard of conduct. Standards of conduct though are subject to personal and professional interpretation and lawyers can behave in a completely different fashion involved in a similar case. Seeking "to produce a 'virtuous profession'" (Economides and Rogers 2009: 17), legal ethics literature in the United Kingdom, however, has shown little interest in lawyers who enable corruption and/or crime (accept perhaps the miners' compensation scandal (Boon 2011) and the literature in the USA, as seen above, is concerned mostly with lawyers propriety rather than the interaction of lawyers and crime (Langevoort 2010, 2012). Ethical principles then, depending on the lawyer(s) can be utilized to defend clients' interests even if corrupt; are lawyers then preventing justice and/or conduits of crime?

Are Lawyers a Conduit of Crime?

Before we progress, a definition, even though it can be contested, of organized crime is needed. There is a wealth of literature on what organized crime is and how it can and should be defined; but rather than dwell on it here (see Paoli 2014). I will, however, use the United Nations classification for organized crime. This is that there is a collaboration of at least three people to commit crime, it lasted for a prolonged period, involved offences that meant, or should incur a prison sentence of at least four years, and the central aim of the enterprise was profit.

A Europol Threat Assessment (2013) illustrated that there is a broad consensus on the potential for corruption by lawyers and notes that 'horizontal crime can include…legal business structures, and professional expertise' (Europol 2013: 10). Furthermore, an interest has also developed in the mechanics of the commission of crime and how networks expedite or inhibit pathways to crime (Levi 2012; Paoli 2014) of which lawyers both commit and enable crimes committed by others under the rubrics of 'white-collar' and 'organized' crime. However, as Middleton and Levi (2004: 125) pointed out it might be wise to appreciate the salience of lawyers to the organization of serious crime, and sidestep the term 'organized crime' and instead examine crime as a business; a process that legitimate business needs such as funds, technical expertise, equipment, systems for the distribution of products, protecting business from threats and the ability to hold and transfer currency and documentation, is needed in both legitimate business and illegitimate business.

Some forms of corruption by lawyers are made possible because of access to clients' legal or illegal funds, and lawyers can thus steal from legitimate and 'criminal' clients and also launder and conceal and move funds for the personal benefit of a client(s) (Otusanya 2011). These embezzlements are damaging, particularly to innocent clients, rather than criminal clients and lawyers because their costs fall upon the profession collectively—via the Solicitors' Compensation Fund (SCF) in England and Wales, to which all make an annual contribution. This is a system of collective professional insurance, but if losses exceed contributions because of frauds and/or incompetence, the profession itself is under strain. It can be put under strain because of poor legal practice on which people can claim but also because of criminal acts.

But should we be surprised that individuals or a collection of professional colleagues engage in criminal acts for personal profit or advise organized crime on how to circumvent the law? Entrusted with holding small or substantial amounts of a clients' funds is bound to be a temptation; whilst lawyers talk of professional ethics, and many follow them, are they little more than camouflage to commit crime for those that are corrupt? To steal from a clients' account is theft, but to lawyers/solicitors in England and Wales it can be presented as 'misappropriation' of client funds. This is an example of individuals in a profession laying claim to legitimacy, even though I consider it to be corrupt, to establish the truth. As Foucault (1980: 131) stated (see also Chapter 4) 'Each society has its régime of truth…the types of disclosure which it accepts…the mechanisms and instances which enable one to distinguish…the techniques and procedures accorded value in the acquisition of truth' and the position that lawyers hold affords them the capacity to determine versions of 'truth' and or denial. Misappropriation is I suggest a denial and manipulation of facts, where a discourse of official denial such as spinning a defensive position, a 'literal denial' (nothing happened); interpretive denial (what happened is really something else); implicatory denial (what happened is justified) (Brooks 2016) is what lawyers can do for clients, and so are more than capable of 'spinning a justification' if accused of crime. Bolstered by the 'language of legalism' (Cohen 1996) a 'legal defence', can become an obfuscation of the 'truth' and can help offenders, and lawyers evade a serious criminal justice sanction. This is 'professional capital' (a subset of social capital) (Middleton and Levi 2004: 130) where prestige and background and reputation all help, combined with knowledge and financial resources to thwart criminal sanctions. This is the case the more prestigious the organization; individual and/or rogue lawyers can and do work in notable and esteemed legal businesses, but we should be vigilant regardless of the reputation of lawyers.

The problem is to what extent the internal structure of a legal firm rather than size of an organization has some influence on the potential for corruption. Clinard (1979) claimed that it is the diffusion and decentralization of power where sectional hierarchical 'cliques' in an organization allows the abdication of personal responsibility. Subcultures can thus form in parts an organization with definitions of corrupt acts dismissed and/or justified or seen simply as another routine part of work with no moral significance. Known as 'ethical-numbing' (Brooks et al. 2013) those 'ethically ambitious' lawyers mentioned by Simon (1988: 204–205) at the start of the chapter will, to be successful (secure promotion in an organization) might be 'morally flexible' and partake of criminal acts to secure a lucrative promotion. Braithwaite (1985) has suggested that the type of regulation can effect how an organization may behave; a culture of compliance or culture of resistance can occur depending on the treatment by a regulatory body; if treated in a firm but fair manner (by fair here I mean as seen by individuals and the profession), compliance is possible, but if viewed as intrusive resistance will occur. This is similar to most offenders (see Chapter 2) and how criminal justice is always searching for legitimacy (Beetham 1991), in a democratic nation. The problem with light-touch regulation of organizations, once exposed as such, and particularly in legal services on which we are dependent, seem to be little more than professional but corrosive armour to downplay serious criminal acts. Despite regulation lawyers can avoid serious sanctions, particularly if a substantive organization (Abel 2008: 54) even if involved in crime(s) (Warren 2016).

A sample of the types of crime lawyers commit help highlight this matter. At its most sophisticated lawyers offer services that are legitimately provided to many clients, such as the structure of business organizations and litigation. This knowledge, however, can and is also used by individuals, organizations—legitimate and illegal and also states to commit crime.

However, individual and organized crime has recourse to fraud. Mortgage frauds are one example. This is where borrowing funds from a bank or other financial institutions for a mortgage (or something else), an individual/organization can mislead by exaggerating income, or claiming to occupy the property as a residence, but rent it out instead etc. Such cases might not implicate a lawyer because applications for mortgages are made by borrowers via an intermediary/mortgage broker(s), or direct to institutions, but there is ample room here for applications for a mortgage to be fraud; personal and financial details are incorrect, income exaggerated, assets on which a loan is provided are absent or exaggerated and/or an intermediary assists in manufactured claims. These are only a sample of potential routes to fraud. In a rising market, however, a property portfolio can be built with little risk legitimately or illegitimately, and if aware that an investigation is imminent property can be sold. This type of fraud has attracted the attention of the 'serious crime community' (Middleton and Levi 2015).

Then there is the problem where a lawyer can hold funds in an account, transfer them to a different account with or without clients' knowledge in different jurisdictions—in legitimate bank(s), or in legitimate tax havens. Since the onus is primarily on the lawyer to inform a regulatory body or law enforcement of 'suspicious clients' it is possible that (1) a lawyer informs a regulatory body or law enforcement of clients but will breach 'lawyers ethical' principles (Banks 2017) (2) discount a crime has occurred or is in the process of being committed (a technique of neutralization) (3) knowingly engage in crime or simply (4) steal a clients' funds. This is a rather crude breakdown of what a lawyer(s) might do, and can be built upon, but it is a simple illustration of what lawyers encounter.

The 'serious crime community', is without doubt associated with money laundering. There is a wealth a material on this subject (Levi 2002, 2008; Levi and Gilmore 2002; Reuter and Truman 2004; Levi and Reuter 2006; Chaikin and Sharman 2009; Masciandaro 2017) but little on lawyers' involvement in it with the exception of (Middleton 2005; Middleton and Levi 2004, 2015; Otusanya et al. 2012). The lawyers role(s) here can encompass the creation of commercial vehicles/enterprises, complex legal plans and organization of trusts; buying or selling of property, performing financial transactions (Otusanya 2011), craft false documentation, offer fictitious pledges and security, financial and tax advice and introductions to personal and business institutions. Here we can see how lawyers can be a conduit of criminal corruption, and help thwart, block and obfuscate investigation of organized crime. A note of caution has to be raised here though; legitimate business can behave in an illegitimate and illegal way far beyond aggressively using the international tax system, and organized crime/terrorism can use the legitimate financial sector, with lawyers and bankers assistance. The 'upper-world' and 'underworld' sometimes inhabit and use the same institutions. These above examples, however, are also provided legally. Lawyers can also be used without knowledge by organized crime and legitimate business and can only have limited knowledge of clients' circumstances. This raises the issue of how far should a lawyer inquire into an individuals'/organizations affairs?

In addition there is tax fraud, claims for financial loss, and calculated and planned high yield investment or bank instrument fraud that can utilize lawyers' expertise and knowledge. Fraudsters—criminals or corrupt lawyers—involvement in these types of schemes are invaluable. Knowingly or unknowingly lawyers offer such frauds credibility. For victims of such frauds lawyers offer legal substance, a legitimacy and credibility with lawyers' compulsory indemnity insurance and compensation funds such as in England and Wales, which lend reassurance and integrity to these types of schemes. Funds are placed into what is seen as a legitimate account backed by documentation. This is known as 'the illusion of security' (Middleton and Levi 2004: 139), placing trust in corrupt or incompetent lawyers. The problem for victims here is that whilst a lawyer might be imprisoned for such an offence if knowingly involved, compensation to victims is sometimes refused. This is because the victim(s) are seen as having acted imprudently or to put in bluntly out of avarice to invest in a scheme where returns were completely unrealistic (see the case of Madoff [Henriques 2017]).

Furthermore, there is also legal aid fraud. Legal aid is where payment from public funds is allowed, in cases of need, to help pay for legal advice or proceedings in England and Wales (with different systems of legal aid in Scotland and Northern Ireland). Lawyers have been involved in claiming legal aid for fictitious individuals and/or exaggerating claims (Middleton and Levi 2015). This harms criminal justice as funds are lost that should be used for those most in need, but with a reduction in levels of funds available in England and Wales (The Secret Barrister 2018) other avenues of fraud are more profitable such as immigration fraud. Corrupt lawyers alone or in concert with organized criminal elements can smuggle people, and yet again lawyers offer the thin veneer of legality and respectability in such an enterprise. There is little evidence to substantiate this view but it is possible to manufacture documentation to offer succour for asylum seekers to seek permission to remain in a country out of compassion—misguided or valued—or work with organized crime and brutalize vulnerable people that fear reporting abuse to law enforcement.

Reflecting on the above examples it is noticeable how little evidence of corrupt lawyers is available. As a profession, it as with any profession, deals with corrupt lawyers 'in-house' and via a disciplinary procedure. This is understandable, even if considered unethical, and no organization or public body wants negative publicity that harms the credibility of its members. However, since lawyers have become to some extent 'gatekeepers' (Coffee 2006) with the expectation but not always in practice reporting suspicious clients' acts, particularly in reference to money laundering, is an illustration of a trend towards the 'responsibilization' of civil society in crime control (Garland 2001).

This section highlighted *what* lawyers might and can do and the avenues available to be corrupt and engage in crime alone, with other lawyers or organized crime. I now consider the role of criminal defence lawyers in particular.

Defence Lawyers

The above section concerned itself with crimes committed by lawyers for clients and personal benefit; here attention is specifically on criminal defence lawyers. This section will deal with three issues: should lawyers represent a client(s) that has committed a serious crime, should a witness be subjected to brutal cross examination even if lawyers know they are telling the truth, and what should lawyers do if knowing a witness will commit perjury to benefit a client? These are not exhaustive but are key elements in criminal justice cases, and hence are of importance here.

There is a view held in some western style democratic nations such as the USA that an adversarial system is a bulwark, a protection from a powerful and potentially dangerous bureaucratic state institution, and as such lawyers should represent a clients' interests as effectively as possible based on 'facts'. But what is meant by 'knowledge of the facts' and effectiveness? Lawyers will seldom have all the available facts, particularly in a criminal or complex financial case but perhaps in possession of enough knowledge that a client is definitely guilty. There are rules that a lawyer in court can engage in criminal proceedings to establish that every element of the case is heard. But is the lawyer in an impossible position? If a person has admitted to his/hers defence counsel facts that establish guilt, and independent investigation by defence counsel also established guilt, yet the client insists on standing trial, lawyers should strongly dissuade them from committing perjury in testifying. Further, if in advance of the trial s/he perjures himself or herself when testifying, the lawyer may withdraw from the case and seek leave of the court, but the court must not be advised of the lawyer's reason to withdraw (Banks 2017) in the USA. Some offenders will be undoubtedly guilty and plead innocence but some clients are lying or mentally ill or mistaken.

There are significant differences, however, between a client that is factually guilty and a client who is legally guilty. The standard required by lawyers is that proof of guilt is in a court of law via credible evidence that meets the standard of 'beyond reasonable doubt'. A number of reasons are also put forward defending individuals and organizations that are 'guilty': such as providing those accused of serious crimes with competent counsel, regardless whether they committed a serious offense or are innocent (Gottschalk 2016a). It is not for lawyers to decide innocence or guilt, and should instead ensure that those operating the criminal justice system do so in a proper manner. In the adversarial system lawyers are often expected to present a fearless defense of clients, and it could be suggested are simply fulfilling the aims of that criminal justice system. In this system, which is representative of the USA, the lawyer is seen as a representative of a system, and part of the system of justice.

However, such as system allows lawyers, in USA, to cross-examine a witness with the simple aim of discrediting them to benefit a client. Even if the lawyer realizes the witness is honest (honest in reference to the case) it is down to them to mislead the jury and challenge the credibility of this truthful witness. Whilst legally permissible, is this immoral because it is an effort to obscure the truth and inflicts harm on the innocent witness and thwarts 'justice'? The only purpose of the deception is to obtain an undeserved acquittal for the client. This is only one view, as others see the lawyers' role as one where they should do everything to discredit a witness if it will benefit a client, even if guilty. Is this justice, though? (Bottoms and Tankebe 2012).

This one question has caused much debate in legal literature, which I do not intend to revisit here but raise the issue that if the justice system is seen as bias, prejudicial, it lacks legitimacy (Tyler 1990, 2003; Bottoms and Tankebe 2012), particularly with the public or at least some members of it (see Chapter 2). A lawyer, however, has no claim on absolute knowledge or truth of a witness (but perhaps a clients' guilt) and the truth, or as close to it as possible, is discovered only through cross-examination. Ultimately the resolution of this difficult question is to define the limits of a zealous defense and calls into question conflicts between the lawyers' clients and duty to the court, to the administration of justice and promotion of the truth in criminal proceedings. The notion of truth is perhaps exposed if a witness willingly commits perjury. If a lawyer withdraws from a case, a person willing to commit perjury—defendant or witness—will do so even with a new lawyer. In fact, some states in the USA prohibit the lawyers' disclosure of the clients' perjury (Banks 2017: 135) but elsewhere could be subject to disciplinary action but only if continuing the case without reporting the matter to the court.

Facilitation of serious crime renders the lawyer a party to crime, and legal ethics are insufficient to tackle this problem. 'The problem is that if the threat of criminal punishment does not deter, professional discipline is unlikely to' (Abel 2011: 456). But law enforcement and state prosecution services can, as with all crime, only conduct investigations into and indict a small proportion of serious crime. Obtaining evidence on lawyers' involvement sufficient to lead to a conviction is very difficult; this disincentivises criminal investigations (Middleton and Levi 2015: 649), since the cost of investigation, in England and Wales, is often viewed as a waste of resources unless the chances of conviction or 'significant disruption' of crime are high, which is often not the case.

Lawyers therefore wrestle with ethical issues on a regular basis, as do law enforcement, judges, probation and prison officers; however, *why* are lawyers seduced into breaking ethical standards and/or engaging in criminal acts? This is the subject of the next section.

Why Do Some Lawyers Commit Crimes?

Lawyers without doubt are white-collar employees. However, as with every profession some of its members will commit crime. There is a wealth of material on white-collar crime (Braithwaite 1985, 1988;

Benson 1985; Benson and Moore 1992; Coleman 1992, 1995; Weisburd and Waring 2001; Pontell 2005; Geis 2006; Levi 2008, 2009; Simpson and Weisburd 2009; Smith et al. 2010; Payne 2012, 2013; Gottschalk 2016a, b; Brooks 2016) and is even considered creative (Brisman 2010). I profess to have reservations about the term white-collar crime, as it denotes the position of the offender not the crime. I prefer fraud, and/or criminal corruption (Brooks 2016) that explain the crime rather than position of the offender. However, I offer a brief review here of the main theoretical approaches that explain white-collar crime.

Seen as the catalyst for trying to understand white collar crime, differential association emphasizes that criminality is learned in interaction with others in a process of communication. This process of communication is learned from observations of what are referred to as definitions favourable to violation of law(s). For a person to commit corrupt/criminal acts there needs to be a culture of dominant attitudes that justify and rationalize that corrupt/criminal acts are an acceptable way to behave. This approach, however, could be a universal description of the aetiology of all criminal behaviour but a key point of differential association is that all criminal behaviour is learned in a process of social interaction.

Sutherland (1939) highlighted illegal practices were widely accepted as a way of 'doing business', which depending on the context and environment in which a person was working could lead to future criminal acts. Once inducted and seduced into such a system of behaviour association transforms them from white-collar workers into white-collar criminals. There is some research that offers limited support for this explanation (Cressey 1953) such as embezzlement. Cressey (1953 in Coleman 1992: 57) expanded this approach and stressed that justifications for acts were not ex post facto excuses to rationalize an action already completed but were psychologically present before crime was committed and a major part of the motivation to act. Sykes and Matza (1957) also referred to these rationalizations as 'techniques of neutralization'. However, whilst Sutherland thought that such behaviour was learned from others, Cressey (1953) emphasized the importance of the construction of a social reality and understanding of the world that allowed a person to engage in crime and yet maintain a positive self-concept.

For Ashforth and Anand (2003) a positive self-concept is a combination of institutionalization, rationalization and socialization (also see Chapter 3 and 4). In a model proposed by them the combination of these elements are that institutionalization is where an initial corrupt act becomes embedded in structures and processes, rationalization is a justification(s) put forward to commit a corrupt act, and socialization is where new employees are induced or seduced to view corruption as permissible and part of a routine and way of 'doing business'. The social cocoon of organizational socialization is a powerful 'force' that seduces individuals into acceptance of corruption. Further, socialization practices can themselves become institutionalized and strongly influence new employees that encounter 'indoctrination' of set practices and views of 'how we do business here' by established members of an organization (Brooks 2016).

The aim of success has often been considered causes of white-collar crimes where the demand for profit places individuals and organizations in an inevitable position of trying to achieve unrealistic aims even if representing the law. The culture of competition leads to a strain (Schoepfer and Piquero 2006) but it is not only a question of access to legitimate avenues to success but also the availability of illegitimate avenues to achieve success to which lawyers have access to both. Strain, however, is incapable of predicting crimes only suggesting conditions that might lead to crime.

It is possible to state with some confidence that lawyers, particularly specialist white-collar crime lawyers that represent rich individuals and/or organizations sometimes have an advantage in competition (Gottschalk 2016b) with poorly resourced state lawyers, and with some judges that have only a passing understanding of the complex nature of white-collar crimes. Furthermore, knowledgeable lawyers can potentially ease the pain of confinement if a client is sentenced to prison. Lawyers can and have put forward what is referred to as the 'special sensitivity hypothesis' (Stadler et al. 2013). This is where lawyers claim that incarceration will inflict more pain on a white-collar criminal that a 'street criminal', once imprisoned in a society of captives (Sykes

1958) where physical prowess and criminal connections rather than legal knowledge hold sway. Stadler et al. (2013) also produced research that highlighted how judges failed to impose a prison sentence on white-collar criminals because of the view that prison was unnecessary and unduly harsh. This, however, might be changing perhaps to public outrage and condemnation in Europe and USA of egregious financial crimes (Brooks 2016).

These financial crimes committed with the knowledge of some lawyers harm both the financial sector and criminal justice system, particularly if a financial penalty (Warren 2016) is passed rather than custodial sentence. Whilst organizations with weak or declining profits could break the law, profit, is only one aim an organization will pursue. The environment in which organizations in specific sectors work are important, though; the political power of the organization, its economic strength and networks to elite political power; it capacity to lobby effectively and ability to muster public support and highlight the visibility of such an issue in a way that is 'damaging to interests' even if this is not the case and the climate of public opinion and prevailing ideology it reflects.

Attempting to explain the situational aspects of crime, a routine coincides with time and space as a crucial function of criminal understanding of places of crime. The emphasis on situational aspects state that since illegal acts must prey upon other acts, the spatial and temporal structure of routines should play an important role in determining the location, type and quantity of illegal acts. This is an ecological approach that shows how people interact within an environment but a theoretical framework for understanding white-collar crime on the individual, organizational and societal levels is complex. There are contradictions on all levels—on the individual level there is a conflict for maximum reward and a positive construction of oneself. However, as with all theoretical approaches it has its limitations. The key fact that white-collar professionals have the opportunity to commit crime every day and fail to is one example that opportunity is not a sufficient factor (Abel 2008: 52) in the commission of white-collar/lawyers crime.

The combination of institutionalization, rationalization and socialization has some explanatory value. The problem here though is that of attribution error(s). This is a tendency to attribute events/acts to individuals rather than organizations and situations, particularly if the consequences of the events are severe. The intertwined processes of institutionalization, rationalization, and socialization, however, are a powerful force, and ethical standards of an organization—a legal firm—cannot be owned by management and imposed as a practice. Once corruption sets in, the processes of institutionalization, rationalization and socialization create an unholy trinity that aggressively resists modification to its business practices regardless of the sector but as with criminal justice the impact of corruption is substantial as its legitimacy is harmed and that of our faith in a notion of 'justice'.

Conclusion

This chapter illustrated that whilst lawyers engage in criminal conduct and are a potential conduit of corruption both for organized crime and legitimate business and can act alone or in concert engaging in crime, 'legal ethics' is the dominant discourse in the USA rather than on lawyers enabling crime. However, I suggested here that there is limited information available on lawyers that can and do harm the credibility of the legal profession and the legitimacy of criminal justice. Playing by the rules, a procedural equality is at times a myth; powerful, rich clients and/or organizations can and do utilize all resources—political, social, economic—to prevent investigation and conviction. Lawyers enable such a system of stratified access to justice. This is not a criticism of lawyers, unless they commit crime, since as part of a social structure that offers legal representation this profession is itself part of a system of civil and criminal justice. Finally, some reflection on the competing and sometimes contradictory theoretical approaches of why lawyers commit crime was considered but as with all theoretical frameworks whilst useful, failed to clearly explain why lawyers commit crime.

References

Abel, R. (2008). *Lawyers in the Dock: Learning from Attorney Disciplinary Proceedings*. Oxford: Oxford University Press.

Abel, R. (2011). *Lawyers on Trial: Understanding Ethical Misconduct*. Oxford: Oxford University Press.

Ashforth, B. E., & Anand, V. (2003). The Normalization of Corruption in Organizations. *Research in Organizational Behavior, 25*, 1–52.

Babcock, B. (1983). Defending the Guilty. *Cleveland State Law Review, 32*, 175–187.

Banks, C. (2017). *Criminal Justice Ethics: Theory and Practice*. London: Sage.

Beetham, D. (1991). *The Legitimation of Power*. London: Palgrave.

Benson, M. L. (1985). Denying the Guilty Mind: Accounting for Involvement in White-Collar Crime. *Criminology, 23*(4), 583–607.

Benson, M. L., & Moore, E. (1992). Are White-Collar and Common Offenders the Same? An Empirical and Theoretical Critique of a Recently Proposed General Theory of Crime. *Journal of Research in Crime and Delinquency, 29*(3), 251–272.

Boon, A. (2011). Professionalism Under the Legal Services Act 2007. *International Journal of the Legal Profession, 17*, 195.

Bottoms, A., & Tankebe, J. (2012). Beyond Procedural Justice: A Dialogic Approach to Legitimacy in Criminal Justice. *Journal of Criminal Law and Criminology, 102*(1), 119–170.

Braithwaite, J. (1985). White Collar Crime. *Annual Review of Sociology, 11*, 1–25.

Braithwaite, J. (1988). White-Collar Crime, Competition and Capitalism: Comment on Coleman. *American Journal of Sociology, 94*, 628–632.

Brisman, A. (2010). 'Creative Crime' and the Phytological Analogy. *Crime, Media, Culture, 6*(2), 205–225.

Brooks, G. (2016). *Criminology of Corruption: Theoretical Approaches*. Basingstoke: Palgrave Macmillan.

Brooks, G., Lewis, C., Walsh, D., & Kim, H. (2013). *The Prevention of Corruption: Investigation, Enforcement and Governance*. Basingstoke: Palgrave Macmillan.

Chaikin, D., & Sharman, J. C. (2009). *Corruption and Money Laundering: A Symbiotic Relationship*. Basingstoke: Palgrave Macmillan.

Clinard, M. B. (1979). *Corporate Crime*. Washington, DC: Government Printing Office.

Coffee, J. C. (2006). *Gatekeepers: The Professions and Corporate Governance.* Oxford: Oxford University Press.

Cohen, S. (1996). Government Responses to Human Rights Reports: Claims, Denials, and Counterclaims. *Human Rights Quarterly, 18*(3), 517–543.

Coleman, J. W. (1992). The Theory of White-Collar Crime: From Sutherland to the 1990s. In K. Schlegal & D. Weisburd (Eds.), *White Collar Crime Reconsidered.* Pennsylvania: Maple Press.

Coleman, J. W. (1995). Motivation and Opportunity: Understanding the Causes of White Collar Crime. In G. Geis, R. Meier, & L. Salinger (Eds.), *White Collar Crime* (3rd ed.). New York: Free Press.

Cressey, D. (1953). *Other People's Money: A Study in the Social Psychology of Embezzlement.* New York: Free Press.

Economides, K., & Rogers, J. (2009). *Preparatory Ethics Training for Future Solicitors.* London: Law Society of England and Wales.

Europol. (2013). *EU Serious and Organized Crime Threat Assessment 2013.* The Hague: Europol.

Foucault, M. (1980). *Power/Knowledge: Selected Interviews and Other Writings 1972–1977* (C. Gordon, Ed.). New York: Pantheon Books.

Garland, D. (2001). *The Culture of Control: Crime and Social Order in Contemporary Society.* Oxford: Oxford University Press.

Geis, G. (2006). *White Collar Criminal: The Offender in Business and Professions.* New Brunswick, NJ: Transaction Publishers.

Gottschalk, M. (2016a). The Role of Lawyers as Defenders of White Collar Crime. In M. Edelbacher, P. Kratcoski, & B. Dobovsek (Eds.), *Corruption, Fraud, Organized Crime, and the Shadow Economy.* Boca Raton, FL: CRC Press.

Gottschalk, P. (2016b). *Understanding White-Collar Crime: A Convenience Perspective.* Boca Raton, FL: CRC Press.

Hall, K., & Holmes, V. (2008). The Power of Rationalization to Influence Lawyers Decisions to Act Unethically. *Legal Ethics, 11,* 137–153.

Henriques, D. B. (2017). *The Wizard of Lies: Bernie Madoff and the Death of Trust.* London: St. Martin's Griffin.

Hough, M., Jackson, J., Bradford, B., Myhill, A., & Quinton, P. (2010). Procedural Justice, Trust, and Institutional Legitimacy. *Policing: A Journal of Policy and Practice, 4*(3), 203–210.

Langevoort, D. C. (2010). Chasing the Greased Pig Down Wall Street: A Gatekeeper's Guide to the Psychology, Culture, and Ethics of Financial Risk Taking. *Cornell Law Review, 96,* 1209.

Langevort, D. C. (2012). Getting (Too) Comfortable: In-House Lawyers, Enterprise Risk, and the Financial Crisis. *Wisconsin Law Review, 2,* 495–520.

Lankhorst, F., & Nelen, H. (2004). Professional Services and Organised Crime in The Netherlands. *Crime, Law and Social Change, 42,* 163–188.

Levi, M. (2002). Money Laundering and Its Regulation. *Annals of the American Academy of Political and Social Sciences, 582,* 181–194.

Levi, M. (2008). *The Phantom Capitalist: The Organisation and Control of Long-Firm Fraud.* Andover: Ashgate.

Levi, M. (2009). Suite Revenge? The Shaping of Folk Devils and Moral Panics About White Collar Crimes. *British Journal of Criminology, 49*(1), 48–67.

Levi, M. (2012). The Organisation of Serious Crimes for Gain. In M. Maguire, R. Morgan, & R. Reiner (Eds.), *The Oxford Handbook of Criminology* (5th ed.). Oxford: Oxford University Press.

Levi, M., & Gilmore, W. (2002). Terroist Finance, Money Laundering and the Rise and Rise of Mutual Evaluation: A New Paradigm for Crime Control? *European Journal of Law Reform, 4*(2), 337–364.

Levi, M., Nelen, H., & Lankhorst, F. (2005). Lawyers as Crime Facilitators in Europe: An Introduction and Overview. *Crime, Law and Social Change, 42*(2/3), 117–121.

Levi, M., & Reuter, P. (2006). Money Laundering. *Crime and Justice, 34*(2), 289–375.

Masciandaro, D. (Ed.). (2017). *Global Financial Crime: Terrorism, Money Laundering and Offshore Centres.* Abingdon: Routledge.

Middleton, D. J. (2005). The Legal and Regulatory Response to Solicitors Involved in Serious Fraud Is Regulatory Action More Effective Than Criminal Prosecution? *British Journal of Criminology, 45,* 810–836.

Middleton, D. J. (2008). Lawyers and Client Accounts: Sand Through a Colander. *Journal of Money Laundering Control, 11,* 34.

Middleton, D. J., & Levi, M. (2004). The Role of Solicitors in Facilitating 'Organized Crime': Situational Crime Opportunities and Their Regulation. *Crime, Law and Social Change, 42,* 123–161.

Middleton, D. J., & Levi, M. (2015). Let Sleeping Lawyers Lie: Organized Crime, Lawyers and the Regulation of Legal Services. *British Journal of Criminology, 55,* 647–668.

Nelen, H., & Lankhorst, F. (2008). Facilitating Organised Crime: The Role of Lawyers and Notaries. In D. Seigel & H. Nelen (Eds.), *Organised Crime—Culture, Market and Policies.* London: Springer.

Oliver, C. (1992). The Antecedents of Deinstitutionalization. *Organization Studies, 13*(4), 563–588.
Otusanya, O. J. (2011). The Role of Multinational Companies in Corrupt Practices: The Case of Nigeria. *International Journal of Critical Accounting, 3*(2/3), 171–203.
Otusanya, O. J., Lauwo, S., & Adeyeye, G. B. (2012). A Critical Examination of the Multinational Companies' Anti-corruption Policy. *Nigeria Accountancy Business and the Public Interest, 11*, 1–52.
Paoli, L. (Ed.). (2014). *The Oxford Handbook of Organized Crime*. Oxford: Oxford University Press.
Payne, B. K. (2012). *White Collar Crime: A Text/Reader*. Thousand Oaks, CA: Sage.
Payne, B. K. (2013). *White Collar Crime: The Essentials*. Thousand Oaks, CA: Sage.
Pontell, H. N. (2005). White Collar Crime or Just Risky Business? The Role of Fraud in Major Financial Debacles. *Crime, Law and Social Change, 42*(4), 309–324.
Reuter, P., & Truman, E. M. (2004). *Chasing Dirty Money: The Fight Against Money Laundering*. Washington, DC: Institute for International Economics.
Schoepfer, A., & Piquero, N. L. (2006). Exploring White Collar Crime and the American Dream: A Partial Test of Institutional Anomie Theory. *Journal of Criminal Justice, 34*, 227–235.
Simon, W. (1988). Ethical Discretion in Lawyering. *Harvard Law Review, 101*(6), 1083–1145.
Simpson, S. S., & Weisburd, D. (2009). *Criminology of White Collar Crime*. New York: Springer.
Smith, G., Button, M., Johnston, L., & Frimpong, K. (2010). *Studying Fraud as White Collar Crime*. Basingstoke: Palgrave Macmillan.
Stadler, W. A., Benson, M., & Cullen, F. T. (2013). Revisiting the Special Sensitivity Hypothesis: The Prison Experience of White-Collar Inmates. *Justice Quarterly, 1*, 1–25.
Sutherland, E. H. (1939). *Principles of Criminology* (3rd ed.). Philidelphia: Lippincott.
Sykes, G. (1958). *The Society of Captives*. Princeton, NJ: Princeton University Press.
Sykes, G. M., & Matza, D. (1957). Techniques of Neutralization: A Theory of Delinquency. *American Sociological Review, 22*, 664–670.
Taylor, N. (1988). *The Guide to the Professional Conduct of Solicitors*. London: The Law Society.

The Secret Barrister. (2018). *The Secret Barrister: Stories of Law and How It's Broken*. London: Macmillan.
Tyler, T. (1990). *Why People Obey the Law*. New Haven: Yale University Press.
Tyler, T. R. (2003). Procedural Justice, Legitimacy, and the Effective Rule of Law. *Crime and Justice, 30,* 283–357.
Tyler, T. (2011). Trust and Legitimacy: Policing in the USA and Europe. *European Journal of Criminology, 8*(4), 254–266.
Tyler, T. R., & Huo, Y. J. (2002). *Building Trust in the Law*. New York: Russell Sage Foundation.
Warren, E. (2016) *Rigged Justice 2016: How Weak Enforcement Lets Offenders of Easy*. Washington, DC: Office of United States Senate and Office of Elizabeth Warren.
Wasserstrom, R. (1986). Lawyers as Professionals: Some Moral Issues. In M. Davis & F. Elliston (Eds.), *Ethics and the Legal Profession*. Buffalo: NY Prometheus Books.
Weisburd, D., & Waring, E. (2001). *White-Collar Crime and Criminal Careers*. New York: Cambridge University Press.

11

Conclusion: Equality in Criminal Justice—An Ideal We Are Still in Search Of?

Final Reflections

In the introduction to this book it was made clear that it was concerned with corruption in criminal justice systems and has hopefully produced a text that is useful and broad in thought, but also accessible for those with knowledge of criminology and corruption, but rarely both. A common theme in this book is that corruption is committed by individuals, specific units such as narcotics or vice in law enforcement and organizations. These—individuals, units, organizations—reflect the literature on corruption regardless of the sector (Johnston 2005; Rothstein 2011; Brooks et al. 2013; Graycar and Prenzler 2013; Heywood 2015; Hough 2015; Brooks 2016; Banks 2017; Miller 2017). I also highlighted the 'collusion' between different parts of the criminal justice system such as law enforcement and private and/or public science (see Chapter 3). Corruption in criminal justice is thus achieved by individuals or units or institutional acts alone or in concert with one another. A victim of criminal justice corruption then can thus encounter corruption with law enforcement, a judge, a bias and prejudicial jury, or at least some members of a jury, smuggling contraband and violence in prison

G. Brooks, *Criminal Justice and Corruption*,
https://doi.org/10.1007/978-3-030-16038-8_11

and perhaps a manufactured or ignored breach of probation conditions under some private sector organization in the community.

Each chapter considered a specific agency of criminal justice but where possible I made connections to other chapters. As such, it is hoped that the issues, debates and examples used increase the analysis and criticism of criminal justice corruption beyond law enforcement and consider the judiciary, prison sector, probation services and corrupt lawyers far more worthy of in-depth analysis. A special plea was raised that we—in sociology, criminology, law, psychology—need to consider private sector corruption and the harm it causes to the legitimacy of criminal justice in democratic nations, particularly at and after negotiating a contract, and that poor state regulation and oversight can embolden corruption. We should move beyond the criticism of contracts based on ethical issues and treatment of offenders and examine avenues of corruption managing criminal justice via outsourced services. Here we can see that whilst individuals, specialized units and/or the criminal justice system itself can victimize both offenders and victims, it is itself also a potential victim via private sector corruption. This is not simply via a private contractor that breaches the conditions of its contract, private individuals also (see Chapter 10) such as lawyers can corrupt criminal justice as well (Middleton and Levi 2015).

I therefore suggest that we should also, sometimes, see the criminal justice system, as well as individuals as a victim of corruption. This is the heart of the matter; if criminal justice, in democratic states is seen by some as corrupt its legitimacy to punish is diminished (Bottoms and Tankebe 2012). This to some extent will have already happened and will always be a part of the problem of trying to deliver 'justice' to a population. Prejudicial views held by some that work in criminal justice will manifest in personal conduct, and supported by a culture that socializes and rationalizes behaviour (Tonry 2011; Tyler 2014).

However, if the level of corruption in democratic states is allowed to flourish we could reach a tipping point where the majority of a population see the criminal justice system as bias, and/or incompetent and ineffectual in preventing crime. I have some sympathy here for those that work in criminal justice; public expectation of what individual members of a criminal justice agency and/or institution can do is often beyond what is possible in a democratic system. The criminal justice system and individuals are often having to address public expectation as well as enforce the law/pass sentence often in a hostile public environment.

There is also a potential problem that public pressure—known or imagined—leads to the corruption of criminal justice (see Chapter 6) where prosecutors might engage in tactics to secure a conviction. In a system where judges/prosecutors are elected the potential for corruption, I suggest, is increased as the financial rewards of such a system encourage people to be unnecessarily punitive and withhold and manipulate 'evidence' to secure a conviction and appeal to the public. This could embolden people to act in a corrupt way—unethical and/or criminal—but a different system that excludes election to 'high office' in criminal justice is still vulnerable to this type of corruption as well.

Preventing Corruption in Criminal Justice Systems

To advance any strategy and in this case, analysis of avenues of potential corruption, some understanding of the size of the problem is needed. As illustrated it is difficult to define, measure and therefore assess the extent of criminal justice corruption (see Chapter 3) in democratic states. The issues raised here are ongoing; they are, however, in need of systematic analysis if we are to prevent corruption to some extent. There are numerous books and articles explaining and highlighting the key elements of an anti-corruption strategy and the need to prevent and reduce corruption, and these that are useful were referred to in this book. The strategic list of key elements in this literature is not exhaustive. It is, however, underpinned by a growing body of work. The problem, however, is that anti-corruption strategies have so far been unsuccessful (Heywood 2015; Hough 2015; Brooks 2016) and are at best patchy and sporadic, depending on the political will of an incumbent administration and organization, and whether it is expedient to endorse or block and obfuscate a change in working practice in criminal justice. Much of what passes to reduce criminal justice corruption, is often sound bites, promises of change to come, and the development of 'new' bodies to deal with criminal justice corruption such as IOPC (see Chapter 3) but which simply replaced a previous body tasked with a similar remit.

However, rather than dwell on criminal justice anti-corruption methods it is best to see criminal justice as a business. Its business is 'justice' with sometimes competing and complementing organizations. Business, however, is often seen as inherently criminogenic (Brooks 2016) and it appears that the criminal justice system is no different where organizational culture can enable 'workplace crime and corruption' (Beare 2017). Corruption is enabled depending on whether there are clear messages about what is acceptable and unacceptable conduct, and depends on factors such as the attitudes of colleagues, the example set by the top management, internal practices, but also by the limited sanctions, if applied for acts of corruption.

Furthermore, but applied to criminal justice here, major business aims are often linked to a plethora of impossible objectives such as order maintenance and security and yet retain ethical standards and notions of justice. Many of the acts of corruption mentioned in this book have a structural problem; that is they are part of a worldwide problem and system that contributes to corruption. It is these structural issues rather than condemnation of a few that need attention.

As mentioned in this book this is difficult to achieve. However, preventing corruption is the responsibility of all; the anti-corruption units of some criminal justice bodies make an admirable attempt at preventing corruption, but as with the public and private sector it is often key individuals, in a suitable political climate, which effect change. This is not an indictment of anti-corruption/integrity units but an understanding of the limits with which they can influence practice (Hough 2015), as vested powerful interests will oppose change that might encroach on the power and authority they presently possess (Brooks et al. 2013).

Any organization, which attempts to prevent corruption, or is in the process of developing a strategy, is to be commended. The development of an anti-corruption and ethics committee culture is of limited value if employees have no clear direction as to what corruption is, or might possibly emerge. A codified set of guidelines regarding risks, ethical behaviour, code of conduct, response plan(s) and anti-corruption strategy alone are insufficient. If they fail to educate and hold those to account who break or circumvent codes of conduct in law enforcement, the judiciary, state and/or private prosecutors, prison officers, attitudes are unlikely to change. A strategy needs direction, leadership and codes of conduct, which need to be enforced if it has any chance of success, and organizations and state representatives need to be held to account if laws are expected to have meaning beyond political mission statements.

The criminal justice system is more a business with its product that of justice. The measure of its success is often how it deals with crime and punishment of offenders. The measure of an organization's success outside of criminal justice is often its size, and the pursuit of expansion pursued with sometimes risky human, financial, environmental costs. However, this is where the business of criminal justice is, or should be different: rather than welcome expansion of the prison sector, punishment in the community (see Chapter 8) and law enforcement, and privatizing of criminal justice services I raise the question here 'who really benefits from criminal justice?' It is clear that it is the public and victims, if living in a democratic state, but this book also highlighted those that work in criminal justice benefit both legally e.g. a wage, but also via corruption.

I do not suggest retrenchment of criminal justice nor accept that its expansion is simply in reaction to a rise in crime in some jurisdictions, as crime can fall but state and private penal expansion continues unabated. Democratic western political systems have to tread carefully here; promising justice but delivering no or little justice or injustice harms the legitimacy of criminal justice. If this is lost, as it is in some states around the world, violence instead of a rule of law dominates what little is left of criminal justice systems. It is naive to suggest that corruption *in* and *of* criminal justice in democratic states is a blot on the landscape and at an acceptable level for criminal justice systems to dispense notions of justice. Corruption is a flexible beast and attempts to prevent and/or reduce it must also be the same. This is not to dismiss it completely but reflect on what is of use and how it can be combined with successful preventive approaches. All approaches—practical and theoretical—must be realistic in that change in practice or sanction(s) are beneficial to justice.

Finally, and illustrated in this book, unless sanctions have some power to deter, the current approach to corrupt individuals, units and organizations, will simply reassure them that the consequences for such acts are often, but not always, minimal, with regulatory bodies and sanctions often ineffective. Further research needs to be conducted on sanctions and deterrence in cases of corruption on those that work in the criminal justice system instead of on offenders on the outside of the justice system and seek to understand what can prevent law enforcement, judges, prosecutors, prison officers and lawyers abusing the system for personal benefit and enrichment.

References

Banks, C. (2017). *Criminal Justice Ethics: Theory and Practice*. London: Sage.

Beare, M. E. (2017). The Failures of Police Legitimacy: Attacks from Within. In V. Mitslegas, P. Alldridge, & L. Cheliotis (Eds.), *Globalisation, Criminal Law and Criminal Justice*. Oxford: Hart Publishing.

Bottoms, A., & Tankebe, J. (2012). Beyond Procedural Justice: A Dialogic Approach to Legitimacy in Criminal Justice. *Journal of Criminal Law and Criminology, 102*(1), 119–170.

Brooks, G. (2016). *Criminology of Corruption: Theoretical Approaches*. Basingstoke: Palgrave Macmillan.

Brooks, G., Lewis, C., Walsh, D., & Kim, H. (2013). *The Prevention of Corruption: Investigation, Enforcement and Governance*. Basingstoke: Palgrave Macmillan.

Graycar, A., & Prenzler, T. (2013). *Understanding and Preventing Corruption*. Basingstoke: Palgrave Macmillan.

Heywood, P. M. (2015). *Routledge Handbook of Political Corruption*. Abingdon: Routledge.

Hough, D. (2015). *Corruption, Anti-corruption and Governance*. Basingstoke: Palgrave Macmillan.

Johnston, M. (2005). *Syndromes of Corruption: Wealth, Power, Democracy*. Cambridge: Cambridge University Press.

Middleton, D., & Levi, M. (2015). Let Sleeping Lawyers Lie: Organized Crime, Lawyers and the Regulation of Legal Services. *British Journal of Criminology, 55*, 647–668.

Miller, S. (2017). *Institutional Corruption: A Study in Applied Philosophy*. Cambridge: Cambridge University Press.

Rothstein, B. (2011). *The Quality of Government: Corruption, Social Trust and Inequality in a Comparative Perspective*. Chicago: Chicago University Press.

Tonry, M. (2011). *Punishing Race: A Continuing American Dilemma*. New York: Oxford University Press.

Tyler, J. C. (2014). Blind Injustice: The Supreme Court, Implicit Racial Bias and the Racial Disparity in the Criminal Justice System. *American Criminal Law Review, 51*, 689–713.

Index

G. Brooks, *Criminal Justice and Corruption*,
https://doi.org/10.1007/978-3-030-16038-8

FSC
www.fsc.org
MIX
Papier | Fördert gute Waldnutzung
FSC® C083411

Kolibri 360 GmbH
Ferdinand-Jühlke-Straße 7
99095 Erfurt, Deutschland
produktsicherheit@kolibri360.de